T. S. Eliot's Negative Way

Eloise Knapp Hay

HARVARD UNIVERSITY PRESS

CAMBRIDGE, MASSACHUSETTS

AND LONDON, ENGLAND   1982

Publication of this book has been aided by a grant from the
ANDREW W. MELLON FOUNDATION

Library of Congress Cataloging in Publication Data

Hay, Eloise Knapp.
    T. S. Eliot's negative way.

    Includes bibliographical references and index.
    1. Eliot, T. S. (Thomas Stearns), 1888–1965—
Philosophy.   2. Negativity (Philosophy) in literature.
I. Title.
PS3509.L43Z6817   821'.912   81-23747
ISBN 0-674-24675-6   AACR2

To Edward

Acknowledgments

This book began as a paper invited by the Institute of Religious Studies at the University of California, Santa Barbara, and was completed after a session at the university's School of Criticism and Theory in Irvine. My starting point was a problem in comparative religion; my conclusion emerged in following T. S. Eliot's "way" as poet, moving toward a vanishing point on the human horizon. The Senior Fellows of the School of Criticism and Theory confirmed my understanding that the high sophistication of current literary theory is valuable to the extent, and only to the extent, that it encourages the best possible reading of literature. To this end, the work of Wayne Booth, René Girard, J. Hillis Miller, and Michael Riffaterre—all Fellows present at the 1979 session of the Irvine School—proved to be exemplary.

The original occasion in Santa Barbara was a conference in honor of Raimundo Panikkar, a creative religious thinker with a special interest in literature and problems of language. What better way to honor this poetic theologian than to remind him of his affinities with one of our language's most theological poets, T. S. Eliot? Since my own interest in Eliot was primarily literary, I soon found that the concepts I wished to understand in his poetry—for instance, "the way up and the

way down," or "attachment ... detachment ... and indifference"—
were ones that speak to us first by way of the senses and only much
later in religious terms. Raimundo Panikkar showed me that this is
indeed the way to read any language, and that Eliot's striving for a poetry that would not be "violated" by ideas is an aim no less in religious language than it is in the language of poetry.

My thanks for helpful discussion of my manuscript (as well as of
Eliot's work) go to many individual colleagues, especially to Raimundo Panikkar himself and to Raymond Preston, but also to William R. Harmon, Lyndall Gordon, Priscilla Martin, Donald Pearce,
Robert A. Potter, Balachandra Rajan, and Georg B. Tennyson. I must
also acknowledge two works by A. D. Moody and Edward Lobb,
whose admirable *Thomas Stearns Eliot, Poet* and *T. S. Eliot and the Romantic Critical Tradition* appeared too late to be fully integrated into
my readings. Like my study, Lobb's discovers in Eliot's unpublished
Clark Lectures of 1926 a crucial turning point in Eliot's career. I see
the lectures as the first fruits of Eliot's conversion from one kind of
negativity (skepticism) to another—the Christian *via negativa*. Lobb,
with equal justice, sees them as the culmination of Eliot's long-standing rejection of Western epistemology, or "psychologism," as Eliot
called it.

In a more personal way, I wish also to thank Rodney Dennis and
his staff at Harvard's Houghton Library for courtesies far beyond their
required duties. For the same helpfulness, I am grateful to Donald
Fitch and his staff at the Library of the University of California, Santa
Barbara. To Donald Gallup and Mary de Rachewiltz, as well as the librarians of the Beinecke Library at Yale, I owe special thanks; also to
the librarians of the Bodleian Library at Oxford, at King's College Library of Cambridge University, and at the Berg Collection of the New
York Public Library.

I am grateful for permission to quote from Eliot's works, as follows:
Reprinted by permission of Faber and Faber Ltd. and Harcourt
Brace Jovanovich, Inc.: *Collected Poems 1909–1962, Selected Essays, Murder in the Cathedral, The Family Reunion, The Cocktail Party, The Confidential Clerk, The Idea of a Christian Society, After Strange Gods,* and *The
Waste Land: A Facsimile and Transcript of the Original Drafts.* Copyright 1932, 1935, 1936, 1950 by Harcourt Brace Jovanovich, Inc.:

copyright 1939, 1943, 1954, 1960, 1963, 1964 by T. S. Eliot; copyright 1967, 1971, 1978 by Esmé Valerie Eliot.

Reprinted by permission of Faber and Faber Ltd. and Farrar, Straus and Giroux, Inc.: *On Poetry and Poets,* copyright © 1943, 1945, 1951, 1954, 1956, 1957 by T. S. Eliot; *The Elder Statesman,* copyright © 1959 by Thomas Stearns Eliot; *To Criticize the Critic,* copyright © 1965 by Valerie Eliot.

Excerpts from Eliot's previously unpublished prose are reprinted by permission of Mrs. Valerie Eliot and Faber and Faber Ltd. Copyright © 1982 by Valerie Eliot.

Other acknowledgments, for instance to Eliot's uncollected essays, appear in my footnotes. I must also stress my debt to all the writers whose essays and books I have recognized in my text and notes, as well as to the many excellent writers whose work I have perhaps failed to mention simply because it did not come to mind at the point of setting my thoughts on paper.

Finally I must thank the student assistants who have greatly lightened the task of preparing my manuscript—in particular, Jodi Patterson, John Stephens, Thomas Lockwood, Lynn Zinberg, John Rose, Diane Siegal, and Leslie White.

And to Stephen Hay, my fellow student and colleague, I am grateful as always for his supporting presence.

Contents

The contemplation of the horrid or sordid or disgusting, by an artist, is the necessary and negative aspect of the impulse toward the pursuit of beauty. But not all succeed as did Dante in expressing the complete scale from negative to positive. The negative is the more importunate.

—"DANTE," 1920

Introduction

The single volume that makes up the "complete poems and plays" of T. S. Eliot presents an enormous challenge to critical theory. My proposal is that we consider this challenge under two headings, both signaled by the poetic phrase "the negative way," which James Johnson Sweeney taught us to take as the key to Eliot's culminating poem, *Four Quartets.* In my rereadings of Eliot's poems and plays, this phrase has come to have as much importance for the early works as for the late ones, though in very different senses. The two theoretical problems implicit in "the negative way" are of course the problem of *negativity* and the problem of *the way* (as path, direction, mode, method, and finally as ultimate goal). "The negative way" is an oxymoron. Is all going or making, arriving or finding—everything implicit in "way"—nullified when the word is prefixed by "negative"? Eliot's early poems focused on this tension, long before he made the Christian *via negativa* the matrix of his late poems and plays. Sometimes the early poems take both images together, as when Prufrock summons us to go a certain way with him and then takes us nowhere. Sometimes the two images of void and path are separated, as when "Gerontion," with its rhythmic denials, projects stasis with no direction but that of a "gull against the wind," or when "Lune de Miel" traces a honey-moon tour without a single negative, yet charts the perfect vacancy of the lovers' vacation. My interest has been to pursue the scope and meanings of these recurring themes, linguistically and tropologically, as developing patterns that reveal a striking design in Eliot's entire poetic corpus.

It was only in the middle of his career that Eliot arrived at the conviction that "the way up and the way down are the same" (as his second epigraph quoting Heraclitus reads in *Four Quartets*) and that Heraclitus's vision of cosmic order in chaos was an appropriate metaphor for the Christian "way." Tempting as it may be to read the early poems in this light, nothing could be more damaging to our understanding. Too many readings, even some of the best, have taken Eliot's early volumes and *The Waste Land* as poems already leading through death to the promise of new life—written as if under the sign of St. Augustine's words in the *Confessions* (IV, 19): "Descend that ye may ascend." Each successive reading has convinced me, to the contrary, that Eliot's poems before "Ash-Wednesday" have the opposite matrix within them. "Ascend that ye may descend" is a better interpretant of his early poetry.

Exploration of the void, either as a stasis or as a "way," was already a project of Eliot's during his philosophical studies and in his first poetry notebook, before he began to publish professionally, as Lyndall Gordon has recently shown. His resolute turn from Western forms of "affirmative" religions to the study of Buddhism and primitive religions paralleled philosophical movements in the first two decades of the twentieth century which also were probing the uses of negation.

Critics have often observed that American writers before Eliot were disposed, by the very conditions of being American, to write "deconstructively" or negatively. J. Hillis Miller considers the tendency a mark of the Protestant heritage, inherited from the Old Testament's assailing of human constructs and institutions. Terence Martin cites examples of nineteenth-century novelists who prided themselves on negative stances as a badge of Americanism. Citing one reviewer's national pride, Martin comments:

> Let us note that the reviewer proceeds by negation, that he tells Americans what they are not, what they do not have; he is congratu-

lating Americans on their freedom from the past. The passage prefigures later statements by Margaret Fuller, James Fenimore Cooper, Nathaniel Hawthorne, and Henry James, who in describing the America of the 1830's and 40's employed the same negative rhetoric (in each case, however, with a degree of unfavorable meaning) . . .

It is, I believe, precisely because Americans defined themselves negatively that they caught so hungrily at such a conservative body of thought as [Scottish] Common Sense philosophy. For when all the negatives were postulated and applauded, one had finally to consider what was left.[1]

Martin presumably has in mind the famous negatives declaring the deficiencies of "our dear native land" in the opening pages of Hawthorne's *The Marble Faun* and Henry James's exuberant expansion of Hawthorne's list in his study of Hawthorne. Eliot often associated his own view of America with Hawthorne's and James's, but his early poetry hardly chides America for its cultural barrenness. To the contrary, it is not the absence of American culture that oppresses Prufrock and Mr. Appollinax but the heavy weight of overrefinement they encounter on the American scene. Eliot's most appealing images for America appear in his uncultivated landscapes of Cape Ann with the open space of sea surrounding it. Nevertheless, Eliot, too, defined his years as an American negatively, as a ceaseless voyage "to no end" in the phrasing of "The Dry Salvages," and his native legacy supported him in the process. Despite his readiness to shed his American Unitarian origins, was he not repeating that tradition of vigorous rejections?

Another force directing Eliot's thought toward negativity was the German philosophical tradition as it influenced his Harvard studies (and as it had influenced the American literary heritage beginning with Emerson). Though it has not been part of my task to consider Eliot's relation to other writers in detail, a striking parallel can be found between his work and that of at least one of his contemporaries trained in this tradition. Martin Heidegger, born in Germany in 1899, believed that German Idealism was the only modern philosophy (1) to see Being as always a Transcendental and (2) to dare thinking of negation as comprehended in Being.[2] Heidegger very early gave up his commitment to Catholic theology, because he rejected a metaphysics claiming to grasp positive concepts of Being, and turned toward a metaphysical viewpoint that he described as the experience of "Being in Nothing."[3] Describing the "dread" or "anxiety" occasioned by the "withdrawal of Being" felt at various periods of history, including our own, he noted that the phenomenon of anxiety in the face of Nothingness had first become a central concern among Christian theologians, especially St. Augustine, Luther, Pascal, and Kierkegaard. Both Eliot and Heidegger began their major work listening to what Heidegger called "the soundless voice which attunes us to the horrors of the abyss [of Nothing]."[4] Like Eliot, too, Heidegger fastened on images of "the way" as the clearest expression of human experience in time. In 1959 Heidegger wrote, "I have abandoned an earlier standpoint, not so that I might adopt a different one in its place, but because even that earlier standpoint was a halting place in a thinking that is on its way. The way is what is enduring in thought."[5] But unlike Jean-Paul Sartre, a later prominent philosopher of Being and Nothingness, both Eliot and Heidegger declared that the philosophy of Humanism (man-centeredness) is not only a failure "to inquire into the relation of Being to man but is even a hindrance in the way of such inquiry," as Heidegger said in his 1946 "Letter on 'Humanism.' "[6] Eliot's view was already established in his essay "The Humanism of Irving Babbitt" in 1927. In "Burnt Norton," V, he speaks of love experienced in time as "Caught ... / Between un-being and being," thus finding its center only in relation to another (nonhuman) center.

Heidegger differed from Eliot, however, in severely refusing to identify this Being with any name given to it by any church, preferring "now to be silent about God in the sphere of thinking."[7] While the movement of Eliot's thought was away from Unitarianism and philosophy to Catholicism and poetry, Heidegger's was away from Catholicism to a philosophy that deferred to poetry in search of expression: "To sing, truly to say worldly existence ... means: to belong to the precinct of beings themselves. This precinct, as the very nature of language, is Being itself. To sing the song means to be present in what is present itself. It means: *Dasein,* existence."[8]

Eliot, both early and late, rejected such tendencies, as he found them in Shelley and Matthew Arnold, to make poetry a substitute for religion. His relinquishing of philosophy for poetry was nevertheless a step along the same negative way in thought expressed by Heidegger. The pure presence that Eliot described for the first time in "Marina" in

1930 exactly coincides with a statement Heidegger made in 1946 on the same subject. Eliot's Pericles asks:

> What is this face, less clear and clearer
> The pulse in the arm, less strong and stronger—
> Given or lent? more distant than stars and nearer than the eye
>
> Whispers and small laughter between leaves and hurrying feet
> Under sleep, where all the waters meet.

"Being," says Heidegger, "is farther away than all that is, and nevertheless is nearer to man than any thing, whether it be a rock, an animal, a work of art, a machine, an angel, or God. Being is the nearest, and yet the nearest is what remains remotest from man."[9]

If Heidegger is right, the philosophical negatives that Eliot studied as a student form a separate tradition from the mystical "way" found in the Pseudo-Dionysius and the Christian mystics. We should therefore defer consideration of the mystical strain in Eliot's poetry till we meet it in *Four Quartets* and the plays, beginning with *Murder in the Cathedral*. Since Eliot's distrust of mysticism was evident in his essays (as well as in his poems on pathological saints) before 1927, I have maintained a neutral (nonreligious) use of the phrase "negative way" before discussing the later works. This neutral usage seems warranted by the prominence of the image long before he gives it a Christian emphasis in the poems. Heidegger's insistence on such a nonmystical neutral interpretation to the end of *his* life seems clear. His discussions of mankind's "waymaking" remind us that Eliot's image of "exploration" has the widest, least sectarian, basis. Thus at the end of "Little Gidding" (1942) Eliot writes:

> With the drawing of this Love and the voice of this Calling
>
> We shall not cease from exploration
> And the end of all our exploring
> Will be to arrive where we started
> And know the place for the first time.

And in 1946 Heidegger, answering the question "What Are Poets For?," writes:

> The venture sets free what is ventured, in such a way indeed that it sets free what is flung free into nothing other than a drawing toward

the center. Drawing this way, the venture ever and always brings the ventured toward itself in this drawing ... The gravity of the pure forces, the unheard-of center, the pure draft, the whole draft, full Nature, Life, the venture—they are the same.

He seems further to echo Eliot's thought in "Language" (1950) when Heidegger says, "We do not aim at advancing further. All that we want is just really to get where we already are."[10]

Philosophy rather than theology directed Eliot's first steps along the negative way, and we should be wary of matching the design of his poetry with Dante's, as many readers have done. Ever since Douglas Bush spoke poetically, at the Harvard memorial service for Eliot, of *The Waste Land,* "Ash-Wednesday," and *Four Quartets* as Eliot's *Inferno, Purgatorio,* and *Paradiso,*[11] readers have hunted in his poetry for counterparts to Dante's descent and ascent in the *Commedia,* despite the anomalies this view creates in reading the poems before "The Hollow Men." If Eliot had been retracing Dante's design in the *Commedia,* descending into Hell inspired by a glimpse of the earthly Paradise and with a classical humanist (Virgil) for a guide, why did his *Poems* of 1920 level broadsides against the Christian legacy of Dante, and not merely against the degradations of that legacy?

Reading these poems, one may question Lyndall Gordon's conclusion that they reflect a "dream of sainthood," implicit from the earliest period.[12] If any such dream can be found reflected in the poems before 1925, it was pure nightmare. Gordon cogently argues that the extraordinary blasphemies and obscenities found in many of the early poems are examples of the "partial belief" that Eliot attributed to Baudelaire. But the argument loses some of its force when we consider that Eliot's recurrent statements on blasphemy—in 1928, 1931, and 1933—all came in the years soon after his conversion. Before that, his poems on neurotic saints and poems like "Mr. Eliot's Sunday Morning Service" testify to a powerful resistance to Christian belief, and indeed mercilessly ridicule such belief. Though he wrote in defense of preserving London churches before 1927, such an effort was hardly more in the way of Christian commitment than his support of Charles Maurras and the Action Française.[13] Eliot's essays on these subjects show him subscribing to social, political, and aesthetic programs without spiritual engagement. In fact, the papal condemnation of the Action

Française in 1926—because the movement had shown itself to be politically rather than spiritually motivated—exactly coincided with the change on Eliot's own part from a spiritually uncommitted stand on Christianity to one of spiritual assent. At this point, as I shall hope to show, the contradiction between his defensive prose (defending the Christian *tradition*) and his offensive poetry (satirizing the Christian tradition) was closed. At this point he could say, as he did in 1933, "that in one's prose reflections one may be legitimately occupied with ideals, whereas in the writing of verse one can only deal with actuality."[14]

The blasphemous poems are also, of course, the *jeux d'esprit* of a savage wit—expressions of the negative way followed after 1910. But only ten years after writing *The Waste Land* did Eliot refer to his state of mind while writing it as comparable to Baudelaire's "spiritual sickness." He had spoken in "Tradition and the Individual Talent" of writing poetry as an "escape from personality," but in 1933 he described his experience while writing poetry as "the sudden lifting of the burden of anxiety and fear," and he added that "what happens is something *negative* . . . the breaking down of strong habitual barriers." I am less interested here in the question of illness than in Eliot's emphasis on the phenomenon of negation. In his 1920 essay on Dante he had seemed to speak for himself when he said that "not all succeed as did Dante in expressing the complete scale from negative to positive. The negative is the more importunate."[15]

The "way down" for Eliot did not begin, then, as a descent with a foreshadowed sequel. By observing the drama of negations in all his poems, we can discern a point at which the "burden of anxiety and fear" departs. A new kind of negation then appears, finally most completely expressed in "Burnt Norton," II:

> Neither flesh nor fleshless;
> Neither from nor towards; at the still point, there the dance is,
> But neither arrest nor movement. And do not call it fixity,
> Where past and future are gathered. Neither movement from
>   nor towards,
> Neither ascent nor decline. Except for the point, the still point,
> There would be no dance, and there is only the dance.
> I can only say, *there* we have been: but I cannot say where.
> And I cannot say, how long, for that is to place it in time.

The long-finished peasant dance to appear later in "East Coker," recollected on a *vacant* hillside, is here first presented as a metaphor—or rather a catachresis, since the image of the dance and the still point are so hard to fuse. The catachresis succeeds through the merging of negative semantic and semiotic elements, affecting us through rhythm and meaning simultaneously. Thus the repetition of negative signs (neither/nor, not, no) orders the semantic elements (arrest, decline, fixity, movement, ascent)—which are themselves divided between positive and negative significance—to produce the paragraph's rise to a climax: "There ... there ... / ... *there*". And this is framed at the end again with a repeating negative: "I cannot say ... / ... I cannot say." Such passages show the uses Eliot made of negation to achieve the

> sentence that is right (where every word is at home,
> Taking its place to support the others,
>
> .   .   .   .   .
>
> The complete consort dancing together)

as he concludes in "Little Gidding," V.

Reading the published poems sequentially, we see that Eliot gradually endowed negativity with more and more personal relevance, until in *The Waste Land* and "The Hollow Men" there is a decisive shift from dramatic monologues, locating the voice outside the implied author's, to interior monologues, identifying it clearly as the author's own voice. The plays, of course, progressively dramatize thought and feeling, but writing plays was no exercise in depersonalization, as Eliot pointed out to Donald Hall in his 1958 interview. The plays in fact helped him, he said, to develop the everyday *personal* idiom that he achieved in *Four Quartets*. If the early poems, through 1924, spoke "in different voices" like Dickens's Sloppy—commemorated in one title of *The Waste Land*'s first draft[16]—the late poems speak in one voice that is unquestionably the poet's own.

My object in offering a new reading of the poems and plays, then, is to trace one significant pattern, certified by Eliot, that illuminates important features of his individual poems and also the design of his whole creative work. Central among these considerations is the important step he took in the late twenties to incorporate the poet's "way" into the vision of St. John of the Cross. Unlike St. John, however, Eliot kept to the poet's way, recognizing that it was not "the saint's way." "A saint limits himself by writing poetry," he said in *After Strange Gods*. No one has sufficiently emphasized the distinction he made here. In my Chapter 6 it will be necessary to trace some rather difficult theology, as Eliot himself did, to clarify his point that he was not to be considered a "religious poet." The adjective, in his view, could only narrow the poet's activity. But paradoxically it is only through understanding his broad theological bearings—Buddhist as well as Judeo-Christian—that we can understand his dedication to the whole of life rather than to any self-limiting part of it.

In 1933 Eliot noted that one reason for the difficulties of "modern poetry" is "caused by the author's having left out something which the reader is used to finding; so that the reader gropes about for what is absent . . . for a kind of 'meaning' which is not there, and is not meant to be there."[17] By noticing the stress he placed on such absences, and on negativity in general as "the more importunate" impulse in his poetry, we listen in a new way to the "different voices" leading through his personal waste land to a crisis generating a fresh "impulse toward the pursuit of beauty." The passage in his 1920 essay on Dante, which I cite as epigraph for this book, might suggest that his poetry would eventually respond to some "positive" impulse in the "pursuit of beauty" that radiates in poems like "Marina" and "Little Gidding." In fact by 1930 he had fully vented his early preoccupation with "the horrid or sordid or disgusting." But as he discovered the new impulse and was drawn compellingly to Dante's vision of Paradise, he also made clear that Dante's world afforded no substitute for his own. Dante's serenity might have lured him only to "a deliberate hebetude," he suggests in "East Coker." As a twentieth-century poet, he found himself "In the middle, not only in the middle of the way / But all the way, in a dark wood, in a bramble, / . . . where there is no secure foothold." Warding off the temptation followed by other writers enchanted with Dante's vision in our century, he moved not from "negative" to "positive" celebrations of the world but toward celebrations of experience in which negation redefines itself in a wholly new role. Following the poet's way from "Ash-Wednesday" on, he scrupulously acknowledged his earlier design while transforming its motifs to shape a "pattern new in every moment," finally to offer one poet's "Valuation of all we have been."

Though it may be argued that Eliot, like another Dickens character—the junior Bailey in *Martin Chuzzlewit*—"rendered [himself] somewhat obscure . . . by reason . . . of a redundancy of negatives,"[18] few poets in the end have been clearer in their vision. And our lucidity in reading him depends finally upon our understanding his ways of negation.

1   The Way of
J. Alfred Prufrock

T. S. Eliot was the first English poet who fully explored the desert places of negativity as a new domain of poetry. If our literary period remains "the age of Eliot" (in Allen Tate's phrase), it is largely because Eliot provided for poetry and drama an idiom and form for investigating negation in ways hardly anticipated by the "masters of suspicion" of the age preceding Eliot's.[1] Suspicion concerning the illusions of consciousness had found its voice among English speaking poets from Tennyson, Arnold, and Dickinson to Hardy. All had *used* negation as a means of rejecting false consciousness, but none had prescribed negation itself as a way to move "between two worlds, one dead, / The other powerless to be born," in Arnold's phrase. In the 1940s Eliot acknowledged Jean-Paul Sartre as another master of negation, but a generation earlier he himself had rung out the old skepticism as forcefully as he rang into English poetry the waste land's "dead sound on the final stroke of nine."

His essay of 1920 on Dante showed that he was initially strongly attracted to the negative aspects of even this most affirmative poet, as we have seen. A postscriptive note after the essay concedes that he rather eccentrically singled out a passage from Landor to make his point:

"Dante is the great master of the disgusting."[2] Thus, in an essay designed to argue that philosophical poetry was still possible, an essay given privileged place as the culmination of his first book of prose, Eliot chose to stress a little-remembered side of Dante's *Commedia*—his power of ordering negative emotions. We shall see the effect Eliot achieved by prefacing his first book of poems, *Prufrock and Other Observations,* with two epigraphs from Dante's *Commedia.* Yet we should recall that because of the "more importunate" appeal of negation, Eliot had begun his career as poet under the influence of more recent poets. His last essay on Dante in 1951 pointed to this fact:

> Jules Laforgue . . . was the first to teach me . . . the poetic possibilities of my own idiom of speech.
> . . . from Baudelaire I learned first a precedent for the poetic possibilities, never developed by any poet writing in my own language, of the more sordid aspects of the modern metropolis, of the possibility of fusion between the sordidly realistic and the phantasmagoric . . . From him, as from Laforgue, I learned that the sort of material that I had, the sort of experience that an adolescent had had, in an industrial city in America, could be the material for poetry; and that the source of new poetry might be found in what had been regarded hitherto as the impossible, the sterile, the intractably unpoetic.[3]

Among French poets he also found another way of exploring "the negative aspect of the impulse toward . . . beauty," and this way, too, had its influence on *Prufrock and Other Observations.* It was the way of Rimbaud and Mallarmé, the French Symbolists. In pursuit of "pure poetry," Mallarmé had written in 1866: "I have been for a month among the purest glaciers of aesthetics," and "after reaching the Void [*le Néant*], I have found Beauty."[4] Like the Symbolists' poems, the poems of *Prufrock and Other Observations* often move from a world of precise sensory images toward one in which sensation is annulled or obliterated.

Eliot did not need to *seek* the void, however, in order to find the creative "derangement [*dérèglement*]" of all the senses that attracted Rimbaud and the later Symbolists. Much as he learned aesthetically from these French poets of *le Néant,* the derangement of the senses (or "dissociation," as he called it) was a condition he found present everywhere in the modern world, one for which he hoped to find a *cure* in poetry. His creative probing of such negativities as urban dissolution, dissociation of the senses, and spiritual emptiness would lead him eventually to the *via negativa* of the Christian saints—the way of Becket in *Murder in the Cathedral*, Henry Monchensey in *The Family Reunion,* and Celia Coplestone in *The Cocktail Party,* as well as the way of the poet's journey through time in *Four Quartets.* None of the French Symbolists, much less Baudelaire, had turned into this way. It was a path that finally isolated Eliot from most of the generation of poets who followed him, resulting in the steep decline of his popularity after his death. Nevertheless, as Denis Donoghue and Graham Hough have observed, Eliot's choice has determined the reactions both for and against him.

Samuel Beckett (whose "dramaticule" *Come and Go* hints at Prufrock's women "talking of Michelangelo") evidently exploited the resources of negativity in his own way. One can imagine him pondering the antithetical "shape of ideas" in Eliot and Sartre when he says, "There is a wonderful sentence in Augustine. 'Do not despair: one of the thieves was saved. Do not presume: one of the thieves was damned.' I am interested in the shape of ideas, even if I do not believe in them . . . That sentence has a wonderful shape."[5] Some such shape seems to have loomed up when Beckett read in Eliot's "Little Gidding," "Where is the summer, the unimaginable/ Zero summer?" In *Endgame,* to Hamm's question, "What time is it?" Clov answers, "Zero." Hamm responds, "It'd need to rain." (Hamm resembles Gerontion, also attended by a boy, waiting for rain.) Like Sartre's artist and man of good faith, Beckett's Hamm resigns himself to creating his world ex nihilo. Such "plot," such beginning and end as the world may have, Hamm intends to give it. Not entirely fancifully, one can see Clov as imitating Eliot's tuxedoed Time at the end of *Sweeney Agonistes.* Like him, Clov sets his alarm clock for the end of Hamm's world—to end with a ring, not a bang or a whimper. Clov stands as the curtain falls, nattily dressed to meet another world beyond the catastrophic end of Hamm's game. Eliot recognized the antinomies between himself and Sartre and acknowledged them in *The Cocktail Party.* There Edward Chamberlayne remarks that "Hell is oneself . . . the other figures in it/ Merely projections." Eliot commented on this as "Contre Sartre."[6]

To the published text of *Endgame* Beckett added a pantomime, however, which shows the matching absurdity of Clov-Eliot's theological via negativa, based (in popular, cheery terms) on faith that God's in His Heaven; all's right in a seemingly hideous world. In the pantomime, a Clov-like man is hurled into a desert beside a single tree— suggesting the wilderness and the world tree of religious anthropology, and indeed of Eliot's first and last long poems, *The Waste Land* and *Four Quartets*. From "nowhere" above this tree a carafe is lowered, announced by a whistle (the divine breath, blown a good bit in the previous play by Hamm, who finally threw his whistle into the audience). Each time the mime reaches for the carafe, it is withdrawn, until he wearies of reaching for it. A rope and scissors—also announced by the whistle—are then lowered, but when the mime is driven to the point of deciding to hang himself or cut his throat with the scissors, these things too are withdrawn. The whistle that has conditioned him to reach keeps sounding, but finally it sparks no response from the solitary mime. Beckett's comic portrait of a desert sage, literally *lost* in contemplation as the curtain falls, cancels the compliment to Eliot hinted in *Endgame*. Undoubtedly the later Eliot enjoyed Beckett's mastery and gamesmanship in negative philosophies, though, we we shall see, Beckett seems to have delivered a further salvo against Eliot in his novel *The Unnamable*.

I have suggested that Eliot's first steps along the negative way were stimulated by both personal and aesthetic considerations. These were hardly distinguishable from his involvements in philosophical issues during the years 1909–1927; therefore, personal, aesthetic, and philosophical concerns must be kept in a single focus. The point that has seldom, if ever, been made is that Eliot's embracing of the austere regimens of the Christian via negativa was possible only because he began by taking a way of even more appalling rejections. A vast tract had to be crossed before "the way upwards and downwards" came to be "one and the same" in his middle years.

Negativity is of course a consideration in any system of thought— mathematical, linguistic, or physical, to mention three. In Western philosophy, the concept of the human mind as a tabula rasa, or empty slate, underlies the main stream of thought from the pre-Socratic Parmenides onward, though negation *antecedent* to human thought has been most commonly identified with Evil, or the absence of God. Judeo-Christian and Greek thought after Socrates both posit a good Being that either creates the world out of nothingness (as in Genesis) or withdraws itself, leaving mere copies and illusions in its wake (as in Plato, the Jewish Kabbala, and Gnosticism—a belief system holding that the God of creation is evil). Though in the East the Hindu Vedas and later Buddhism posited a negation fundamental to the very act of creation, it was not until Spinoza that Western philosophers could think of ultimate Being as itself *comprehending* negation. Spinoza's intuition was developed by Leibniz and the German Idealists (whose tradition Eliot studied), but it was obscured until the early twentieth century by the shift in philosophical studies from ontology to epistemology, where to some extent negation had already been accepted as "original" in the tabula rasa theories of Aristotle, Aquinas, and John Locke.

With the diversion of attention to epistemology, accelerating since the time of Descartes and Locke, interest shifted from the emptiness before creation to the empty tablet of the mind at birth and the process of writing upon it. Jean-Jacques Rousseau's ecstatic reflections on "le néant" are directed only at the empty page, which (as Paul de Man has observed) becomes for him a kind of banquet board, inviting the imagination to fill or stock it. Thus in *La Nouvelle Héloïse* the heroine, Julie, takes Being for granted, as only parenthetically important, while she thrills to contemplate the space existing before the mind begins to think. She writes to St. Preux: "the land of illusions is the only place in this world worth living in, and the emptiness of human affairs is such that apart from Being existing by itself, there is nothing beautiful except that which is not."[7] Here the human mind wants to return as if to the moment it was created, to *imitate* God in creation, but on the plane of imagination, not of atoms and molecules.

After Rousseau, other philosophers of negation were similarly fascinated with the emptiness existent after creation, and with man's terror or longing or heroism in the face of it. Kierkegaard and Nietzsche were the most influential of these before Heidegger and Sartre, but some focused often (as Nietzsche too did in part) on a simpler, do-it-yourself individualism exemplifying "nothingness" in living circumstances, disregarding the question of existence before and after human life. Americans, in their "New World"—and preeminently Emerson—provided models for practical application of such thinking. Eliot's training as a philosopher at Harvard in the beginning of the twentieth century predisposed him both to such pragmatism and to post-Hegelian idealism, in which, as in Rousseau, Being is posited as an unrealized Absolute drawing the human mind from negation as a starting point. But being an American also gave Eliot an unusually skeptical approach to all systems, including Idealism. Like Emerson feeling the oppression of other men's systems, Eliot was disinclined to make a system of his own (as Blake, for instance, decided he must do in self-defense). It was Emersonian of Eliot to reject Emerson, of course. The idealist Emerson wanted a constant writing of new "scriptures" on the tabula rasa. He wanted a continuous news report on the findings of the "transparent eyeball," meaning human vision without medium or system. But by 1914 Eliot recognized that this too was a system,[8] blocked at an impasse, and even Irving Babbitt's recourse to a systemless but affirmative Buddhism, which Eliot as his student accepted to some extent, seemed merely therapeutic. The self without system pointed in every direction to the annihilation of self, since every particular becomes meaningless alone. Exactly here Eliot found himself situated by his dissertation on F. H. Bradley; and it was just here that he began to move resolutely toward representation of the dilemma in poetry, rather than to continue with analysis of the dilemma in philosophy.

That he chose to make "The Love Song of J. Alfred Prufrock" the starting point of his first book of poems is of some importance in this respect. It was not his first poem in order of composition. "Portrait of a Lady" (written some months before "Prufrock" in 1910) was earlier, and "Conversation Galante" came first of all among the published works. Either of these poems might have begun his volume, and indeed "Conversation Galante" would be an appropriate title. "Prufrock," however, fixes upon a voice and a theme which connect everything that came after—even beyond the first volume, as perhaps he dimly foresaw. B. Rajan has noted that the "overwhelming question" and the never perfectly effective man who asks it (in a "love song"!) are prominent no less in the last works than in the first.

Yet there is more to the primacy awarded to "Prufrock." A curious narrative unfolds if we look at the whole story told by the many voices of the text, beginning even before the poem properly appears. First the title page speaks of matters impersonally observed: *Prufrock and Other Observations*. Immediately following this, however, comes an epigraph that is anything but impersonal, one which clearly refers to these "observations" as vanities (in a citation from Dante that implicitly excludes them with a purgatorial renunciation). We then turn the page to the first poem: "The Love Song of J. Alfred Prufrock," with an epigraph of its own that degrades Prufrock still further, suggesting that his confession is the account of someone eternally damned.

More specifically, read as the start of a continuing series of confessions, the title page tells that the "Observations" are "For Jean Verdenal, 1889–1915, mort aux Dardanelles." The simple fact of a friend's death is given as it appeared in an official army report. (Verdenal, a young doctor, lived in Eliot's boarding house in Paris while Eliot was writing "Prufrock.") Then the epigraph from *Purgatorio,* XXI, given in Dante's Italian, seems to be spoken both in Dante's voice and in Eliot's. No speaker is identified (nor is the source), but one soon recognizes the lines as Dante's if one can read them at all. They appear to be spoken to Verdenal, coming right after the account of his death and the notice that what follows is "for" him: he is the only natural referent for "you." Translated, the lines read: "Now you can understand the measure of love that burns in me when I forget our vanity, treating shadow as if it were a solid thing."[9] The intertextuality toward which one is drawn in search of sense leads further. Not only does Eliot borrow Dante's voice to address Verdenal but, we are made to consider that Dante is speaking in the voice of Statius, addressing Virgil. Thus Eliot (like Statius) declares his love for one who was his guide, Verdenal (like Virgil), whose beloved shade appears deceptively "solid." Since the epigraph points to the volume that follows, "our vanity" points toward the poems that were the shared activity of Verdenal and Eliot (and also of Statius and Virgil). It is the poems, rather than the man addressed (as in Dante), whose solidity Eliot calls into doubt. By dedicating the volume "for" Jean Verdenal rather than "in memory" of him, Eliot implies that Verdenal is no more a "shade" than he is himself—cast as Eliot is here in the role of the shade Statius. A further comic element may be intended, since Statius, Virgil, and Dante in the *Commedia* are all together mounting the steps of Purgatory, and, as we shall see, many of the figures in the *Prufrock* poems are also engaged in ascending stairs.

The title page locates everyone near the high and hopeful ledges of Purgatory, and the reader turning the page is prepared to hear the "love song" (announced as the first poem), for we have just been told of "the measure of love" remembered for Verdenal. That the singer of this song should be named J. Alfred Prufrock, however, reminds us

[17]

more particularly of "our vanity"—another comic twist, especially when "Prufrock's" epigraph reverses our direction and plunges us back into Hell. Coming after the "love song's" title, and before a first-person narrative, this second epigraph from Dante appears to be spoken by Prufrock: "If I believed that my answer were given to one who would return to the world, this flame would stand without moving. But because no one ever returned alive from this depth, if I have heard the truth, I answer you without fear of infamy."[10] The fact that Prufrock's answer is all about his failure to find an answer to an unstated question will later, retrospectively, be the crowning negation of the title. The first two lines of the epigraph address a "person" who can be no beloved but only himself or the reader, drawn by the epigraph and by the first line of the poem into the streets of Hell: "Let us go then, you and I." Dante's speaker in the *Inferno*, XXVII—Guido da Montefeltro indicating the corruption of Florence—both parodies and is parodied by Prufrock, lamenting his situation in a modern city. The negative charge directed at, and drawn from, Dante's passage also attracts more recent intertextualities: the evening walk of Romantic literature and the twilight, here not peacefully recumbent like Michelangelo's "Dusk" but flat out on an operating table—dying (for the patient is "evening," which of course will not survive the coming of night).

The whole of *Prufrock* as book, like "Prufrock" the poem, thus begins and continues the pattern of a negative way—confessing failure but ventriloquizing the confession, producing an effect of understatement gained from hiding behind another poet's (Dante's) confession (in a foreign language), which is at the same time an overstatement as the contrast between the *Commedia*'s souls in torment and Eliot's timid temporizers develops from poem to poem.

As the volume proceeds, another pattern is perceptible which makes "Prufrock" still more magisterial as the master key. This is the pattern of self-sacrifice—not in the obvious religious sense of denying oneself for others but in the alternative religious sense of killing a victim in order to end a crisis. Prufrock feels himself singled out as a victim, singled out for sacrifice, but cannot keep his mind on the "matter":

> Should I, after tea and cakes and ices,
> Have the strength to force the moment to its crisis?
> But though I have wept and fasted, wept and prayed,

Though I have seen my head (grown slightly bald) brought in
   upon a platter,
I am no prophet—and here's no great matter . . .

The crisis that is the subject of the poem already exists at the opening,
when Prufrock takes us "to make our visit." Something is expected of
him, an undifferentiated imperative issuing from an undifferentiated
group that is vaguely female, and his response to the imperative is
supposed to end the crisis, even though he is branded as a failure. He
knows that his failure to fulfill the feminine imperative will turn him
either into a Hamlet—indecisive and therefore destroyed—or into
someone like John the Baptist, destroyed because he is *too* decisive in
bringing an unmistakable message. Yet it is not the martyrdom he
fears—only the inefficacy of his response. Alluding to the gospels of
John and Luke, especially the latter where Jesus says that even if the
dead were to return the people would not believe, Prufrock asks:
"Would it have been worth while"

To say: "I am Lazarus, come from the dead,
Come back to tell you all, I shall tell you all"—
If one, settling a pillow by her head,
   Should say: "That is not what I meant at all.
   That is not it, at all."

. . . . .

No! I am not Prince Hamlet, nor was meant to be;
Am an attendant lord, one that will do

but "will do" so little that the poem itself reads as his only expiatory
act. Its last words lead to total self-effacement. The "crisis" is ended
when Prufrock resorts to the seashore and mythical dreams to escape
his treacherous society.

I shall wear white flannel trousers, and walk upon the beach.
I have heard the mermaids singing, each to each.

I do not think that they will sing to me.

Without saying how he makes the transition from standing on the
beach watching the mermaids, in the last strophe he attains the refuge
of total immersion in dream that is the "singer's" perfect self-immola-

tion. And as in a ritual sacrifice, he takes "us" and our communal wrongs with him:

> We have lingered in the chambers of the sea
> By sea-girls wreathed with seaweed red and brown
> Till human voices wake us, and we drown.

The poem published next to "Prufrock" enacts the same scene: the diffident man confronted with a social crisis—expressed in terms of a nameless woman's unstated demands upon him—whose failure to solve the problem leads to an act of self-nullification. "Portrait of a Lady" is trimmer, allowing for less slippage in reading, though its imaginative range is narrower than that of "Prufrock." Again the confessional voice (here unnamed) admits defeat when confronted with the "lady's" reliance on him for heroic action. She says,

> "You are invulnerable, you have no Achilles' heel.
> You will go on, and when you have prevailed
> You can say: at this point many a one has failed.
> But what have I, but what have I, my friend,
> To give you, what can you receive from me?
> Only the friendship and the sympathy
> Of one about to reach her journey's end.
>
> I shall sit here, serving tea to friends . . ."

And the narrator tells us:

> I take my hat: how can I make a cowardly amends
> For what she has said to me?

The speaker's sense of guilt is vastly out of proportion to the harm he is capable of doing, and this is the point. The vaguely sensed crisis he faces is so undifferentiated that he dimly identifies his own part in it with murder. Being beyond the circle of desire and passion which have brought on the crisis, he can only dimly distinguish its pattern by way of newspaper stories he stumbles on amid the sports pages and comics:

> You will see me any morning in the park
> Reading the comics and the sporting page.
> Particularly I remark

An English countess goes upon the stage.
A Greek was murdered at a Polish dance,
Another bank defaulter has confessed.
I keep my countenance,
I remain self-possessed
Except when a street-piano, mechanical and tired
Reiterates some worn-out common song
With the smell of hyacinths across the garden
Recalling things that other people have desired.

The lady on his conscience is a counterpart for the "English countess," frustrated into sensational conduct. He "particularly" remarks acts of vengeance (like the Polish murder of a Greek) and of confession (like the bank defaulter's) which offer counterparts to his own intensifying resentment and guilt as he encourages overtures that he despises in the lady. Only the waking of emotion by stimuli equal to his own inane feelings, such as the "mechanical and tired" street piano and the hyacinth smell, can stir the sap in him. But these undo him by drawing him into the vicious circle of other people's desires, so that he persists—from December to April to August—mounting "the stairs" of the lady's flat. It is an ascent that is no ascent at all but a continual evasion. Though the lady admires him because he has "no Achilles' heel," he submits to her maneuvers, tending toward the kill: a death that will finish them both as the only possible conclusion to this endgame.

Well! and what if she should die some afternoon,
Afternoon grey and smoky, evening yellow and rose;
Should die and leave me sitting pen in hand

  .   .   .   .   .

Would she not have the advantage, after all?

The crisis, thus unresolved, directs him away from her death to foretelling his own as the poem ends. The music mentioned in the last three lines "is successful with a 'dying fall'" presumably because it is his own death knell, echoing Prufrock's. The quotation marks evidently point not to Shakespeare's lovesick Orsino but back to "Prufrock," where the voices of others that finally occasioned his drowning were heard first mingled with music:

> I know the voices dying with a dying fall
> Beneath the music from a farther room.
>   So how should I presume?

The music mentioned repeatedly in "Portrait of a Lady" also mingles with the voices but then merges with the anxiously confessional voice ("Inside my brain a dull tom-tom begins / Absurdly hammering a prelude of its own, / Capricious monotone / That is at least one definite 'false note' "—"Among the windings of the violins.") So the "dying fall" is a reprise, and its success can only mean that the confession has accomplished its purpose, readying the speaker not for the lady's death but for his own. The smile that has marked his self-possession throughout the poem is of questionable propriety on the face of the victim, and so the poem ends:

> This music is successful with a "dying fall"
> Now that we talk of dying—
> And should I have the right to smile?

After the peculiarly negative journeys of "Prufrock" and "Portrait of a Lady," nine poems follow that bring us back to the volume's title and its focus on "observations." A genre popular among empirically minded essayists of the nineteenth and twentieth centuries, "observations" call attention both to things the essayist has seen in the physical world and to his reactions by way of feeling and thought. What unifies the random poems that come under Eliot's title is, appropriately, first a sequence of four scenes visited by the Prufrockian observer, and then four portraits of women and men encountered, the ninth poem (eleventh in the volume) presenting a "Conversation Galante" that begins, "I observe." Read as observations made on what I calling Eliot's negative way, this sequence begins with "Pre-"—an itinerary through a repellent city landscape, whose title ts a musical antithesis to the offensive sensory images based on ouch, taste, and sight. We are led through and out of the the title's nexus with (as "prelude" to) another musical title t poem, "Rhapsody on a Windy Night"—the title again

]

negated by the sordid impressions of the itinerant observer. A time sequence, beginning on a winter evening in "Preludes," also leads us from 6 P.M. to dawn after a night of "sordid" dreams (in "Preludes") and then in the "Rhapsody" to further waking reflections on the remembered night walk ("I could see nothing behind that child's eye. / I have seen eyes in the street / Trying to peer through lighted shutters"), which end like "Prufrock" and the "Portrait" in an imagined death of the observer-victim: " 'sleep, prepare for life.' / The last twist of the knife." The next poem, "Morning at the Window," brings the observer to life again, but only such life as one feels who is imprisoned upstairs, out of reach of humanity below:

> The brown waves of fog toss up to me
> Twisted faces from the bottom of the street,
> And tear from a passer-by with muddy skirts
> An aimless smile that hovers in the air
> And vanishes along the level of the roofs.

This upstairs-downstairs image is a marker[11] in five of the twelve poems, always marking (as in "Prufrock" and "Portrait") a futile effort at communication. Here the observer sees a lady below whose smile annihilates him (it is "aimless" though directed at him) and then suggests that the smiler too (like Carroll's Cheshire cat) is annihilated, as the smile "vanishes along the level of the roofs."

The portrait sequence is introduced by "The *Boston Evening Transcript*," a poem which also ends the itinerary sequence, since it takes the "observer" to the door of his Cousin Harriet, characterized only by the observer's remark that arriving at her house effects a change in him tantamount to another self-annihilation, or at least a self-induced transformation. Again it is signaled by the climbing of the stair:

> I mount the steps and ring the bell, turning
> Wearily, as one would turn to nod good-bye to La
>   Rochefoucauld,
> If the street were time and he at the end of the street,
> And I say, "Cousin Harriet, here is the *Boston Evening
>   Transcript*."

(The imagined turning on the stair is another marker—suggesting "visions and revisions"—for we find it in "Prufrock" and "Ash-

Wednesday" in equally characteristic moments. Prufrock says "there will be time / . . . / Time to turn back and descend the stair," and the poet of "Ash-Wednesday" speaks of "turning" on three stairs, although he does "not hope to turn again.") Here the lady's imperatives, thematic in "Prufrock" and the "Portrait," make her visitor abandon his spirit companion La Rochefoucauld, in another act of comic self-dispossession, accomplished on another mock Dantean ascent as the "observer" forgoes the company of one he cannot admit to the ennervating earthly paradise—beyond time—of Cousin Harriet.[12]

The portrait poems—"Aunt Helen," "Cousin Nancy," "Mr. Apollinax," and "Hysteria"—all focus on acts of dispossession or destruction, mostly on the part of the observer himself—destroying images of proper Bostonians (if "Cousin Harriet" is a key to their company). These iconoclastic "speech acts" thus have the force of negations turned against others, instead of against the observer himself as in the earlier poems. "Aunt Helen" performs, or observes, the parodic ritual burial of "my maiden aunt":

> Now when she died there was silence in heaven
> And silence at her end of the street.
> The shutters were drawn and the undertaker wiped his feet—
>
> . . . . .
>
> And the footman sat upon the dining-table
> Holding the second housemaid on his knees—
> Who had always been so careful while her mistress lived.

"Cousin Nancy" seems to be herself a New England iconoclast. She

> Strode across the hills and broke them,
> Rode across the hills and broke them—
> The barren New England hills—

To her aunt's perplexity, she smoked and "danced all the modern dances." More vigilant than the aunts, however,

> Upon the glazen shelves kept watch
> Matthew and Waldo, guardians of the faith,
> The army of unalterable law.

The observer's humor situates him, through an intertextual reference to George Meredith's sonnet "Lucifer in Starlight," beyond the universe of both the shenanigans of Cousin Nancy and the guardians of New England morality, Matthew Arnold and Emerson. Just as in Meredith's poem the implied poet moves into the position of God, watching Satan humbled before the stars ("the army of unalterable law"), so the implied poet here observes the humbling of Cousin Nancy. Unlike Meredith, however, he also humbles the guardians of the law.

"Mr. Apollinax"—a dubious compliment to Bertrand Russell and his shattering descent into the academic complacency of the Harvard community in 1914—is again iconoclastic both to the "gods" of New England and to the God who put them to flight:

> In the palace of Mrs. Phlaccus, at Professor Channing-Cheetah's
> He laughed like an irresponsible foetus.
> His laughter was submarine and profound
> Like the old man of the sea's
> Hidden under coral islands
> Where worried bodies of drowned men drift down in the green
> silence,
> Dropping from fingers of surf.
>
> I looked for the head of Mr. Apollinax rolling under a chair

The Proteus who can undergo decapitation and revive, and hide beneath the sea where (in "Prufrock") "human voices wake us, and we drown," would be indestructible but for the negative way of the observing poet's deft and all-encompassing put-downs. Not only the overthrow of idols (the theme of the sequence of portraits) but the imagery connects this poem with others in the volume: the surface of tea party vanities, adrift on a devouring sea, and the automatic laughter (or perfunctory smiles):

> Would it have been worth while,
> To have bitten off the matter with a smile[?]
>
> ("Prufrock")

> I feel like one who smiles, and turning shall remark
> Suddenly, his expression in a glass.
>
> ("Portrait")

[25]

> Wipe your hand across your mouth, and laugh;
> The worlds revolve like ancient women
> Gathering fuel in vacant lots.
>
> ("Preludes")

There are many such images to call in question the laughter of Mr. Apollinax, most effective of all being the laughter which is the very subject of the "observation" immediately succeeding "Mr. Apollinax"—"Hysteria": "As she laughed I was aware of becoming involved in her laughter and being part of it, until her teeth were only accidental stars with a talent for squad-drill." Here is another tea party and another shattered social event, immediately followed (in the second-to-last poem of the volume) by a full treatment of levity as the social glue that will not stick. "Conversation Galante" takes a passing swipe at the image of chamber music which satirically connects the violent visions of the volume, but then focuses on laughter as the greater target:

> And I then: "Someone frames upon the keys
> That exquisite nocturne, with which we explain
> The night and moonshine; music which we seize
> To body forth our own vacuity."
> She then: "Does this refer to me?"
> "Oh no, it is I who am inane."
>
> "You, madam, are the eternal humorist,
> The eternal enemy of the absolute,
> Giving our vagrant moods the slightest twist!

Put down by this piece of levity, the lady ends the poem by falling into the "observer's" trap: "Are we then so serious?"

The unity existing in (and between and among) the twelve poems of the *Prufrock* volume, all stages on an observer's negative way, is nowhere more apparent than in the observer's final self-revelation in the last poem—"La Figlia Che Piange"—another interior flight from an encounter with a lady. "La Figlia" recalls "Prufrock" first in beginning as a "love song," addressed to a histrionic woman by a man who is deserting her. As it closes, it is again like "Prufrock" in silencing—this time finally—all human voices including its own.

In the first strophe we seem finally to have arrived at the love song we never heard in "Prufrock." The observer has given up his voyeuristic position for one of direct and passional communication with the "lady." Though he is leaving her for the last time, her resentful gestures appeal to him and he begs her in parting to "weave, weave the sunlight in your hair." To our amazement, then, the next strophe shifts back to voyeurism and to monologue. The man is *imagining* the whole incident: "So I would have had him leave," and the sadistic motives behind the scene emerge: "So he would have left / . . . / As the mind deserts the body it has used." Then with a shift of pronouns in mid-strophe (from "him" and "her" to "we"), the monologuist shifts again. He tentatively offers the scene, as a way of parting, to a woman he knows. The scene painted is a mental rehearsal for an actual desertion he is contemplating. Now we perceive the scene as anteced- ent to the opening: "I should find/ Some way incomparably light and deft" to desert the woman effectively. The underlying theme or matrix of the poem comes out as "effective desertion," with the word "effec- tive" (implied rather than stated) meaning both efficient and aestheti- cally right. In the third and last strophe, then, the pronouns shift dis- turbingly again—from "you" and "we" back again to "she" and "I."

> She turned away, but with the autumn weather
> Compelled my imagination many days . . .

Now again he resorts to fantasy, but this time it is after the parting has been accomplished *in fact* ("She turned away"). His fancy now re- verses its direction. It is not how he would have had her look and how he would have wanted to desert her but how they might have been together if he had not let her go. She simply turns and goes. It is he who is left with the "pained surprise":

> I wonder how they should have been together!
> I should have lost a gesture and a pose.
> Sometimes these cogitations still amaze
> The troubled midnight and the noon's repose.

So the poem ends, leaving it uncertain whether he has deserted the woman or she has deserted him. The one definite fact given is that "she turned away," leaving the Prufrockian figure spinning the wheels of thought. All his worry about the "gesture and a pose" merely em- phasizes the ridiculous vacillations of a monologuist who cannot make a decision even in imagination. The lady has clearly turned away in boredom, and the purely imagined opening "love song" was the nearest he could come to effecting a real attachment. Furthermore the poet, like Pygmalion, is fantasizing upon a statue (as Helen Gardner and Kristian Smidt have noted). But in the end he *refuses* life instead of summoning it forth.

Those, like Mario Praz,[13] who read the poem as imitating a Pre-Raphaelite love song appear to miss the point that it is the antithesis of a love song. It is the volume's final variation in the negative mode. The lover is only nostalgic for a literary pose, and this nostalgia breeds anguish in him not because it is literary rather than real but because his fantasy has forced him to take a stand. When he is forced to the stand of losing the woman, he reverses it: "I wonder how they should have been together!" So the "cogitations" that "amaze" his midnight sleep and noonday naps are *not* (as we supposed at first) his indecisions relative to a woman, but his inability to find any pose or footing of any kind in the flux of his interior mind.

As the last poem in the *Prufrock* volume, "La Figlia Che Piange" perfectly sums up the theme of the anesthetized aesthete's plight. The epigraphs from Dante foretold at the beginning of the volume that the "observer's" dilemma would be to live where solid things evaporate, and to perceive this only in a mirror darkly—the mirror of literature—as Hell. Each poem moves toward a condition of vacuity, the common denominator of them all. The "way" is down, though nearly half the poems enact the mounting of stairs, toward a brilliantly dramatized nothing. We seem very near *The Waste Land*, but Eliot had another book of poems and another passageway to explore on his via negativa before that further descent.

2 "I Pray You Remember My Anguish": *Poems* of 1920

The volume of poems that followed *Prufrock* three years later also followed the First World War. Its poems adverted plainly to the period's armed belligerencies, to the postwar dislocations of personal and public life, and to another struggle—an intensifying moral anguish of Eliot's own which broke loose in the poems, making Prufrock's perplexities appear lighthearted, or like those merely "bewildering minutes" which Eliot later compared with "moments of moral and spiritual struggle": "It is in fact in moments of moral and spiritual struggle depending upon spiritual sanctions, rather than in those 'bewildering minutes' in which we are all very much alike, that men and women come nearest to being real."[1] Many of Eliot's best readers, like Elisabeth Schneider, find the people in *Prufrock* much more real, engaged in more important struggles, and the poems correspondingly better. Yet is this not perhaps because Prufrock and the others are in their "bewildering minutes" so much like what we think ourselves superficially to be, and what we certainly imagine Eliot, on the surface, to have been? The figures in the *Poems* of 1920, by contrast, are most real in being grotesques, with and against whom we struggle at a very deep level: the played out Gerontion, Burbank the tourist and his more potent fellow travelers, Bleistein, Sweeney, Pipit, the flea-bitten honeymooners, Grishkin, and "Mr. Eliot" himself, who for the first time shows his own face unmasked at a "Sunday Morning Service." Schneider notes that Eliot reveals in these poems a ferocious arrogance and contempt for humanity, as compared with the *Prufrock* poems: "a harsh tone prevails, one that repels as the tone of no others of his poems do before or after. Whatever the poet approaches seems to revolt him, not the sordid and false in modern civilization only but the human race itself: the reader finds himself repelled by humanity along with the poet, but also quite separately repelled by the spirit in which the poet writes." She notes a bit later that Eliot's words about Sacheverell Sitwell in 1916—that a poet may achieve "a distinguished aridity . . . in the inevitable dry times" of his life—applied as much, if not more, to Eliot in those years.[2]

The title he gave to the volume's British edition, *Ara Vos Prec* [Now I Beg You], intimated strongly that the writer did not stand aloof in arrogance but associated himself with the grotesques in his poems. In this volume he set out again, as in *Prufrock*, with a passage from Dante as a lens through which to view his world. But this time Eliot's citation (to which the title alone directs us) calls attention to the *suffering* ahead for us: "I pray you now by the Goodness which guides you to the summit of the stair, be mindful of my anguish in due time."[3] Poet and reader here would identify with Dante's interlocutor, the poet Arnaut Daniel (being cleansed by fire for his sexual—or bisexual—vices), even though the "stair" to which Eliot points in the volume ahead can only be the "waterstair" up which the voluptuous, vulpine Princess Volupine entices Sir Ferdinand Klein. The American edition's more neutral title—retained for *The Complete Poems*—withdraws the Dante quotation (with its reference to a sick and suffering poet). By then Eliot was on the verge of finishing his first long poem, and the "Ara vos prec" passage was to hold a still more privileged place—in the conclusion of *The Waste Land*. In both editions of 1920, at any rate, the leading poem, "Gerontion," determines our view of the whole volume, much as Tiresias was to provide a voice (as Eliot intended) for the whole of *The Waste Land*. It is Gerontion's attitude toward postwar Europe that governs both the new poems of 1920 and the superadded (or republished) *Prufrock* poems which end the volume. Reading the latter in their new context, one would view the

American scene they represent as all the more bemused, provincial, insubstantial, and isolated—as America itself must have appeared at the time to young exiles in revolt like Eliot and Ezra Pound.

The twelve new poems of the American edition were forged to technical perfection under the eye of Pound, as his marginalia in the manuscript poems suggest. Indeed this volume, as much as *The Waste Land,* might have been dedicated to this Arnaut Daniel, "the better craftsman" in Dante's *Purgatorio,* XXVI, whom Eliot identified with Pound in 1922. Pound must have encouraged, too, Eliot's ruthless airing in the new poems of animosities against religious, philosophical, and sexual habits. Readers too seldom remember that his racial slurs in the volume are only a fraction of the violent assaults on humanity's *idées reçues* and mores in this period.

No one can miss the shaping structure of negations in the volume. Here everything that Paul Ricoeur says concerning Freud's theory of negation and its relevance to poetry seems to apply. Freud had said that poetic symbols of negation allow thinking to free itself "from the restrictions of repression." Such symbols allow thinking to enrich itself "with material that is indispensable for its proper functioning." One does not need Freud to know that such symbols belong "to the instinct of destruction," but in view of Eliot's extraordinary (and anti-Freudian) views throughout his life on the pernicious effects of "desire," it is interesting to recall Freud's words: "The general wish to negate . . . is probably to be regarded as a sign of defusion of instincts that has taken place through a withdrawal of the libidinal components." Eliot's continuing interest in Buddhism (as we shall see) had predisposed him from his student years to an anti-Freudian position in this regard. Ricoeur adds to these comments of Freud his own view of poetic symbols: "To play with absence is already to dominate it and to engage in active behavior toward the lost object as lost. Hence . . . do we not discover another aspect of the death instinct, a nonpathological aspect, which would consist in one's mastery over the negative, over absence and loss? And is not this negativity implied in every appeal to symbols and to play?"[4]

In the 1920 poems, Eliot appears to do just this—to "play with absence" and to move thus toward mastery over it. He spoke in these years and later of poetry as a confrontation of the faceless and nameless, or deprecatingly of "the relief of a personal . . . grouse against life."[5] In 1953 he wrote that the poet "is oppressed by a burden he must bring to birth in order to obtain relief. Or, to change the figure of speech, he is haunted by a demon, a demon against which he feels powerless, because in its first manifestation it has no face, no name, nothing; and the words, the poem he makes, are a kind of form of exorcism of this demon."[6] Earlier, on Shrove Tuesday 1928, he had written to Paul Elmer More, contrasting himself to most people "who are unconscious of any void" and saying that for him the void existed "in the middle of all human happiness and all human relations."[7]

Gerontion, whose voice Eliot would have made the first in *The Waste Land* if Pound had not performed surgical service, speaks authoritatively of the void. He ruminates disconnectedly on his deficiencies, sensory and mental, as he counts through a litany of losses and failures, inspired by what a boy is reading (just such a boy as Beckett would find for other self-paralyzing thinkers). Gerontion's negatives construct a grid for these thoughts:

> I was neither at the hot gates
> Nor fought in the warm rain
> Nor knee deep in the salt marsh . . .
>
> .   .   .   .   .
>
> I have no ghosts,
>
> .   .   .   .   .
>
> Neither fear nor courage saves us.
>
> .   .   .   .   .
>
> We have not reached conclusion . . .
>
> .   .   .   .   .
>
> I have not made this show purposelessly
> And it is not by any concitation
> Of the backward devils.

The redundancy of negatives, once so amusing to Dickens, here threatens to lose the reader (especially in the last lines quoted), but they achieve their rhythmical and semantic effects finally because redundancy is just the point. Against these echoing negations run four series of positive insistences: "Think now . . . Think now . . . Think . . . Think at last . . . Think at last." And "[History guides] . . . gives . . . gives . . . giving . . . Gives . . . Gives." And "I have lost . . . I have lost." Finally comes a series of four questions, all expecting a negative answer: "After such knowledge, what forgiveness?" None. "Why should I need to keep [my passion] / Since what is kept must be adulterated?" You should not. "How should I use [my senses] for your closer contact?" You cannot. "What will the spider do, / Suspend its operations, will the weevil / Delay?" No.

By these linguistic reiterations, the presence of absence (as Heidegger would say) is poetically established. The poem's "plot" comes through the crooning of a one-man chorus. Singing of his pathetic, or absurd, loss of any chance to come "near your heart," Gerontion tells of propagated fear and terror, attenuated by "small deliberations" into a "chilled delirium." The poem focuses on the loss of the feeling of loss and presents all its dramatis personae in such a way as to account for it.

Gerontion molders in a decaying boardinghouse, like one of Faulkner's, against a windswept hill. The house reminds us of Prufrock's "one night cheap hotels" or the room looking out on smoky rooftops in "Portrait of a Lady" or the "furnished rooms" of "Preludes" or "the numbered door" of "Rhapsody on a Windy Night." But a note never struck in *Prufrock* becomes a dominant chord here. This decrepit figure is worse than an older Prufrock, for the land before him and the history behind him have nothing amusing about them. There is no gentle self-irony here. The rain that will follow the "dry season" will fall only on stonecrop, and as in *The Waste Land*, the trouble is so far back in history that there is no place to look for help. In fact the Savior toward whom the world looked is seen in this poem as the chief destroyer.

From his draughty windows Gerontion looks up a barren hill: once again the eye ascends in order to descend into an abyss, reversing the motion of Dante and the Christian saints who followed St. Augustine's "Descend that ye may ascend." Gerontion's *mind* wanders backward, however, not upward—as far back as 480 B.C. and the battle of Thermopylae (which translates as "hot gates"), then forward through a series of wars that Gerontion feels would have compensated him if he had been there to fight. He thinks of history as a system of corridors ingeniously contrived to confuse and finally to corrupt the human race. History is a "she"—like his old housekeeper, poking a clogged drain; also like Fräulein von Kulp (for *culpa?*) who turned seductively in the hallway; or the mystical Madame de Tornquist (a tourniquet, or screw for stopping blood?). Like these women, history leads nowhere but to corruption. She "gives too late or too soon," like a frustrating woman, and she leaves her lover not only ill-at-ease but frightened. Heroic efforts to satisfy the unclear demands of history have led to nothing but cruelty and hate. And into this history "Came Christ the tiger."

Gerontion thinks of the coming of Christ in two ways, first as a useless infant and then as a hunted tiger. This part of the poem is usually misread because no one notes that Eliot pointedly left the phrase borrowed from Lancelot Andrewes with "the Word" uncapitalized. Thus in "Gerontion" we read only of "The word within a word, unable to speak a word." Eliot knew what he was about when he restored the capital in "A Song for Simeon" and "Ash-Wednesday" (1930): "The Word within [the biblical] word, unable to speak a word." As Gerontion reflects, the answer to the Philistines' cry for a "sign" was *disappointingly* a speechless child, who passed from winter darkness and swaddling clothes into a "depraved" spring, when he was transformed into a ravening tiger—a sacrificial beast which in contemporary life is hunted and *eaten* by bloodless transients like the boarders Silvero, Hakagawa, Fräulein von Kulp, and Madame de Tornquist. "The tiger springs in the new year" makes "springs" a syllepsis, or pun, meaning both "arises like a rejuvenating spring" and "pounces like a murderous animal."[8] In John 6:52–58, Jesus says that those who take his body and blood to become one with him in communion will live eternally, while those who reject him will die. Gerontion concludes that this death-dealing doctrine came to devour those who do not devour "the tiger," as do Gerontion's fellow boarders. To them the ritual meal is no "communion" but a cannibal "dividing." "After such knowledge," indeed, "what forgiveness?"

Knowledge here includes the decay of Christianity into hyprocrisy, the decay of Judaism into exploitativeness (like his landlord's), and the decay of European art in museums, like the one here through which the Japanese Hakagawa comes bowing after the war. "Vacant shuttles weave the wind" that blows through the corridors of history, no yarn being left in the shuttles to continue any pattern, much less to begin a new one. Whether the corridors are in history, or in the museums of Venice, in Gerontion's boarding house, or in the winding pathways of his brain, there is nothing to resist the wind that blows destructively through time, though not "before and after time" as later in "Burnt Norton," II. Here there is nothing beyond the vortex that "whirls" beyond the stars, to vanish in "fractured atoms," leaving (below on earth) white feathers in white snow.

As the initial poem of the 1920 volumes, "Gerontion" signals not only the negative way Eliot himself was following at the time but also what Harold Bloom calls "the secret path from one poem to another." It leads toward the eleven poems that follow as insistently as "Prufrock" led into the poems of 1917, but now Eliot is preoccupied with "the way" as baffled *itinerary* in history, as a poetic *method* to express total inanition of thought and feeling, and as the *way-lessness* of European and American energies. He is no longer wondering "how should I presume," as in the beginning of *Prufrock,* or worrying about his "gesture and a pose," as at the end. The ending of "Gerontion" accommodates itself to the extravagant metaphysics of four other poems in the volume—"A Cooking Egg," "The Hippopotamus," "Whispers of Immortality," and "Mr. Eliot's Sunday Morning Service"—where pathway, method, and ultimate "way" are lampooned until again (as in "Gerontion") they are recognizable only by their absence.

The poem immediately following "Gerontion" connects with his boarding house somewhere in Europe rather than with his apocalyptic vision, however. "Burbank with a Baedeker: Bleistein with a Cigar" takes us to Venice by way of an epigraph made up, indeed, of "fractured atoms" in the form of a literary splattering from Gautier, Mantegna, Henry James, Shakespeare, Browning, and John Marston (as Grover Smith points out), preparing us for the jostle of ill-assorted visitors to Venice we meet in the poem. Here the house is a "small hotel" where Burbank woefully fails to entertain Princess Volupine (though he falls, he cannot rise). "Defunctive music" reminds us again of the "dying fall" heard in "Prufrock" and "The Portrait"; here it is heard undersea as Burbank plays out his strength. Now we follow an actual itinerary, not a mental one, as Princess Volupine leaves Burbank to cruise through Venice in her "shuttered barge," picking up

Bleistein ("Chicago Semite Viennese") along the way. "Bleistein's way" is her way, we learn, but she leaves him for a tryst with "Sir Ferdinand / Klein" at the summit of a "waterstair" we cannot help connecting with the many sordid or substanceless stairs in the *Prufrock* volume. The strength lost by the Anglo Burbank has been inherited by "the jew" who is "underneath the lot" like Webster's rats, but here of course meaning underneath Europe's real estate. Burbank's Bank of England once backed "the lot" now controlled by Sir Ferdinand. Conscious of his own lost potency (for he would be beneath the lot if he could), Burbank reflects self-consolingly on the "smoky candle end of time" declining in Venice. Its emblem is the Lion of San Marcos:

> Who clipped the lion's wings
> And flea'd his rump and pared his claws?
> Thought Burbank, meditating on
> Time's ruins, and the seven laws.

Ruskin's laws in *The Seven Lamps of Architecture* are as profound as Burbank's idea of laws can be, and it is Ruskin who has brought him, presumably, to Venice. The three tourists and the "phthisic" Italian princess are, thus, all pursuing four different negative ways, which come in the end to pretty much the same thing.

The prostitute's house in the next poem, "Sweeney Erect," introduces once more the theme of inmates in the house of Europe, if we read it in the volume's context. The poem's own mock-heroic similes, comparing Sweeney and his woman to Theseus and Ariadne, support such a context, though Sweeney (Eliot later said) was based on a Boston pugilist he admired, and though he is compared to Emerson's ideal man:

> (The lengthened shadow of a man
>   Is history, said Emerson
> Who had not seen the silhouette
>   Of Sweeney straddled in the sun.)

If I am right in reading the *Poems* of 1920 as having an integral order, then Sweeney appears here—and in the last poem of the new group— as a returning American soldier making himself comfortable in the European houses where he is most at home. In *Ara Vos Prec* the two Sweeney poems appear together at this point, but in the American and later editions of the poems, "Sweeney Among the Nightingales" is placed last, the American hero thus providing a transition back to the American scene following in the *Prufrock* poems, suggesting perhaps what other Americans will return to after the war. When the latter poems come first, as in *The Complete Poems,* the second Sweeney poem gives a strikingly elegiac ending to the 1920 volume's meditations on Europe. In the last lines, we are made to suspect that the naive Sweeney will be murdered by order of the "host" in collusion with the residents of the brothel. This house is then suddenly juxtaposed with a convent next door, and the nightingales heard are both the sentimentally admired birds of ancient poetry and the nuns (coarsely called "nightingales," an old term for prostitutes). Finally, in a stunning shift, the last quatrain focuses on another credulous strong man coming back from a war to his death, not Sweeney but Agamemnon. The closure lends dignity—and tragic dimension—to all the volume's distasteful scenes, impressing Eliot himself that with Sweeney he had produced two "intensely serious" poems, "among the best I have ever done," as he wrote to his brother right away.[9] The volume that began with "Gerontion" thus ends:

> The host with someone indistinct
> Converses at the door apart,
> The nightingales are singing near
> The Convent of the Sacred Heart,
>
> And sang within the bloody wood
> When Agamemnon cried aloud
> And let their liquid siftings fall
> To stain the stiff dishonoured shroud.

The last line of "Sweeney Among the Nightingales" thus circles back to the epigraph—Agamemnon's cry in Aeschylus, "Alas, I am stricken by a mortal wound from within!" And "from within" refers both to the house (Agamemnon's own household or Sweeney's bordello) and to the heart wound (more cruel than any blow), felt by the Greek in contrast to Sweeney, who will never feel anything, presumably, "from within."

Following the "secret path" that connects the poems of 1920, one finds that this last epigraph—about death—also points back to the first epigraph, "Gerontion's" from *Measure for Measure:*

Thou hast nor youth nor age
But as it were an after dinner sleep
Dreaming of both. *{sic}*

The epigraph is usually misread as if it were addressed to Shakespeare's Claudio and therefore to Eliot's Gerontion. In fact it is addressed (by Shakespeare's Vincentio) to *life,* and it appears that Vincentio's view at this point very closely parallels Gerontion's. Vincentio is telling the imprisoned Claudio to be "absolute for death," since life "exists on many a thousand grains / That issue out of dust." When *life* is old and rich, he goes on, it "has neither heat, affection, limb nor beauty" to make its riches pleasant (Act 3, Scene 1). Gerontion's own mono- logue exactly expresses this *tedium vitae,* illustrating the transference of a death wish into the poetic symbols described by Freud and Ricoeur. I have noted the grid of negative signs on which "Gerontion" is con- structed. These contrast absolutely with the concluding Sweeney poem, where not a single negative appears, suggesting that Sweeney (though no Agamemnon) was "absolute" for life before his untimely death. In "Sweeney Erect," too, the only negatives are associated with Sweeney's antagonists—Emerson ("Who had not seen the silhouette / Of Sweeney straddled in the sun") and Mrs. Turner with her "ladies," who "find themselves involved, disgraced" and "deprecate the lack of taste" in the razor-wielding ape and his hysterical compan- ion. This is life in the 1920 poems, and the rest of the volume con- tinues the contrast thus erected between the mindless but vital Sweeney and the mind-ridden but deadened Gerontion. The new poems also present a continuing contrast between youth and age, both equally deprived though in different ways, so that both together express life "as it were an after dinner sleep"—drugged, effete, inane. After the first Sweeney poem (where the epigraph and first lines, taken together, suggest that Sweeney has turned his back on a "desolation," to find his retreat with a latter-day Ariadne), the 1920 *Poems* present a series of portraits contrasting youth and age.

First we meet the wearisome Pipit in "A Cooking Egg." Grover Smith reminds us that a cooking egg is one no longer fresh enough to be eaten raw or singly—good only when combined in cooking. Pipit is such an egg. Time has run down in her presence, as in Gerontion's, though it is only her companion who is aware of it. Whether he is her former lover or just a childhood friend isn't clear, but the epigraph from Villon's "Le Testament" suggests that in the thirtieth year of his life (as Eliot was in 1918) he has "drunk up all his shame," and, regretting his own wasted youth, he sits in the crumbled world of Pipit's parlor, looking at her keepsakes: *Views of the Oxford Colleges,* ancestral silhouettes, and an old dance invitation. He reflects that he will not need Pipit in his heaven, for he has other saints (also relics of the postwar world, like the outmoded heroes of the classics, Sir Philip Sidney and Coriolanus, like the financial wizard Sir Alfred Mond, and the theosophist Madame Blavatsky) to compensate him for losing Pipit along with the rest of "the penny world" he remembers buying and sharing with her "behind the screen."

A new dimension—otherworldly—enters Eliot's world for the first time in four stanzas midway through the poem repeating variations on "I shall not want . . . in Heaven." These are set off in ellipses, as if the speaker's mind had flown for relief to some absurd height. Again the "ascent" is a "descent," however, for the poem reaches a new low in this shift of consciousness. The shift is remarkable for its scornful treatment of a compensatory heaven, and Dante's share in the invention of it comes in as its final note:

> I shall not want Pipit in Heaven:
>   Madame Blavatsky will instruct me
> In the Seven Sacred Trances
>   Piccarda de Donati will conduct me.

In the Berg manuscript after this last line, Eliot added a gross slur on the Eucharist, which will be worth considering in the light of the blasphemous elements that loom large in the volume. Here I need only add that Pipit's two worlds of paralyzed adulthood and dreamy childhood are separated by a burlesque flight to Heaven, echoing the Twenty-Third Psalm in four stanzas ("I shall not want . . .") and suggesting that at least *there* one will not want any such "life" as Pipit offers. Meanwhile outside, as the poem ends, await the "red-eyed scavengers" and cheap restaurant meals to which the speaker must descend in leaving Pipit.

Another poem contrasting youth and age, along with two more views of unlivable life, follows. "Le Directeur" is the first of four French poems in the volume, the foreign tongue diverting us perhaps from its focus on the director of *The Spectator* and his politics. The "reactionary" commercial agents of *The Spectator* go touring arm-in-arm past a small girl, Tamise, pug-nosed and in rags. Here is another "tour" with landscape, recalling the recurring motifs in the *Prufrock* volume, others in this volume (like "Burbank with a Baedeker" and the two French poems that follow), and the far more interesting per- ambulations in the landscapes of *The Waste Land* and *Four Quartets.* "Le Directeur" is otherwise simply a comic exercise in repeating rhymes. In the English edition it was titled "Le Spectateur," calling attention to the doubling of the little girl as spectator and the director of the "conservator" periodical whom she encounters:

Une petite fille
En guenilles
Camarde
Regarde
Le directeur
Du Spectateur
Conservateur
Et crève d'amour.

The child thus returns love for nothing on another negative way.

I have said that Eliot begins to speak in his own voice in this vol- ume in ways unprecedented in *Prufrock,* and surely we may read the next French poem, "Mélange Adultère de Tout," as an amusing self- portrait, or anyway as a sort of music-hall burlesque of Eliot's own qualities. This "adulterated mixture of everything" is a prototype of Saul Bellow's Henderson. He is a professor in America, a journalist in England, a lecturer in Yorkshire, and "a bit of a banker" in London. He has his hair done absurdly in Paris, stops in Germany for stirring philosophical debates, wanders East and West, and ends his song glancing at his birth and death: "I celebrate my birthday in an African oasis, dressed in the skin of a giraffe. My cenotaph will be exhibited on the burning shores of Mozambique."

After this vagabond's portrait comes another French poem, one that lets down the barriers of disgust for the rest of the volume. In "Lune de Miel" two nameless honeymooners begin another "ascent" which is a fall. They have seen the Low Countries, and now they return to the "high land" of Italy, arriving in Ravenna by night to take their ease "between two sheets, among two hundred bedbugs." This drama for "four soft legs, swollen with bites" is enacted "less than a mile from the basilica of Saint Apollinaire in Classis," a fifth-century church, ad- mired for the acanthus leaves (symbols of immortality) "that turn in the wind" on its capitals. The honeymooners have no time to stop, though, for they leave at eight "to prolong their miseries from Padua to Milan," where they will find a cheap restaurant—and Da Vinci's Last Supper. The groom thinks about tips, and does his accounts. By the end of the honeymoon, they will have seen Switzerland and crossed France. The poem ends with another juxtaposition of youth and age, and again two examples of the dust of which both are composed in this volume's view of life. After the young honeymooners have departed, the speaker of the poem reflects as the poem ends:

> Et Saint Apollinaire, raide et ascétique,
> Vieille usine désaffectée de Dieu, tient encore
> Dans ses pierres écroulantes la forme précise de Byzance.

Reading the lines today, we may miss the force they carried in 1920. Saint Apollinaire is "ugly and ascetic, an old factory abandoned by God, [which] keeps in its crumbling stones a Byzantine precision of form." The penultimate line in French can be read either as just translated or as "an old abandoned factory of God," laying the stress rather on humanity's loss of interest in the basilica than on God's. The ambiguity in French leans toward the absence of God, and this is important when seen in the context of the whole volume, for as the next poem reveals, Eliot's attitude toward the Church as a whole is anything but nostalgic.

"The Hippopotamus" begins with two epigraphs, one in Latin from St. Ignatius to the Trallians, the other in English from St. Paul (Colossians 4:16), both together implying—when read in the light of the poem that follows—that "there is no Church" surviving which is *not* "abandoned by God." St. Ignatius's words demand reverence for churchmen (a reverence which of course the poem destroys) saying that without these churchmen, nothing is left: "In like manner, let all reverence the Deacons as Jesus Christ, and the Bishop as the Father, and the Presbyters as the council of God, and the assembly of the Apostles. Without these there is no Church. Concerning all which I am persuaded that ye think in the same way." The poem leaves no doubt that Eliot thinks "in the same way" and that therefore the Church's doctrines are as void as the men who hold them. (I must reemphasize that Eliot's essays at this time, as he said, expressed an "ideal" that conflicts with the "actuality" he expressed in the poems,[10] and the actuality is as much a matter of his own feeling as of that of the churchmen he is lampooning.) The poem reaches limits far beyond the malpractices of living exemplars. So Paul's words too, presumably, include the author among the Laodiceans in the second epigraph: "And when this epistle is read among you, cause that it be read also in the church of the Laodiceans." Mr. Eliot's own church is seen two poems later.

The parallel between "the true Church" and the "broad-backed hippopotamus" is funny, first because it notes the absurdity of the doctrine that "flesh and blood" may err like the hippo—and the churchmen—but that still "the True Church can never fail / For it is based upon a rock." Only after five stanzas contrasting the weakness of those who must preach the word of God with the invulnerability of the "rock" on which they are based do we see, in the sixth stanza, that, like the hippo, this base is really mud and that there is very little difference between the hippo and the Church. As Cowper's hymn had sung, "God works in a mysterious way His wonders to perform":

> The hippopotamus's day
> Is passed in sleep; at night he hunts;
> God works in a mysterious way—
> The Church can sleep and feed at once.

The predatory nature of the Church is matched only by its power to sleep while feeding its flock—and growing fat itself simultaneously. (But then we remember, from "Gerontion's" epigraph, that all life is like "an after dinner sleep.") Predictably, perhaps, the hippo *ascends* at the end of the poem, which we thought in the beginning that only the True Church could do; and the final comic focus is on the *fallen* Church, which has descended that the hippo might ascend in one of the witty reversals of the via negativa so common in this volume:

> I saw the 'potamus take wing
> Ascending from the damp savannas,
> And quiring angels round him sing
> The praise of God, in loud hosannas.
>
> . . . . .
>
> He shall be washed as white as snow,
> By all the martyr'd virgins kist,
> While the True Church remains below
> Wrapt in the old miasmal mist.

Eliot seems to have been conscious of striking out at Christianity more intensely than he wished to be apparent (indeed, along with all the other gripes that sharpened his humor in the 1920 *Poems,* his savaging of Christianity is almost as striking as his more celebrated anti-Semitism), for he separated "The Hippopotamus" from the other poem written entirely against Christian teaching and practice—"Mr. Eliot's Sunday Morning Service." Intervening between the two come the last French poem, "Dans le Restaurant," and "Whispers of Immortality." The French poem gives us another age-versus-youth contrast, this time between an old waiter and his memory of himself as a seven-year-old, tickling a younger girl after they were caught in a spring rain, and then being frightened off by a playful dog. As I read this poem, the disgust roused in the reader should fall less on the waiter than on the speaker, who repels the sentimental waiter's attempt to confide in him, calling the waiter "lubricious" and giving him an insulting ten sous to finance a bath. The poem's last stanza, made famous by the transference of its image to *The Waste Land's* "Death by Water," seems to superadd a corrective voice, chiding the angry and penny-pinching diner as a commercial traveler like Phlebas, "who forgot the cries of gulls and the storms off Cornwall, and the profits and losses, and the cargo of tin. A current undersea carried him far, passing through the stages of his anterior life. Think, therefore, of that dreadful fate . . . this was once a handsome man, and tall." The tone—following the contrasts earlier—for the first time introduces into the volume (and into Eliot's poetry as a whole) a new kind of negativity—one that is neither gently ironic nor venomously wry but deeply engaged with the tragedy behind the restaurant scene as it reflects in its tawdry way the fate of all mankind.

The tone is not sustained until *The Waste Land,* and in the following poem "Whispers of Immortality," Eliot's mordant humor returns, this time (perhaps picking up the image of the child at seven) mocking the romantic Wordsworth. Here are your "Intimations of Immortality," and your daffodils. Indeed no such immortality preoccupied Webster, who "was much possessed by death"—and sexual violence—as the end to which all men come, and the way they come to it.

> Daffodil bulbs instead of balls
> Stared from the sockets of the eyes!
> He knew that thought clings round dead limbs
> Tightening its lusts and luxuries.

Webster's negative way is subtly played off against Wordsworth's affirmative way, as Webster shows the tenacity of the mind's attachment to the flesh, eschewing "Abstract Entities." The poem reminds us that Eliot was writing his essays on Donne and the metaphysical poets at about this time, and the poem offers a case of the inconsistencies between Eliot's early prose and poetry that I have discussed—and that Paul Elmer More noted in 1932.[11] In the essays (including the one on Marvell), Donne is equated with Dante, and both are seen as "explorers of the soul," capable of uniting sense and thought, as overcoming the "dissociation of sensibility" toward which the seventeenth century moved.[12] Yet I see no way to read "Whispers of Immortality" except as a reminder that Webster and Donne laudably expressed the refusal of the soul to venture beyond "the fever of the bone."

> Donne, I suppose, was such another
> Who found no substitute for sense,
> To seize and clutch and penetrate;
> Expert beyond experience,
>
> He knew that anguish of the marrow
> The ague of the skeleton;
> No contact possible to flesh
> Allayed the fever of the bone.

Was it not the idealizing tendency of Eliot's prose (as he himself suggested) that counterbalanced the unrelieved "actuality" here expressing itself in verse? Later, in the Clark Lectures of 1926 (as yet unpublished), Eliot would criticize the very limitations of Donne that are praised in this poem. In the lectures he would include Donne with all poets after Dante who *failed* to achieve a poetry uniting sense and spirit. The actuality expressed in "Whispers of Immortality" then did appear in prose.

In this poem the subject is precisely the disunified sensibility, accentuated by the ellipsis separating the stanzas on Webster and Donne from those on Grishkin. Grishkin (and possibly the whole poem) seems drawn from ironic speculation on two lines from Gautier, which Eliot cited in his essay on Marvell: "Le squelette était invisible / Au temps heureux de l'art païen! [The skeleton was invisible / In the happy time of pagan art!]." In Grishkin the skeleton is well concealed, whereas for Webster and Donne it was an ever haunting presence. The death toward which Grishkin compels "the scampering marmoset" is also unsuspected, for Grishkin "is nice," and her "uncorseted" frame promises "pneumatic bliss," disguising "the fever of the bone." Like another such Russian consoler, Helena Hahn Blavatsky, she draws about her "Abstract Entities" that promise immortality in the "arborial gloom" of her drawing-room. The poem ends as the speaker recognizes that most of us feel neither the fevered sensuality of the seventeenth century nor the circuitous feline magnetisms of the twentieth, since "our lot crawls between dry ribs / To keep our metaphysics warm."

Once again Eliot's "way" has risen in order to fall, here rising from the "breastless creatures underground" up to the nubile Grishkin's "maisonette," only to fall back to a lustless intellectual's limbo. We are not far from the dead center between the devouring tiger of Gerontion's memory and the coughing goat "above" him in the present. Again images of an undercut youth and vitality (in Grishkin as in Sweeney) glow for an instant only to die on the cooling embers of "our metaphysics." In the margin of the Berg manuscript, Pound's handwriting suggests a different first two lines for the last quatrain. Instead of "And even Abstract Entities / Circumambulate her charm," Pound suggested that the Holy Spirit did not despise copulation in fleshly form, before the last lines: "But our lot crawls between dry ribs / To keep our metaphysics warm." The crude blasphemy somewhat clarifies where the poem's tension belongs—that is, between the appeals of two kinds of sensuality against a vapid but restraining "metaphysics."

The next poem, next to the last, drives the nail home still further. "Mr. Eliot's Sunday Morning Service" is seldom if ever remarked upon as part of the sequence where Eliot placed it, and this is a pity because it comes between two poems contrasting Sweeney's animality on one side and Grishkin's on the other, thus accentuating "Mr. Eliot's" Sunday morning dilemma all the more. Even in the very different arrangement of the *Ara Vos Prec* edition, "Mr. Eliot" set himself between them, there placing both the Sweeney poems beforehand and setting "Whispers of Immortality" afterward. In the American *Poems* (where Grishkin precedes and Sweeney follows), the "Sunday Morning Service" is even more aptly placed, for it is followed by the intimations of Sweeney's downfall, which end the new poems.

The other striking fact relating to Eliot's perspective in the "Sunday Morning Service" is that "Mr. Eliot" is not going to church with the congregation described but appears to be outside the church; and not only outside but also inside another house—viewing the "avenue of penitence" through a window-pane. The precisely imaged scene in its impeccably metered and rhymed quatrains is an eloquent—and also very funny—dramatization of Eliot's chilled metaphysics, as he holds himself aloof, musing on the idiocy of the Christian Church. It is not his own metaphysics, of course, but the metaphysical theology of St. John's Gospel, chapter one, and its development by the third-century Origen, that runs through his mind. The title makes plain that "Mr. Eliot" chooses also to muse on his own idiocy, however, since it would appear that he is writing the poem as *his* Sunday morning service. He is perhaps not inside the poem at all in his own character, for when we ask *whose* "window-panes" it is that "the sapient sutlers of the Lord / Drift across," we are led to focus on Sweeney's bathroom—the only other location given. Since the point of view cannot be Sweeney's in his own voice at the end, however, "Mr. Eliot" is either outside the poem or, like Sweeney, a boarder in some house across from the church.

The poem is technically—both in sound and in sense—one of the most expert in the volume, setting a vivid scene, presenting a devastating but assured commentary, and making the most of its juxtapositions. As a procession of affluent, self-regarding churchmen move in solemn ritual toward the church doors, "Mr. Eliot" recalls a painting that shows "the Baptized God" in a "cracked and brown" waste land, his "unoffending feet" merely the extremities of a simple man, above whose head the painter has set a nimbus topped by "The Father and the Paraclete." The "sable"-dressed presbyters are set off against "red and pustular" children (youth against age again), and the tormented children against "staring Seraphim." A marvelous simile compares the clergy to bees who make honey out of mating parishioners that would (*mirabile dictu*) remain infertile without them:

> Along the garden-wall the bees
> With hairy bellies pass between
> The staminate and pistillate,
> Blest office of the epicene.

This stanza, set off in turn against Sweeney in his bath, brings us to the fully sexed man who needs no such go-betweens. There is surely a *dedoublement* here such as Eliot said he learned from Laforgue for the split consciousness of Prufrock, for the last two lines of the poem perfectly merge Sweeney's point of view with "Mr. Eliot's." Sweeney is no worse off "stirring the water in his bath" than the "masters of the subtle schools / . . . controversial, polymath" whose inane theology (so the poem implies) created the disjunction between the sensuous Sweeney and the "epicene" Church. The contrast is crystallized in the implicit comparison between the baptism of the simple, unoffending *man,* Jesus, and the immersion of Sweeney. The latter's ruminations, as he "shifts from ham to ham" and stirs the water, suggest an implicit rejection of the "metaphysics" represented in the ritual across the street. There are again no lexical negations here, but Sweeney's posture and nudity make the dressy procession of peddling savants ("sapient sutlers") into a distinct reminder of all the negative itineraries in the volume. And the implied poet's thought moves, as always before, by way of a comic ascent (here toward the starry regions of the Creating Word, the Trinity, and Seraphim) to an equally comic descent, passing by the bees to Sweeney in his bath.

The last poem in the new poems of 1920 takes us away from metaphysics and theological disputes, but not away from Sweeney. As already discussed, in "Sweeney Among the Nightingales" he is (perhaps again) housed across the street from an ecclesiastical house—the Convent of the Sacred Heart—but the more important juxtaposition is between Sweeney and another pagan hero. Ending with a dirge for Agamemnon, this last poem grotesquely foreshadows the death of Sweeney, fallen not in Argos or on the Maginot Line, but in the house away from home that is the volume's overarching image for the dwelling of modern man.

3   *The Waste Land's* Roadway to Nowhere

The Waste Land, Eliot's first long philosophical poem, can now be read simply as it was written, as a poem of radical doubt and negation, urging that every human desire be stilled except the desire for self-surrender, for restraint, and for peace. Compared with the longing expressed in later poems for the "eyes" and the "birth," the "coming" and "the Lady" (in "The Hollow Men," the Ariel poems, and "Ash-Wednesday"), the hope held out in *The Waste Land* is a negative one. Following Hugh Kenner's recommendation, we should lay to rest the persistent error of reading *The Waste Land* as a poem in which five motifs predominate: the nightmare journey, the Chapel, the Quester, the Grail Legend, and the Fisher King.[1] The motifs are indeed introduced, as Eliot's preliminary note to his text informs us, but if (as this note says), "the plan and a good deal of the incidental symbolism of the poem were suggested by Miss Jessie L. Weston's book on the Grail legend," the plan can only have been to question, and even to propose a life without hope for, a quest, or Chapel, or Grail in the modern waste land. The themes of interior prison and nightmare city—or the "urban apocalypse" elucidated by Kenner and Eleanor Cook—make much better sense when seen as furnishing the centripetal "plan" and "symbolism," especially when one follows Cook's discussion of the disintegration of all European cities after the First World War and the poem's culminating vision of a new Carthaginian collapse, imagined from the vantage point of India's holy men.[2] A passage canceled in the manuscript momentarily suggested that the ideal city, forever unrealizable on earth, might be found (as Plato thought) "in another world," but the reference was purely sardonic. Nowhere in the poem can one find convincing allusions to *any* existence in another world, much less to St. Augustine's vision of interpenetration between the City of God and the City of Man in *this* world.[3] How, then, can one take seriously attempts to find in the poem any such quest for eternal life as the Grail legend would have to provide if it were a continuous motif—even a sardonic one?

It seems that only since Eliot's death is it possible to read his life forward—understanding *The Waste Land* as it was written, without being deflected by our knowledge of the writer's later years. Before Eliot's death the tendency was to read the poem proleptically—as if reflecting the poems of the later period. This is how Cleanth Brooks, writing the first fully elucidative essay on *The Waste Land,* read it, stressing the Grail legends, the longing for new life, rather than the purely negative aspects of the theme. Thus Brooks interpreted the Sibyl's appeal for death at the beginning of the poem as exactly parallel to the Magus's appetite for death in the Ariel poems (the Magus's, of course, filled with the pain of knowing that Christ had subjected himself to weak mortality and not knowing yet of the Resurrection).[4] To make the Sibyl and the Magus parallel was to read Eliot's development backward—perhaps an irresistible temptation when the pattern in his life was so little known and when (as then in 1939) Brooks was acquainted with the man at work on *Four Quartets,* who had recently produced the celebrated *Murder in the Cathedral.* It was also irresistible, in a culture still nominally Christian, to hope that *The Waste Land* was about a world in which God was not dead. But the poem was not about such a world.

Within ten years after finishing *The Waste Land,* Eliot recognized that the poem had made him into the leader of a new "way." His own words of 1931, however, require us to read the poem as having pushed this roadway through to its end—for him. It was no Grail quest. Those who followed him into it, and stayed on it, he said in

"Thoughts After Lambeth," "are now pious pilgrims, cheerfully plodding the road from nowhere to nowhere." There could be no more decisive reference to the negative way he had followed till 1922, and also to the impasse where it ended.

A good reading of *The Waste Land* must begin, then, with recognition that while it expressed Eliot's own "way" at the time, it was not intended to lay down a way for others to follow. He did not expect that his prisonhouse would have corridors connecting with everyone else's. "I dislike the word 'generation' [he said in "Thoughts After Lambeth"], which has been a talisman for the last ten years; when I wrote a poem called *The Waste Land* some of the more approving critics said that I had expressed the 'disillusionment of a generation,' which is nonsense. I may have expressed for them their own illusion of being disillusioned, but that did not form part of my intention."[5] Dismay at finding his personal, interior journey (which he later called "rhythmic grumbling") converted into a superhighway seems to have been one of the main impulses toward his discovery of a new way after 1922.

If we listen attentively to the negations of *The Waste Land,* they tell us much about the poem that was missed when it was read from the affirmative point of view brought to it by its early defenders and admirers. Ironically, it was only its detractors—among them Eliot's friend Conrad Aiken—who acknowledged its deliberate vacuity and incoherence and the life-questioning theme of this first venture into "philosophical" poetry on Eliot's part. Aiken considered its incoherence a virtue because its subject was incoherence, but this was cool comfort either to himself or to Eliot, who was outraged by Aiken's opinion that the poem was "melancholy."[6] It was far from being a *sad* poem—like the nineteenth-century poems that Eliot had criticized precisely because of their wan melancholias, based as he said on their excesses of desire over the possibilities that life can afford.[7] Neither Aiken, who found the poem disappointing, nor I. A. Richards, who was exhilarated by its rejection of all "belief," spotted the poem's focus on negation as a philosophically meditated position.

Like "Prufrock," "Gerontion," and many other early poems, *The Waste Land* presents its whole world in its epigraph's grain of sand: Eliot gives only the Latin from Petronius's *Satyricon,* but he may have read it also in Dante Gabriel Rossetti's translation:

I saw the Sibyl at Cumae
  (One said) with mine own eyes.
She hung in a cage, and read her rune
  To all the passers-by.
Said the boys, "What woulds't thou, Sibyl?"
  She answered, "I would die."[8]

Eliot would have remembered Michelangelo's fierce Cumaean Sibyl—mannish with aged female breasts—on the ceiling of the Sistine Chapel when he saw the link between her and Tiresias, the androgynous prophet who had once "walked among the lowest of the dead" in the *Odyssey* and who became "the most important personage" in *The Waste Land*, as Eliot's note announced. Petronius's Sibyl hangs in a cage in the bazaars of a populous city, negating the specious life force which Eliot found so odiously celebrated by Bergson, Shaw, and the "two depressing life-forcers" Bertrand Russell and Aldous Huxley.[9] If Tiresias's voice merges with the other reflective voices in the poem, it is because like them and the Sibyl he has resolved that "We who were living are now dying / With a little patience." The poem is most centrally a repudiation of what the world has called "life," and its crowning negation is the rejection of "the Resurrection and the life"—at the heart of the Grail legends. I anticipate, but one should bear the end of the poem in mind when re-reading the beginning, recalling that in "What the Thunder Said" Eliot leaves no doubt in his allusions to Christ: "He who was living is now dead." In a preliminary draft, he made the pastness of the Christian past—and its failure to survive in the present—so explicit as to be banal:

After the ending of this inspiration
And the torches and the faces and the shouting
The world seemed futile—like a Sunday outing.
                                    (Facsimile, p. 109)

In the same rejected section, citing a famous passage from St. John's Gospel (11:25), he tried out another parody, this time (as Valerie Eliot notes in the Facsimile) ringing Emerson as well as the Bible with his noose. The fragment is again too flaccidly comic in tone to be appropriate for *The Waste Land*, as Eliot decided. It runs:

> I am the Resurrection and the Life
> I am the things that stay, and those that flow.
> I am the husband and the wife
> And the victim and the sacrificial knife
> I am the fire, and the butter also.

In the finished manuscript, Eliot used comic parody only for sexual abuses (for instance, "When lovely woman stoops to folly ..."), maintaining a seriously philosophical tone for all passages on spiritual disorders. The Sibyl and Tiresias (who reminds one also of Tennyson's Tithonus and Eliot's own Gerontion) together offer a resounding negation: the examined life is not worth living.

Earlier Eliot had said the same with another epigraph. Craig Raine and others have remarked on Eliot's original choice of Kurtz's death scene in Conrad's *Heart of Darkness* for *The Waste Land*'s title page, noting that Eliot was right when he argued with Pound that the Conrad passage was "the most appropriate I can find, and somewhat elucidative." (Pound had doubted "if Conrad is weighty enough to stand the citation."[10]) To see all the elucidative features of the passage is also to see in a new light the whole "plan" of Eliot's poem. The passage Eliot would have used is preceded in *Heart of Darkness* by Kurtz's saying, " 'I am lying here in the dark waiting for death,' " at which Marlow notes a contradiction: "The light was within a foot of his eyes." In other words, Kurtz's vision "of an intense and hopeless despair" is impervious to ordinary light. Eliot's epigraph would have been from the following paragraph.

> Did he live his life again in every detail of desire, temptation, and surrender during that supreme moment of complete knowledge? He cried in a whisper at some image, at some vision—he cried out twice, a cry that was no more than a breath—
> "The horror! the horror!"

What Kurtz sees is what Tiresias and Eliot see—a quest that began as a travesty of the Grail quest by a knight of nothingness (to use Sartre's phrase). Kurtz sees that the quest he began as a torchbearer into darkness, as a defender of Europe's high Christian legacy of humane political conduct and controlled sexuality, has been only a shell covering a void, into which every corruption has rushed. The fertility rites he has participated in, including those of Frazer's "Hanged God" (so often taken in readings of *The Waste Land* to point to renewal and resurrection), are *worse* than cannibal rites because Kurtz has perverted every code that sustained him. His sexual exploits—with the Harlequin (whose eyes he opens to new possibilities) no less than with his African bushwife—might well "elucidate" the fertility rites of Eliot's Mr. Eugenides, for Kurtz too was a trader; and like Phlebas the Phoenician sailor, he would have carried knowledge of secret cults back to Europe if he had lived. Moreover, as Conrad's tale reflects the collapse of European political codes at the time of the Boer War, imaging London and Brussels against the memory of Rome, so Eliot sets his scenes of London against fractured glimpses of Europe in shambles after "the Carthaginian peace" he agonized over in the postwar years. As Eleanor Cook has shown, *The Waste Land*'s references to Munich and Russian refugees in "The Burial of the Dead" point forward to the "falling towers" and constant failures of hope for peace in a whole civilization when the poem's last part focuses on "the present decay of Eastern Europe":

> What is that sound high in the air
> Murmur of maternal lamentation
> Who are those hooded hordes swarming
> Over endless plains, stumbling in cracked earth
> Ringed by the flat horizon only
> What is the city over the mountains
> Cracks and reforms and bursts in the violet air
> Falling towers
> Jerusalem Athens Alexandria
> Vienna London
> Unreal

Eliot's view of the void thus sets off his London scenes against the desert places of his poem's last part just as Conrad (who had much to say of Eastern Europe) set the cities of Europe against the dark heart of Africa. Both visions negate every hope on which their readers in 1899 and 1922 might rely.

Adding these comments to Raine's on the discarded Conrad epigraph by no means diminishes his chief insight that the Conrad passage appealed to Eliot because Kurtz's "supreme moment of complete knowledge" came as he "live[d] his life again in every detail of desire, temptation, and surrender." *The Waste Land* is indeed, as Raine argues, a poem about reenactment. It is a despairing visionary's appalled memory—extending over twenty-five centuries—of reliving the same scenes over and over. And the direction Eliot's recollection takes—insofar as it is voluntary—is not toward the Fisher King's desire for renewed life but toward hope for cessation of this cycle of rebirths. The first part's focus on springtime's "breeding . . . out of the dead land"—like Gerontion's recoil from a "depraved May," and the spring remembered by the pathetic waiter of "Dans le Restaurant," or even the summer of the vapid honeymooners in "Lune de Miel"— makes clear that the primitive fertility rites symbolized by Madame Sosostris's "wicked pack of cards" are better off forgotten. Little wonder that Pound, in Canto LXXX, associated Eliot with the "prince of morticians."[11] *The Waste Land* might be called a song in praise of winter, for "Winter kept us warm, covering / Earth in forgetful snow, feeding / A little life with dried tubers."

The poem is about the "feeding of a little life." As the reflecting voice mixes memory and desire, it calls for an explanation but also for a description of recurring life: "What are the roots that clutch, what branches grow / Out of this stony rubbish?" And the answer comes in negation and warnings:

> You cannot say, or guess, for you know only
> A heap of broken images, where the sun beats,
> And the dead tree gives no shelter, the cricket no relief,
> And the dry stone no sound of water. Only
> There is shadow under this red rock

And there we will be shown "fear in a handful of dust." This too, surely, echoes Conrad, grimly reversing the line in *Youth* where Marlow, remembering a great adventure, recalls finding "the heat of life in a handful of dust."[12] The biblical prophecies of Ecclesiastes 12, which Eliot also recalls in this passage (as his note says), spoke in negations too when it was a question of asking more of life than dust with a little breath in it. The ensuing memory of desire in the poem's next lines again repeats the movement of desire toward silence, negation, and emptiness. The memory of a moment without issue in a garden is associated with the last solitude of Tristan.

—Yet when we came back, late, from the hyacinth garden,
Your arms full, and your hair wet, I could not
Speak, and my eyes failed, I was neither
Living nor dead, and I knew nothing,
Looking into the heart of light, the silence.
Oed' und leer das Meer.[Desolate and empty the sea.]

The lexical negatives that structure these two passages also govern the
next two verse paragraphs, closing the poem's first section. Madame
Sosostris, a hollow replica of the Sibyl and the poem's other "real"
prophets, produces the card of the drowned Phoenician sailor, which
she says is "your card"—identifying the speaker of the poem at this
point with Phlebas. Though it may seem idiosyncratic to insist, there
is much in the poem to persuade us that the "I" who appears in "The
Burial of the Dead" and "A Game of Chess" is principally the sailor
who remembers another sailor's song in Part I and ends the poem's
first pragraph with "Desolate and empty the sea." The importance of
the troubled mariner was clear in the original manuscript, not only
from Marlow's words in the epigraph but also from Eliot's long passage on a disastrous voyage from the Dry Salvages that preceded the
lines as now published in "Death by Water." If Pound had not canceled the voyage verses, we would see the Phoenician Sailor as also a
modern Ulysses, reenacting the voyage of Dante's Ulysses, who was in
Hell because he treacherously tricked the Trojans but also because he
left his homeland to sail beyond the known world, a daring prohibited
by the gods. With this added dimension (if the poetry had been adequate), the poem's first protagonist would have stood out more clearly
as a traveler in a world abandoned by God. In the canceled voyage, the
reenactment of Ulysses' drowning clearly recalled the doom foreshadowed in the "desolate and empty sea" of the earlier line:

> One night
> On watch, I thought I saw in the fore cross-trees
> Three women leaning forward, with white hair
> Streaming behind, who sang above the wind
> A song that charmed my senses, while I was
> Frightened beyond fear, horrified past horror, calm,
> (Nothing was real) for, I thought, now, when
> I like, I can wake up and end the dream.
> —Something which we knew must be a dawn—

A different darkness, flowed above the clouds,
And dead ahead we saw, where sky and sea should meet,
A line, a white line, a long white line,
A wall, a barrier, towards which we drove.
My God man there's bears on it.
Not a chance. Home and mother.
Where's a cocktail shaker, Ben, here's plenty of cracked ice.
Remember me.

And if *Another* knows, I know I know not,
Who only know that there is no more noise now.[13]

The passage is elucidative as further evidence that the "quest" journeys in the poem are all abortive, and like this one (if the whole section is read) undertaken with no recognized purpose. The last lines here quoted further clarify the irony beneath all the ironies of the poem, the fact that human life in general is plotless. The "dead" speaker of the poem—*unlike* Dante's pagan Ulysses in Hell—acknowledges no Other. (Ulysses had understood that his drowning within sight of Purgatory was "as Another willed"; *Inferno, XXVI.*)

The Tarot cards, then, identify the first protagonist of the poem, along with all the others represented in the deck, as empty figures, galvanized into meaningless action. Belladonna, the man with three staves, the Wheel of life, and the one-eyed merchant, are all—as Eliot wrote in 1921—relics "of that vanished mind of which our mind is a continuation."[14] But look closely at this remark. The primitive "mind" that evolved the myths of fertility ritual is "vanished." There is no survivor of any sort to carry it on. "Our mind" must then perpetuate an absence, as a fossil continues a lost species or as the vestigial appendix "continues" the second stomach of an earlier species. To read *The Waste Land*'s allusions sensitively, as I have said, we must take the *negations* as the authoritative clues. When Madame Sosostris shows "the sailor" the card of the one-eyed merchant, she notes that the blank card next to this "is something he carries on his back, / Which I am forbidden to see." As others have noted, she is forbidden to see the arcana of the mystery rites that (as Jessie Weston says) were carried by Syrian merchants around the Mediterranean Sea. Nor can Madame Sosostris find the card of the Hanged Man, which Eliot's note associates with Christ. An irony always missed is that Eliot, not Madame Sosostris, associates the Christian mysteries in this poem with the vanished species of which our mind is a fossil.

For the auditory imagination, these negations (the forbidden vision, the missing Hanged Man) and the fortuneteller's concluding counsels of fear ("Fear death by water" and the paranoiac message for Mrs. Equitone) exactly echo the negations and fears recurring in the previous verse paragraph: "You cannot say . . . for you know only / A heap of broken images . . . / And the dead tree gives no shelter, the cricket no relief / . . . the dry stone no sound of water . . ." culminating in the vision of fear in a handful of dust. And in the following section, the last of "The Burial of the Dead," negation and fear recur in a different key. The sailor (in my reading) goes out into the London streets. It is not yet April, for there is still "the brown fog of a winter dawn," and seeing the crowds of people foretold by Madame Sosostris, he reflects (as well "the drowned" sailor might), "I had not thought death had undone so many"—Dante's words in Hell (*Inferno*, IV). This traveler who (we see later in the person of Tiresias) has "sat by Thebes below the wall / And walked among the lowest of the dead," is qualified to terrify an old acquaintance encountered in the street, rising up like a ghost and saying:

> "You who were with me in the ships of Mylae!
> "That corpse you planted last year in your garden,
> "Has it begun to sprout?"

He insinuates both that a murder has been covered up and that the buried life might be his own. The last line suggests that the buried life, asking to remain buried before, has now risen to confront us all, for the "hypocrite lecteur . . . mon frère" is suddenly identified with Stetson as one who has buried a corpse that may rise to undo him. Like Kurtz, the Sibyl, and later the voice crying "We who were living are now dying / With a little patience," this voice in Part I charges all those with hypocrisy who deny their roles as "buriers of the dead" and live in hope of rebirth.

In Part II, "A Game of Chess," the presiding *revenant* relives one of his many lives as a tormented city-dweller, first as the upper-class husband of a neurotic wife, herself a reincarnation (the images reveal) of Dido, Cleopatra, Hérodias, and Emma Bovary. We have seen such passages before (in verses on Burbank, Bleistein, and Sweeney, for instance) written all in affirmatives but signifying lives that come to nothing. It is only when the truth comes out that the negatives again recur: " 'I never know what you are thinking. Think.' " And " 'What is the wind doing?' / Nothing again nothing. / 'Do / 'You know nothing? Do you see nothing? Do you remember / 'Nothing?' " He remembers his own death: "Those are pearls that were his eyes," for surely this is the ghost of the Phoenician, wishing for a death that will *not* give him back to life, while his wife taunts him with it: "Are you alive, or not? Is there nothing in your head?"

Just before their conversation (if one can call it that, considering that the husband's answers are all unspoken) the marker of the stairway, which we have learned to expect in the early poems, recurs as a transition (from the passage evoking ladies of bygone days) to the domestic game of chess. "Footsteps shuffled on the stair" outside the boudoir where the scene is set, outside their "room enclosed" —isolated and isolating. Again the stairway signals an ascent just before plunging us into horror, crystallized in the last lines of the scene:

> And we shall play a game of chess:
> The ivory men make company between us
> Pressing lidless eyes and waiting for a knock upon the door.

The middle line, so distressing to Vivien Eliot that she called for its removal, will surely be restored eventually now that it can no longer hurt. As Eliot's widow notes, he had already restored it in 1960, thirteen years after Vivien's death.[15] The line is essential to the poem's unified vision of interior prison and exterior waste land. It also dramatizes the devastating contrast between this couple—with no children but chessmen—and the succeeding scene in a pub, where a lower-class woman tells Bill, Lou, and May about her friend Lil (dreading her husband's return from the war), who has five children and is sick from aborting her sixth—another buried corpse.

After this the third part, "The Fire Sermon," can tell us little more about loveless sexuality except the perfunctory coupling snatched in any city. Echoes of Spenser's *Epithalamion* establish the mood of the first scene—the banks of the Thames, emptied even of trash, the old river still running softly while the *revenant* hears at his back the cold blast, rattle of bones, and hellish, disembodied chuckle of a *danse macabre*. Insistent negations—evacuation and emptiness—again create the tone of solemn reflection:

> The wind
> Crosses the brown land, unheard. The nymphs are departed.
>
> .   .   .   .   .
>
> The river bears no empty bottles, sandwich papers,
> Silk handkerchiefs, cardboard boxes, cigarette ends
> Or other testimony of summer nights. The nymphs are departed.
> And their friends, the loitering heirs of City directors;
> Departed, have left no addresses.

"The river's tent is broken," but foggy drizzle rather than Spenser's stubborn sun appears when the clouds break. Farther within the Unreal City, spring will soon bring Sweeney to his brothel, and even now on "a winter noon," Mr. Eugenides propositions the speaker for a lunch and weekend at two disreputable hotels. Like Madame Sosostris, we are forbidden to understand what mystery this Smyrna merchant may carry with his currants, but clearly the "vanished" cults are blank to him as well.

The introduction of Tiresias at this point makes a distinct transition from the first half of the poem, which dealt—however negatively—with the "normal" world of births (and abortions), marriages (sterile ones), and deaths (however doubtful in "The Burial of the Dead"), to the second half of the poem where all the Western world collapses in images of falling towers and bridges. Just before Tiresias enters in "The Fire Sermon" section, the "I" of the poem (which had been associated with the Phoenician sailor in lines 6–8) becomes associated for the first time with "the man with three staves," or the Fisher King (the two identified with each other "quite arbitrarily," as Eliot's note says). Thus in the passage just preceding Tiresias's entry we read

> A rat crept softly through the vegetation
> Dragging its slimy belly on the bank
> While I was fishing in the dull canal
> On a winter evening round behind the gashouse
> Musing on the king my brother's wreck

This last line leads me to believe that Eliot's first intention .as to have the long shipwreck scene—finally reduced to the ten lines of "Death by Water"—come *before* the shift of perspective to the Fisher King and Tiresias. Since in the typescript "The Fire Sermon" (whose perspective is also that of the Buddha's fire sermon) is not assigned a part number, we are free to think it may have been Eliot's first thought for a conclusion—before he went to Lausanne and wrote "What the Thunder Said." In either case his plan would have been to end the poem with allusions from a non-Western sacred poem. By preceding "The Fire Sermon," the drowning of the Phoenician sailor would not only account for the change of narrative point of view but would also take us to the underworld of the *Odyssey*, where the sailor Ulysses met Tiresias. We must recall that "Death by Water" originally had the long passage leading to a shipwreck and ending with the adventurer's *death*—as Dante invented it, but without Dante's faith in "the will of Another." Once Eliot decided upon a different Part V (based on the *Upaniṣads*), he would have seen that "The Fire Sermon" could be made Part III, continuing the vision of degraded sexuality begun in "A Game of Chess," and that the sexually tormented Tiresias could both deliver the last word on lust and also merge with the Fisher King in his (anti-Grail legend) renunciation of hope for renewed life. This renunciation is, to my mind, the final stage of the poem's negative way.

Reading "The Fire Sermon" this way thus solves several problems, including the loss of the hopeful line "These are pearls that were his eyes!" which had first accompanied the dirge for Phlebas in "Dans le Restaurant." It was appropriate for Madame Sosostris to say it, for she makes a business of pandering to hope, while the message of "Death by Water" is that *this* corpse will suffer no better sea change than a ghastly recapitulation of "his age and youth." Pound wanted to excise the Ariel line from Madame Sosostris's speech, but Eliot insisted on retaining it.[16]

When the "I" of "The Fire Sermon" passes from the Fisher King to Tiresias, in any case, the poem situates us clearly between two worlds—"throbbing between two lives"—as Tiresias describes his fate. Though Eliot's note refers only to the sexual dilemma of this "old man with female breasts," his privileged place in the poem also suggests that he is caught between our life on earth and his life among the shades of Hell. On earth, his punishment for knowing too well the secrets of lust was to be blinded by Juno (as Eliot's citation from Ovid certified), but Zeus rewarded him with prophetic powers so great that he was "forever charged with reason even among the dead," as Ulysses learned when told to seek his help in the underworld of the *Odyssey*. "To him alone, of all the flitting ghosts, Persephone has given a mind undarkened."[17] This may explain why Eliot's note endows him with a clairvoyance capable of revealing not only the depraved coupling of the typist and "the young man carbuncular" but also the entire vision of *The Waste Land*: he is "the most important personage in the poem, uniting all the rest ... What Tiresias *sees*, in fact, is the substance of the poem." The fact that in most of the old myths Tiresias's rewards include a special staff to guide him in his blindness may further connect him with "the man with three staves" (Eliot's Fisher King) in the Tarot pack.

Tiresias twice describes the hour of his entry into the poem as "the violet hour," an insistence that carries over into "What the Thunder Said," where two stanzas connect the seer's vision with images from Hieronymus Bosch's hell scenes.[18] Here again the violet light twice signals an infernal landscape:

> What is the city over the mountains
> Cracks and reforms and bursts in the violet air
> Falling towers
> Jerusalem Athens Alexandria
> Vienna London
> Unreal

> A woman drew her long black hair out tight
> And fiddled whisper music on those strings
> And bats with baby faces in the violet light
> Whistled, and beat their wings ...

And in the typist's teatime seduction scene, Tiresias watches her young man ascend and descend a stairway that we have learned to associate in Eliot's early poems with a descent into one kind of hell or another. The lexical negations show Tiresias too to be a master of negativity. (My italics show the grid.) The small house agent's clerk, after tea with the typist,

> Endeavours to engage her in caresses
> Which still are *unreproved, if undesired.*
> Flushed and decided, he assaults at once;

> Exploring hands encounter *no defence;*
> His vanity requires *no response,*
> And makes a welcome of *indifference.*
>
> .   .   .   .   .
>
> Bestows one final patronising kiss,
> And gropes his way, finding the stairs *unlit* . . .

Tiresias then himself wanders through the streets of London, his mind drifting back (in time to music heard from a mandoline) to the coupling of Queen Elizabeth with the Earl of Leicester on her river barge—more glamorous, but in context no less sordid than her lower-class counterpart next seen "Supine on the floor of a narrow canoe."

At the end of "The Fire Sermon," Tiresias's voice, as I have said, merges with two voices of non-European holy men, the African Augustine and the Indian Buddha, who both fled from the detritus of their ancient civilizations. The phase of St. Augustine's teachings dramatized in *The Waste Land* is the phase where he tells of his "unholy loves," his rejections, his negations—in the period before he found his ultimate path. Eliot's focus on this earlier phase—when Augustine's mother was distraught with grief while he "fell headlong . . . into the love wherein I longed to be ensnared"—seems to have some biographical interest when one reads Eliot's letters about his own mother while he was working on *The Waste Land* (for instance the letters quoted in the Facsimile, pp. xvi and xviii). The passage he collocates with the Buddha's fire sermon is in Augustine's *Confessions,* III, 1:

> To Carthage I came, where there sang all around me in my ears a cauldron of unholy loves. I loved not yet, yet I loved to love, and out of a deep-seated want, I hated myself for wanting not. I sought what I might love, in love with loving, and safety I hated, hating a way without snares . . . yet, through that famine I was not hungry; but was without all longing for incorruptible sustenance . . . the more empty of it, the more I loathed it.

It is this empty but secret desiring after desire (which Tiresias had the gift to understand in the passage on Juno's lust) that Eliot found "of great anthropological interest" in Ovid, as his note says.

The passage from Augustine is as interesting for what Eliot does not use as for what he does. There is no "longing for incorruptible sustenance" in *The Waste Land.* While visualizing the "Unreal City," as we have seen, the poem presents no image of a real city, much less the City of God. Even where human yearning and fulfillment are evoked, these are imaged only as longing for self-surrender and control of emotion: "the hand expert with sail and oar." The absence of "the hanging man" from Madame Sosostris's deck is an observation rather than a complaint. And the poem's hint of Christ's appearance on the road to Emmaus is a hallucination, as the notes say. Eliot's focus on the Buddha's fire sermon reflects the point his teacher, Irving Babbitt, had made in 1919, that Buddhism wisely remains skeptical on the existence of God. In Babbitt's translation, Buddha says, "the disciple who is fully awakened delights only in the destruction of all desires . . . Even in heavenly pleasures he finds no satisfaction."[19] Thus Babbitt would have approved of Eliot's relating Augustine's *Confessions* to the Buddha's sermon, making the latter the overarching teaching.

For Babbitt, Augustine went wrong when his "way" diverged from the Buddha's: "Our actual attention should be fixed on the step in the 'path' that is just ahead of us," Babbitt said. "We can infer what Buddha would have thought of the Augustinian Christians who would have man turn away from works and brood everlastingly on the mystery of grace. He would have agreed with [Oliver Wendell] Holmes that the only decent thing for a consistent Calvinist to do is to go mad."[20] If Eliot later concluded that grace plays a greater part in life than karma, or the sum of one's past actions, it was directly in opposition to his most influential teacher's views that he did so: for Babbitt sarcastically called grace the "divine *bon plaisir*" while largely approving the Buddha's vision of human life as the total ethical consequences of one's acts.

Eliot's attitude at the time can be guessed from his last two notes for Part III, the one affirming a parallel between the Buddha's sermon and the Sermon on the Mount; the other clarifying that what interested him in the collocation of Augustine and the Buddha was their asceticism (rather than any common beliefs). It is hard to see any parallel between Jesus's sermon (leading up to the prayer to God, "for thine is the kingdom, and the power, and the glory, for ever") with the Buddha's sermon:

All things, O priests, are on fire . . . The eye, O priests, is on fire; forms are on fire: eye-consciousness is on fire; impressions received by the eye are on fire; and whatever sensation, pleasant, unpleasant, or in-

different . . . that also is on fire . . . With the fire of passion . . . with
the fire of hatred, with the fire of infatuation; with birth, old age,
death sorrow, lamentation, misery, grief, and despair are they on fire
. . .²¹

This is *The Waste Land*'s message, as the last part (with all its negations) assures us:

> Here is no water but only rock
> Rock and no water and the sandy road
> The road winding above among the mountains
> Which are mountains of rock without water . . .

The "red rock" of the poem's first stanza had at the outset signaled the
burning rock (which in an early draft had been gray²²,) and nowhere
in the poem (early or late) is there any burning with love such as Augustine describes throughout his *Confessions*. For instance, in the same
book Eliot cites, Augustine describes the burning desire which Eliot
reckons *without*: "how inwardly did even then the marrow of my soul
pant after Thee" (III, 10). The "Lord" who "pluckest me out" in *The
Waste Land* is surely more like the Lord Buddha of the "Fire Sermon,"
where there is only a tormenting fire. The poem's next section
quenches this in the grimmest of ways.

"Death by Water" here comes in dramatically, not as a reminder of
a resurrected god on the Nile but as a death without any desired sequel. The wheel, which is both Ixion's and the Buddha's *chakra*—that
is, both the racking instrument of fortune and the law of escape from
it through asceticism—is now the one link between the drowned
sailor and the reader. No longer "hypocrite lecteur," as when the sailor
himself addressed the reader, we are still his "semblable," but we are
addressed in a far different mood than in Part I. Now the poem's more
philosophical voice speaks:

> O you who turn the wheel and look to windward,
> Consider Phlebas, who was once handsome and tall as you.

The voice, as I have said, is that of Tiresias (chastened by the Buddha's) merging with a modern Fisher King, the sailor who has no
hope for cure but can only hope to control the wheel of torment, thus
finding a condition of peace.

The hope of happiness is evidently one that must be stilled if the burning is to cease; and in the last part of the poem, "What the Thunder Said," the modern Fisher King explicitly renounces the Christian promise: "He who was living is now dead / We who were living are now dying / With a little patience." This is the poem's late reflection on the Sibyl's "I want to die." And the rhythmic negations we have come to associate with Eliot's most serious voice continue from the passage on patience:

> Here one can neither stand nor lie nor sit
> There is not even silence in the mountains
> But dry sterile thunder without rain
> There is not even solitude in the mountains
> But red sullen faces sneer and snarl
> From doors of mudcracked houses

The mythical mind of the past may have vanished, but the primitive instincts for violence and hate survive in force. And the way through this wilderness is mocked by delusions of a God who shared the unending human ordeal. "Who is the third who walks always beside you?" Readers are not wrong to latch on to the several associations with Christ in the poem's last part; they are only wrong in missing what Eliot's note clearly says: "the party of explorers, at the extremity of their strength, had the constant *delusion* that there was *one more member* than could actually be counted." (I have stressed "delusion" though it hardly seems necessary.) His first note for the part indeed says that "three themes are employed: the journey to Emmaus, the approach to the Chapel Perilous . . . and the present decay of eastern Europe." But the themes are treated from the standpoint of pure negation. The chapel is explicitly *not* haunted, as in the Grail legends, for the speaker assures us,

> There is the empty chapel, only the wind's home.
> It has no windows, and the door swings,
> Dry bones can harm no one.
> Only a cock stood on the rooftree

No cross. And the cock banishes all ghosts. "Then a damp gust / Bringing rain." But the rain brings no new life, which indeed the whole poem has urged would be only a renewal of destructive desires. Lines 394–396 clearly indicate that rain leads only to the waiting for more rain. The empty chapel reminds us that Eliot is just where he was when he wrote, in "Lune de Miel," of the church as "an old factory abandoned by God." But now the emptiness is the Buddha's *sūnyatā,* an emptiness that brings release from desires which are self-defeating. As one scholar describes this teaching found in Nāgārjuna,

> The apprehension of emptiness was "enlightenment," the recognition of things as they really are ... Ultimate release (*nirvāna*) was the nonreplenishing of fuel for the flames of hate and greed.[23]

. . . . .

> The soteriological importance of this negation is its attempt to divert the religious man from longing after or desiring an eternal, unchanging, self-existent Ultimate ... To see [things] as "empty" is to see them in actuality ... Thus, the expression of "emptiness" is *not* the manifestation of *Absolute Reality,* the revelation of the Divine, but the means for dissipating the desire for such an Absolute.[23]

After the words on the emptiness of the chapel, the thunder speaks, and the wisdom achieved in the poem is revealed. The voice in the waste land recognizes that if he could give more, sympathize more, control his life more, the fires would abate. The insight is the same as the Buddha's vision of enlightenment through compassion, surrender of selfish desires, and self-control. "These are small gains," says Rajan, speaking of *The Waste Land*'s ending, "but their very narrowness suggests their authenticity ... The break-out from sterility is no more than that; it is not a movement into fruitfulness." Compared with Eliot's earlier poems, however, *The Waste Land* moves forward "to the fringe of a world which the poem can formulate but not enter."[24]

As the composite speaker now sits upon a nameless shore, "with the arid plain behind," a life of order and peace seems possible. Though London bridge is still falling down, the poet distractedly recalls other poets with comparable afflictions: Arnaut Daniel, who was refined but not destroyed by cleansing fire; and the lovelorn, disinherited poet Nerval. Also he recalls victims of lust turned into birds, suggesting the power of song to sustain love among the ruins of time. Fragments of poems telling their story are props against his own ruins. Finally a fragment of Kyd's *Spanish Tragedy* recalls Hieronymo's madness, deliberately put on to catch unwary villains. Hieronymo, like Eliot, when young gave his mind "to fruitless poetry," but now his apparent vanities have a deadly aim—at the world of the living dead.

The Waste Land ends repeating the words of the thunder in the *Bṛ-hadaraṇyaka Upaniṣad*: "Datta. Dayadhvam. Damyata. [Give. Sympathize. Control.] / Shantih shantih shantih." Spoken in stark, impersonal severity, the words harmonize well with the Buddha's fire sermon (based on the wisdom on the *Upaniṣads*), but there is no reference as in the *Upaniṣads* to an ultimate union with Brahma. This concluding peace offering has been generally read as evidence that Eliot combined the highest hopes of Christianity with the Hindu vision, but his own words undercut any reading of an affirmatively Christian kind. His last note in the early editions of the poem (1922–1926) identify the last words of the poem as the "formal ending to an Upanishad." He added rather brutally that the Christian " 'Peace which passeth understanding' is a feeble translation of the content of this word."[25]

With this remark, Eliot virtually dismissed the Christian's peace, announced by the angel of the Nativity and again by Jesus, parting from his disciples before the Crucifixion. Here Eliot again echoed Babbitt, who also saw the Buddha's peace as superior to the Christian's. In 1917 Babbitt had written, "One should grant the Buddhist his Nirvana if one is willing to grant the Christian his peace that passeth understanding. Peace, as Buddha conceives it, is an active and even an ecstatic thing, the reward not of passiveness, but of the utmost effort."[26] Eliot's note, ending *The Waste Land,* makes the same invidious comparison.

The poem's nightmare vision of Europe after the Peace Treaty of Versailles helps to explain why no Western formula for peace could satisfy Eliot at the time. Yet the poem is not a political diatribe. It is an expression of horror at the panorama of anarchy and futility within the poet's mind as well as outside in the modern world. In the face of such interior horror, the voice of *The Waste Land* asks relief from consciousness itself, and this is the peace promised by the *Upaniṣads*. As the *Bṛhadaraṇyaka Upaniṣad,* on which the poem's last stanza is based, expresses it: "Arising out of these elements, into them also one vanishes away. After death there is no consciousness"—for the deserving who have reached Nirvana.[27] Many years later, in *Four Quartets,* Eliot would have a very different view, seeing moments of perfect stillness as a liberation *into* consciousness:

> Time past and time future
> Allow but a little consciousness
> To be conscious is not to be in time
>
> ("Burnt Norton," II)

Despite *The Waste Land*'s closing words on such positive virtues as generosity, sympathy, and control, the last line of the poem answers the Sibyl's opening to it: "I want to die." At some subliminal point, release from consciousness is what the poem seeks and finds. All the same, as *The Waste Land* ends, the seer's cage is opened, and the void is freely chosen.

4   Toward Ash-Wednesday

Eliot's choice of emptiness, so central to the tenets of Buddhism, has occasioned much commentary on his Buddhist studies and sympathies. Much more can still be profitably said, for it becomes increasingly clear that if Eliot had not first steeped himself in the negative way of Buddhism, he would not have found his bearings toward the negative way of Christianity. We have seen that "the negative way" imaged in his first three volumes of poetry followed from two vital impulses. One was a personal, idiosyncratic revulsion against the main road taken by Anglo-American poetry. The other was a deeper philosophical issue that had engaged him as a doctoral candidate: What can the human mind know of the absolute ground of all reality, and how can one speak meaningfully about such a ground either in the field of philosophy or in religion? Since his first philosophical poem, *The Waste Land,* presented the conclusion that nothing could be known of this Absolute (a conclusion reached both by the Buddha and by Eliot's skeptical thesis on F. H. Bradley, as its last two chapters show)—we might now look deeper for the roots of Eliot's interest in theological negations and then see where they led when he discovered the reactions of his readers to publication of *The Waste Land.* For these reactions strongly affected his shift to a new vision of the negative way.

Eliot published almost nothing about the religious tradition in which he was raised until 1925, when he engaged in controversy with John Middleton Murry over the possible advantages of disestablishing the English Church. He then wrote to Murry, "I happened to be brought up in the most 'liberal' of Christian creeds—Unitarianism: I may therefore be excused for seeing the dangers of what you propose [abolition of the institutional church] ... If one discards dogma, it should be for a more celestial garment, not for nakedness."[1] Reading this letter as applicable only to the period after he finished *The Waste Land*, we can nevertheless see that the "more celestial garment" had already become visible to him during his studies of Buddhism at Harvard under Irving Babbitt, James Woods, and Charles Lanman.

It was above all Irving Babbitt who directed Eliot to the study of Sanskrit and Oriental religions, as he told an interviewer in 1950.[2] Though the powerful influence of Babbitt has often been noted with respect to Eliot's French preoccupations and the strong bias against Romanticism taught by this polymath (learned in both classical and modern literature), Babbitt's influence on Eliot was equally strong in the fields of religion and Oriental languages, as we have begun to see. This was obscured in 1928, when Babbitt founded the neohumanist movement, which ran diametrically opposite to Eliot's own thought at the time. If we consider Babbitt's religious thought in the earlier period, however, and look particularly at his Buddhist sympathies, we can see that Babbitt found in Buddhism (as Eliot at first also did) just that "celestial garment" which both men felt had been lost in the Christianity of their American traditions.

Babbitt's interest in both Confucius and the Buddha had been developing from the time of his marriage to the daughter of Peking's first American consul. His Buddhist sympathies culminated in a translation he made of the *Dhammapada* and a long essay titled "Buddha and the Occident" which accompanied the translation. The essay stresses the mystical and supernatural aspects of Buddhism and then goes on to describe other characteristics which must have had a powerful appeal for Eliot, especially the Buddha's critical and experimental approaches to ultimate reality. Throughout his essay, Babbitt contrasts Buddhism to Christianity, always to the advantage of the Buddhists.

"Buddha also differs from the religious teachers with whom we are familiar by his positive temper. The idea of experiment and the idea of the supernatural have come to seem to us mutually exclusive. Yet Buddha may perhaps be best defined as a critical and experimental supernaturalist."[3] To Eliot, whose acute reserve and impersonality both as man and as poet won him the name of "the invisible poet," Babbitt's emphasis on control of emotion and "the will to refrain" (p. 102) must have held great appeal. "As a result of the primary emphasis on Law," Babbitt writes, "the temper of the Buddhist is more impersonal than that of the Christian. An effusion like Pascal's *Mystère de Jésus,* profoundly religious in its own way, would have seemed to [the Buddha] to involve a morbid exacerbation of personality" (p. 113).

Two last points on which Eliot's sympathies would have resonated with Babbitt's praise of the Buddha were renunciation and meditation—both appearing to Babbitt as signally lacking among modern Christians. Westerners, said Babbitt, "though resolved to renounce nothing . . . hope to enjoy all the fruits of renunciation." Westerners, being appalled at what technology has done to their society, feel that they "may finally have to choose between Henry Ford and Gandhi . . . Buddha, on the other hand, not only stands for . . . the idea of meditation—but he deals with meditation and the form of effort it requires in a more positive and critical fashion perhaps than any other religious teacher" (pp. 117–118).

Such comments, very ordinary to us now, seemed to Babbitt necessary correctives to the sentimentalizing of Buddhism under the influence of Schopenhauer. It was partly Babbitt's inspiration that made Eliot change his concentration at Harvard from English literature to philosophy, for the year after taking Babbitt's course on literary criticism in France, he enrolled as a graduate student in philosophy, with a special emphasis on the Sanskrit and Pāli scriptures—continuing from 1911 to 1914. In these three years, his Harvard lecture notes show, he did more than scratch the surface of Indian thought. He studied the *Pancha-Tantra* and *Bhagavad-Gītā,* as well as the sacred books of Buddhism—the Jātakas, Buddhaghosa's Commentary on the *Anguttara Nikāya* (Legends of the Buddhist Saints), selected dialogues of the Buddha, Pantanjali's *Sūtras* with the *Bhāshya* and the *Vārttika,* and the Commentary of Vāchaspati-Mishra—all in the original languages. In the last year he took meticulous notes on a full-year course on Buddhism given by one of the world's leading Buddhist philosophers—Masaharu Anesaki. It is hard to realize that when he sat in these classes, he had already written "Portrait of a Lady" and "The Love Song of J. Alfred Prufrock." But at least one of his friends on the *Harvard Advocate* (where his poetry was first published) made the connection. William Chase Greene, who found Eliot "aloof and silent," said, "I used to tell him he reminded me of a smiling and quizzical Buddha."[4] Greene's observation went deeper than surface impressions, evidently, for Stephen Spender came to believe that it was a matter of spiritual commitment: "Buddhism remained a life long influence in his work," Spender wrote in 1975, adding that "at the time when [Eliot] was writing *The Waste Land,* he almost became a Buddhist—or so I once heard him tell the Chilean poet Gabriele Mistral, who was herself a Buddhist."[5]

Whether Eliot's Indian studies were the origin of his developing inclinations to asceticism and meditative poetry, or whether these characteristics were already in his blood and led him to Oriental philosophy and religion, is not clear. One of his earliest unpublished poems—copied in his notebook about the same time as "Prufrock" was begun—was a two-stanza poem called "Silence." Dated "June, 1910," the month when he first went to France after studying with Babbitt, returning a year later to start his studies in philosophy, the poem already centers on feelings of recoil from the noisy swell of life toward a center of ultimate stillness. The poem ends expressing terror in the face of such peace. I do not read this poem the way Lyndall Gordon does,[6] as an inclination toward Christianity. In a poem dated the month before and titled "Easter: Sensations of April," he referred scathingly to Christianity's petty formulations, thus recording an early reflection on the month of the Resurrection—"the cruellest month" in *The Waste Land's* phrase. Clearly the Buddhist peace of emptiness and negation was already more real to him than the Christian peace, however terrifying that emptiness seemed to him at the time.

The other poems in this notebook, which he carried to England with him and showed to Pound when they met in 1914, were mostly fragments—some twenty or so. Many of them take passing shots at Christianity in a far lighter mood than *The Waste Land's*. The notebook contained not only "Portrait of a Lady," "Prufrock," and the first sketches for "Gerontion," but also fragments bizarrely contrasting holy yearnings with sordid motives of men and women living in squalid surroundings.

In one of the 1910 poems a blind old man like Gerontion sits in a vacant square meditating. His futile imaginings are likened to auto-eroticism or the dead residue of sensation. The poem finally hints that the old man is made in the image of the "Absolute" itself, his mind being only a reflection of a reflection. Here and in other fragments (two titled as debates between the Body and Soul), the Absolute recalls Hume's philosophy of impressions, in which all ideas (including the Absolute) are no more than withered sensations. As in Hume, the mind in these poems attains pure thought only as sense decays. The old man, therefore, logically if grimly finds his perfection only as he withers into total extinction. In one poem beginning, "Do I know how I feel? Do I know what I think?" a man considers asking the porter of his lodging house to tell him what he himself feels or thinks. Giving it up, the lodger goes on to imagine his own death. A doctor will come to pronounce on his nameless disease, or madness, and will say that the cause of death was no more or less than the cause of life. In another fragment, which Eliot apparently wrote in Paris at around the time he also wrote "Prufrock," another lodger reflects momentarily on Christ, thinking that His life and death were more impressive than those allotted to an office worker, who will die in an attic over several flights of broken stairs.

While most of these poems alluding to Platonic Absolutes and degraded ruminations on sacred history were not worth saving, several of them found their way, softened, into the volumes of 1917 and 1920. "Conversation Galante" came out in the *Prufrock* volume with its reference to the lady as "eternal enemy of the absolute," but in the notebook fragments the Absolute too is a lethal enemy. In one poem, for instance, the cosmos is seen as a giant spider's web at the center of which the Absolute sits waiting to entangle us all. It seems to make little difference whether the Absolute is masculine or feminine—the seeker will be devoured.

When read as poems reacting humorously against philosophical conundrums, as well as poems experimenting on new idioms for English poetry, these unpublished drafts clearly represent the position of religious and philosophical pessimism Eliot cultivated through the writing of *The Waste Land*. In an unpublished paper he delivered to the

Harvard Philosophy Club (of which he was president) in 1913–14, he made a deliberate point of advocating this form of pessimism. He put down both the mystical idealism popular in some English philosophy and the Christian idealism being revived at Harvard by his teacher Josiah Royce. Thus after a good natured jab at Bosanquet's Absolute, Eliot poked fun also at Royce's efforts in behalf of a defunct Christianity. And alluding to his own family's Unitarianism, he added that its faith in endless progress could hurt no one if limited to inciting personal motivation. The harm would come in formulating a general philosophy upon such faith.[7] *Philosophers* who ride on such stimulants can lead nowhere but to chaos and despair. Among such philosophers he names Nietzsche, a "vicious" intellectualist posing as an exposeur of creeds (p. 13). Nietzsche's voluntarism disposes of the need for rationality, since "the irrational knows so well what it wants." Including Nietzsche with Bergson and the pragmatists, he says, "I feel at the bottom of Bergsonism and pragmatism (as I am convinced in the case of Nietzsche) a fundamental pessimism and despair" (p. 19). But he distinguishes his own position—a dualist position somewhere between materialism and idealism ("for materialism is always the Doppelgänger of idealism")—as a "philosophical pessimism . . . [which] lends itself to cheerfulness" (p. 20).

This paper goes far to explain the comic tones of all Eliot's poetry before the finishing stages of *The Waste Land,* where of course his pessimism loses its cheerfulness. It also clarifies the position from which he could take intense interest in every variety of religious and philosophical speculation while at the same time retaining a cool and distant view of them. In addition to the extensive study of Indian religions he made in his graduate student years, he was also reading exhaustively in the field of mysticism—primitive and modern. As Lyndall Gordon has noted, his Harvard student notes include forty-one cards largely on the subject of mysticism and the psychology of religious experience, indicating that he read some forty-five books and many more articles on these subjects. The latest of these books, Evelyn Underhill's *Mysticism,* was studied by Eliot in an edition of 1912, suggesting that his reading was done chiefly for Josiah Royce's seminar on comparative methodology in the fall and winter of 1913–14. The paper for that seminar (now in the Eliot Collection at Cambridge University) was on primitive religions, and Gordon sums it up as follows:

He criticized the anthropologists—Frazer, Jane Harrison, Durkheim, and Lévy-Bruhl—for giving no explanation of religious ritual "in terms of need." He criticized their "wanton interpretation" based on uninvestigated assumptions, and suggested there was no adequate truth in the study of religion short of an absolute truth. And that would be found, not through methodological inquiry, only through intuitive sympathy . . . Eliot tried to bypass anthropologists' records of behaviour with the question: "What is [the believer] sincere about?" Behaviour is mere mechanism, Eliot added, unless it has some sort of meaning. "The question is, what is that meaning?" Finally . . . Eliot criticized all theories of knowledge for their inability to "treat illusion as real."[8]

The paper on primitive religions and the reading cards are the strongest evidence we have that Eliot was tending toward theology even on the negative path he followed in the years from 1910 to 1922, when he first abandoned literature for philosophy and then abandoned philosophy again for poetry. Much later, in 1952, he could see an affirmative path for philosophy that he might have taken: "The root cause of the vagaries of modern philosophy—and perhaps, though I was unconscious of it, the reason for my dissatisfaction with philosophy as a profession—I now believe to lie in the divorce of philosophy from theology."[9] The point was, however, that in his Harvard years as a philosophy student, Eliot saw no possible marriage between modern thought and "that vanished mind" accessible only to the archaeologists of religion.

When emphasizing that his Buddhist studies gave him a *religious* position that was compatible both with his personal experience and with his philosophical skepticism, I am not forgetting that late in life he also issued a caveat against following the way of Eastern mysticism too blindly. He spoke disparagingly of those "who find their way toward the religious life only through the mysticism of the East," warning against "those universalists who maintain that the ultimate and esoteric truth is one, that all religions show some traces of it, and that it is a matter of indifference to which one of the great religions we adhere."[10] To understand his poems before 1925, we must nevertheless face the fact that if there was any "esoteric truth" behind them, it was not in any understandable sense Judeo-Christian.

He was, in fact, much closer to the position he described as Paul

Valéry's both in 1924 (when Eliot could easily have been describing himself) and in 1947. Thus two years after publishing *The Waste Land,* introducing Valéry's *Le Serpent,* Eliot spoke of the poet's sense of "le Néant," noting how it differed from the philosopher's: "In *La Pythie* I find, not a philosophy but a poetic statement of a definite and unique state of the soul dispossessed."[11] (Dispossession, we will observe, was the first stage of both the Buddhist and the Christian via negativa, and Eliot's words—coming in 1924—are important for focusing on this state.) Later, his words on Valéry were even more closely parallel to the accounts he gave of himself while writing *The Waste Land* (as Valerie Eliot's Introduction to the Facsimile makes evident). Thus, in 1947, he wrote of the difficulties of writing for a poet whose vision cannot break free of "le Néant." At best Valéry was able to play

> an elaborate game ... but to be able to play this game, to be able to take aesthetic delight in it, is one of the manifestations of civilized man. There is only one higher stage possible for civilized man: and that is to unite the profoundest skepticism with the deepest faith. But Valéry was not Pascal, and we have no right to ask that of him. His was, I think, a profoundly destructive mind, even nihilistic. This cannot ... alter our opinion of the poetry ... But it should, I think, increase our admiration of the man who wrote the poetry. For the agony of creation, for a mind like Valéry's, must be very great. When the mind constantly mocks and dissuades, and urges that creative activity is vain, then the slow genesis of a poem ... [is] only possible by a desperate heroism which is a triumph of character.[12]

Eliot's mind was just such a mind—until 1926. As his sympathy with Babbitt showed, it was a mind in tune with civil and intellectual order against any kind of philosophical anarchism, but it was also a mind committed to religious skepticism. Babbitt's influence, in fact, led him to the political idealism of Charles Maurras in the twenties—a political point of view that could harmonize religious unbelief with support for the Christian Church as a barrier against various despotisms. And Maurras's *negative* example—his *failure* to make political order the sine qua non for interior order—became (as Eliot said) one of "the positive forces which oblige the reason [his own reason] to respond to the call of Faith."[13] Before 1926, like Babbitt and Maurras, Eliot valued his skepticism as a perfectly walkable negative way.

In 1914–15, when writing his thesis on F. H. Bradley, Eliot was as skeptical about philosophical idealism as he was about the materialism of Bertrand Russell, which he described in a letter to Pound as "Priapism." In an unpublished essay written at Oxford while he was studying Aristotle, Eliot wrote, "I cannot see my way to the admission that reality is spiritual," adding that this gave him "certain reservations" about Bradley's *Appearance and Reality*. He agreed with Bradley (against the extreme idealists) that appearances are as "real" as what lies behind them, and this contrasts strongly with the "Unreal City" we see later in *The Waste Land*. But his view throughout the years before 1925 was expressed in the same essay: "all faith should be seasoned with a skillful sauce of scepticism. And scepticism too is a faith—a high and difficult one."[14] At the same time he was equally skeptical about the testimonies of mysticism, criticizing Aristotle on this very ground. Reading Aristotle's teaching that life changes on earth reflect stellar motions, Eliot wrote in another essay for Oxford that in this way of accounting for material changes, "we are reduced to mysticism or mythology."[15]

In view of this and other remarks he made on mysticism in passing, I cannot agree with Lyndall Gordon that from 1913 on he "was more concerned . . . with what one of his sources termed 'la vie religieuse normale,' the traditional pattern of progress towards sainthood through phases of awakening, unworthiness, mortification of the senses, and illumination"[16] than he was with the pathologies of mysticism. In the years leading up to *The Waste Land,* indeed, sick mysticism interested him increasingly. He certainly decided early that illusions—and even delusions—were "real," as the essay on primitive religions had maintained. This point, however, had been confirmed even by Bertrand Russell, whose lectures are cited in Eliot's notes for 1914 at Harvard. In one of these lectures, Eliot noted, Russell had said, "Hallucinations are not error. And in a proper physics, they would find their place. They are just as solid as anything else." Russell added, "It is only when you have a description that you have unreality."[17] Russell thus provided Eliot with ammunition for attacking Frazer and the Cambridge School of anthropologists, who attempted to *describe* the religious experiences of a vanished primitive mind. At the same time, we cannot say that Eliot concluded in this period that any mysticism, ancient or modern, corresponded to the *"high dream"* he was to distinguish in Dante in 1929, when he would also say that "the modern world seems capable only of the *low dream.*"[18]

That Eliot was far less concerned before 1922 with "la vie réligieuse normale" than with neurotic religiosity seems obvious from the two saint poems of his poetry notebook. Both of these were evidently written in 1914–15, as Valerie Eliot and Lyndall Gordon have said. One of them, "The Death of Saint Narcissus," was good enough (Eliot at first thought) to be included in *The Waste Land,* and two versions of it are published in the Facsimile edition. Both of the poems show that Eliot was emotionally repelled far longer than we realize by the faith to which he submitted himself rather suddenly. His conversion in 1927 appears to have occurred more as the abject surrender of a twice-thinking intellectual, to an adversary whom he feared might be disabling, than as the victory of a twice-born soul steadily progressing toward a long-foreseen end.

If retained in *The Waste Land,* "The Death of Saint Narcissus" would have introduced a powerful theme of sick spirituality, indistinguishable from sick sexuality, for this poem on the vanished mind of ancient fertility rites. "Saint Narcissus" is equally confused about divine and sexual urges. The poem seems to have been partly inspired by Valéry's "Narcisse" poems and Gide's "Traité de Narcisse" (also, as Helen Gardner suggests, by Gide's *Prométhée mal enchaîné*[19]), and not by the second-century Christian bishop Narcissus. Eliot portrays an aesthete crazed by the beauty of his own body. Confusing this self-intoxication with a longing for divine union, he becomes "a dancer before God." Then, unable to "live men's ways," he withdraws to the desert. There the sun's arrows embrace him, and he dies in voluptuous surrender, his white body "green and stained," "the shadow in its mouth" which corresponds to the shadow in *The Waste Land* that the poet will see under the red rock. As a comment on "The Burial of the Dead," this poem would have added one more longing for annihilation in the waste land.

Another important source suggests itself—one that is unusually elucidative. When Narcissus dies with "the shadow in his mouth," Eliot seems to echo Victor Hugo's famous apocalyptic poem "Ce que dit la bouche d'ombre." "The mouth of darkness" in Hugo's long poem speaks as an oracle out of the heart of dark rock which is matter. Its voice leads the poet to a cave in the rock where he will be shown the terrifying emptiness of matter in relation to the Absolute. Eliot echoes several of its lines in "Narcissus" and in *The Waste Land*. For instance, in "The Burial of the Dead" ("I will show you something different from either / Your shadow at morning striding behind you / Or your shadow at evening rising to meet you"), Eliot must have remembered Hugo's

> Ne réfléchis-tu pas lorsque tu vois ton ombre?
> Cette forme de toi, rampante, horrible, sombre,
> Qui, liée à tes pas comme un spectre vivant,
> Va tantôt en arrière et tantôt en avant.

And Eliot's earlier line, "Son of man, you cannot know," seems to echo Hugo's "Homme, tu ne sais rien." As Eliot's oracular voice says, "(Come in under the shadow of this red rock), / . . . I will show you . . . fear," Hugo's oracle says, "Je viens de te montrer le gouffre. Tu l'habite."[20] It seems curious that Eliot provides no note on these resemblances. The contrast between the romantic Hugo and the modernist (but not Modernist) Eliot could not be more striking, of course. For Hugo, "the mouth of darkness" resoundingly affirms Pascal's God of terrifying, infinite spaces—within which man's sun is a sparkling cinder:

> Ton soleil est lugubre et la terre est horrible.
> Vous habitez le seuil du monde châtiment.
> Mais vous n'êtes pas hors de Dieu complètement.

However, in *The Waste Land*, as in "The Death of Narcissus," the saint dies with no word—no apocalyptic promise beyond death and a life of fear. (Conrad's Kurtz too may have been an ironic comment on Hugo's "mouth of darkness.")

Craig Raine and others are right that the Narcissus poem, had it remained in *The Waste Land*, would have emphasized that poem's theme of transmigration of souls—and hence its Buddhist stress on the burning of desire that perpetuates the "red rock," which is black in Hugo and grey in "Narcissus." In the corrected version as given in the Facsimile, Narcissus (like Phlebas's corpse) goes through earlier stages of his evolution, first sure that he had been a tree, then a fish, then a young girl, before becoming a dancer before God. Eliot's philosophy notes at Harvard refer twice to the Egyptian and Pythagorean belief that transmigration of souls was a judgment imposed on those who had not escaped rebirth. After the death of Eliot's Narcissus, presumably his soul will return to rock, thus beginning another cycle of tormenting rebirths.

The other saint poem in Eliot's poetry notebook—"The Love Song of Saint Sebastian"—presents another case of spiritual neuroses taking the form of crazed eroticism (or vice versa). Gordon has noted that between 1910 and 1914 when the poem was drafted, Eliot studied several Mantegna paintings of the saint riddled with arrows, but Eliot's Sebastian suffers a different ordeal. He flagellates himself at the foot of a stair (the marker I have associated with the hideous ascent and descent motif), a stair presided over by a lady in white. As his blood stains the lamp in his hand, she calls him to her, and he dies with his head between her breasts. Then in the second and last stanza, this reverie is followed by another, still in the saint's mind, which ends the fragment. This time he comes to the lady with a towel in his hands and, bending her back, wins her love in the moment of strangling her. As a crude blasphemy against the third-century Roman martyr Sebastian, the poem makes less sense than if read (shakily I admit) as a symbolist fantasy in the mind of Sebastian Melmoth—the name taken by Oscar Wilde before his conversion to Catholicism (faith of Dante's lady in white) and his early death.

In any case, these two poems about saints form images of sick spirituality suggesting that Eliot was dealing with an "actuality" (as he said poetry must) that deeply probed and criticized Christian spirituality while releasing (the word he used) certain strains in his own deeper psychology. Some of these motifs were released into the published poems of 1920, as I noted in "A Cooking Egg," "The Hippopotamus," "Whispers of Immortality," and "Mr. Eliot's Sunday Morning Service." In addition to what has already been said of this last poem, we should recall here that it also presents a case of erotospiritualism. As the Sunday service begins, Mr. Eliot reflects on the first line of St. John's Gospel—"in the beginning was the Word"—which Mr. Eliot then calls "Superfetation of τὸ ἕν," humorously suggesting that Christ was twice conceived; first in the womb of the Absolute (τὸ ἕν) and then, before ever having been born, again in the womb of Mary. This doctrine of the Catholic church, which Robert

Lowell later described as all too gynecological, was considered just that in Eliot's poem, for he adds: "And at the mensual turn of time / [God] Produced enervate Origen"—the self-castrating theologian. Eliot's manuscript version of these lines confirms one's suspicions. "Mensual" originally read "menstrual," Eliot's point being that the gynecologically precocious First Mover was also able to produce the castrated Origen (as the manuscript also has it) during his mother's menstruation. In subtilizing the language for publication, Eliot lost nothing of his point. The poems he left unpublished in his notebook were censored not because they were obscene or blasphemous but because they were not good poems. When he came to believe in the doctrines he had been ridiculing, he still republished all the poems of 1920—except "Ode." This was a "marriage song" with an implicit sylleptic slur on "hymen." The poem's degraded and degrading view of sexual failure was better put in the less pathological "Lune de Miel," which kept its place in the volume's travelogues for a diseased humanity's negative way.

Whatever Eliot may have been arguing in favor of traditional Christianity in his *essays* before 1927 (when the first version of "Ash-Wednesday" was published), his *poems* bear witness to a struggle against Christianity which is no less dramatic in these poems than in *The Waste Land* and "The Hollow Men." I have said that public reactions to *The Waste Land* precipitated the change in his stance, and I think this can be shown most clearly in the extraordinary responses he made to the admiration for *The Waste Land* expressed by I. A. Richards. This applause, and the reasons Richards gave for it, troubled Eliot far more than Edmund Wilson's review describing the poem as a "rag-bag of the soul," or John Middleton Murry's attack on its "life-denying" qualities, or Aiken's reference to it as an "anatomy of melancholy."[21]

As a Cambridge don, convinced from reading *Ara Vos Prec* in 1920 that Eliot's was the most interesting new voice in poetry of the day, Richards held a mirror up to Eliot, revealing exactly the face he had shown to discriminating readers. Richards sensed the deep philosophical skepticism on which Eliot had prided himself from his student years and applauded it as a remedy for the preoccupations with belief and religion that he felt had plagued English poetry till then. Meeting Eliot in 1920, he began trying to persuade him to apply for the Cambridge Honorary Fellowship in Poetry which had last been held consecutively by Hardy and Kipling. When Richards published the second edition of his *Principles of Criticism,* he appended an essay on *The Waste Land,* pointing out Eliot's "persistent concern with sex, the problem of our generation, as religion was the problem of the last."[22] In this book and two other ones—*Science and Poetry* (1926) and *Practical Criticism* (1929)—Richards was developing his theory that there are two kinds of truth—poetic and scientific (or discursive). The truth of poetry was the truth of human feeling and could only appear as "pseudo-statements," depending on a "neurological jungle" of emotions, expressing themselves in ways very different both from scientific thought and from political or religious belief. Samuel Hynes has summed up Richards's view of *The Waste Land,* saying it

> was a key example and a model, and his interpretation of the poem as a document of unbelief for a time of unbelief very quickly became the common one. Eliot did not protest the interpretation in 1925, when he accepted Richards's essay ["A Background for Contemporary Poetry"] for publication [in *The Criterion* for July, 1925], nor in 1926 when it was reprinted in *Science and Poetry* . . . but one can see why he had to speak up in 1927, for he was then on the verge of conversion . . . Reading over Richards's footnote [to the *Criterion* essay], Eliot must have felt like a general who has lost his artillery to the enemy, and is being shelled by his own guns.[23]

Like Eliot, Richards saw the condition of the modern world as a waste land, but his view of the way out, suddenly in 1926 (earlier than Hynes suggests), appeared alien to Eliot. According to Richards,

> It is very probably that the Hindenburg Line to which the defense of our traditions retired as a result of the onslaughts of the last century will be blown up in the near future. If this should happen, a mental chaos such as man has never experienced may be expected. We shall then be thrown back, as Matthew Arnold foresaw, upon poetry. It is capable of saving us; it is a perfectly possible means of overcoming chaos. But whether man is capable of the orientation required, whether he can loosen in time the entanglement with belief which now takes from poetry half its power and would then take all, is another question.[24]

Making a similar point in an earlier chapter of *Science and Poetry,* Richards appended a footnote referring directly to Eliot:

To those familiar with Mr. Eliot's *The Waste Land,* my indebtedness to it at this point will be evident. He seems to me by this poem, to have performed two considerable services for this generation. He has given a perfect emotive description of a state of mind which is probably inevitable for a while to all meditative people. Secondly, by effecting a complete severance between his poetry and *all* beliefs, and this without any weakening of the poetry, he has realised what might otherwise have remained largely a speculative possibility, and has shown the way to the only solution of these difficulties. "In the destructive element immerse. That was the way."[25]

Eliot's response to Richards came in the first issue of Wyndham Lewis's *The Enemy*—in January, 1927, the same month as Eliot's baptism into the Anglo-Catholic community: "I cannot for the life of me see the 'complete separation' from all belief [in *The Waste Land*]. A 'sense of desolation, etc.' [quoting Richards's text introducing the footnote] (if it is there) is not a separation from belief; it is nothing so pleasant. In fact, doubt, uncertainty, futility, etc., would seem to me to prove anything except this agreeable partition; for doubt and uncertainty are merely varieties of belief."[26] The sick spirituality he had ridiculed in early poems like "The Death of Saint Narcissus" and "The Love Song of St. Sebastian," as well as "A Cooking Egg," "The Hippopatamus," and "Mr. Eliot's Sunday Morning Service," now appeared at least to be the basis for some form of belief; and he returned repeatedly to his quarrel with Richards, first in the Clark Lectures of 1926, then in his 1929 Dante essay, and finally in 1933 in the Charles Eliot Norton Lectures (*The Use of Poetry and the Use of Criticism*). Riveted thus on the point that his own poetry expressed belief of a kind, he had then to compare the *quality* of beliefs held by poets in different ages. In 1925 he had begun studying Dante intensively for the first time in that light for the Clark Lectures, and though these lectures show that he thought Dante's beliefs to be outdated in modern Christianity, some time between 1926 and 1929 he went the further step of identifying his own beliefs at the most fundamental level with Dante's. This step seems to have been taken after what he called a long process of "rejection and elimination"[27] (the essence of the "negative way"), for when he wrote the 1929 Dante essay, he still held that it was possible to appreciate Dante fully *without* sharing his beliefs, as the essay said. Only in adding a long footnote on Richards did

he alter that statement to say, "Actually one probably has more pleasure in the poetry when one shares the beliefs of the poet."[28] The controversy with Richards drove him so far that in *The Use of Poetry* he
would say, "the reason why I was intoxicated by Shelley's poetry at the
age of fifteen, and now find it almost unreadable, is not so much that
at that age I accepted his ideas, and have since come to reject them, as
that at that age 'the question of belief or disbelief,' as Mr. Richards
puts it, did not arise."[29] One may ask whether, if it were not for Richards, "the question of belief or disbelief" in poetry would have arisen
just then for Eliot. As in his arguments with Babbitt, he was most
profoundly influenced by a man whose convictions inspired his complete assent up to a point of crisis, at which point his negative instincts rebelled. To Richards's last point, that poetry "is capable of
saving us," Eliot responded in the Norton lectures by quoting Jacques
Maritain: "It is a deadly error to expect poetry to provide the super-
substantial nourishment of man."[30] But Eliot's poems after 1925 show
a steady, if tormented, inclination to direct the reader toward that su-
persubstantial nourishment.

As his first major poem published in three years (since *The Waste
Land*) "The Hollow Men" deceptively seemed to confirm Richards's
view that a poem could be written without belief of a nonpoetical
kind, and in fact Richards described it in 1926 as "the most beautiful
of Eliot's poems,"[31] possibly because it is the one poem Eliot wrote in
which the failure of belief is explicitly rather than implicitly the subject. In *The Waste Land* it had been taken as axiomatic that Christian
belief was impossible. "The Hollow Men" situates us, as its first epigraph says, in the world *after* the horror of a world without faith has
been seen but has flickered out: "Mr. Kurtz—he dead." Now we are in
a world of children's make-believe, and the second epigraph asks for
"A penny for the Old Guy," for the stuffed effigies of past horrors.
But the poem itself responds to the black boy's comment in *Heart of
Darkness* and the children on Guy Fawkes Day by identifying its
speaker with a stuffed effigy who comes to life and reflects on his condition. It is as though one of the Tarot cards in Madame Sosostris's
pack had been able to see before and after life as it is. This is a new
departure, since even the Fisher King had resigned himself at last to
his waste land, asking for no further vision. That vision *beyond* the
waste land appears for the first time in "The Hollow Men" as "death's

other Kingdom." If *The Waste Land,* in Eliot's words, revealed a "roadway to nowhere," "The Hollow Men" came at the end of that negative way to signal the sight of a possible roadway to somewhere. But it also registered a dread of *being seen* on that road and a search for shelter in the shadows that fall between idea and reality, motion and act, conception and creation, emotion and response. To this extent, "The Hollow Men" is another poem of negativity, but negativity of a new kind, since its rejections are the opposite of those we have seen before. "Let me be no nearer," the speaker pleads, "No nearer — / Not that final meeting . . ." No such meeting has been evoked in Eliot's poems before.

The poem is like a Fifth Monarchist's nightmare. The speaker lives in one "dream kingdom," haunted by fears of another "twilight kingdom" where he dreads some final encounter. The dreams (so much discussed by critics) in the poem become clear if we relate them to an essay of 1937 Eliot wrote on the subject of revelation:

> The human mind is perpetually driven between two desires, between two dreams each of which may be either a vision or a nightmare: the vision and nightmare of the material world, and the vision and nightmare of the immaterial. Each may be in turn, or for different minds, a refuge to which to fly, or a horror from which to escape. We desire and fear both sleep and waking; the day brings relief from the night, and the night brings relief from the day; we go to sleep as to death, and we wake as to damnation.[32]

The dreamer of "The Hollow Men" is presently situated in a "dry cellar," a "hollow valley / This broken jaw of our lost kingdoms" (reminding us again of Hugo's "bouche d'ombre" and its echo under Eliot's "red rock"). He cannot hope for death now, for death too has two kingdoms, and his mind fitfully considers them. One is the Kingdom of Heaven (indicated by the capital "K"), and as Part I ends, he asks those "who have crossed / With direct eyes, to death's other Kingdom" to "Remember us—if at all—not as lost / Violent souls [like Kurtz and Guy Fawkes], but only / As the hollow men / The stuffed men." The scene poignantly recalls Kipling's scene in his poem "The Broken Men" where Englishmen exiled to the Colonies after being "busted" back home—in *that* Kingdom—loiter by the shore, waiting to communicate with passengers of ships from their "lost kingdom." Eliot cited Kipling's poem as his primary inspiration for "The Hollow Men."[33]

Part II reveals that in yet *another* "dream kingdom," no eyes will appear except as "Sunlight on a broken column." The speaker hopes to be admitted there, where he will wear "deliberate disguises," like a scarecrow—"Behaving as the wind behaves / no nearer" to "that final meeting/In the twilight kingdom." The twilight kingdom is no dream but a reality. The speaker fears it as a condition approachable both in life and death, when one is between light and darkness. It resembles Purgatory, where Dante finally saw the eyes of Beatrice reflecting the reality of Christ's divinity—the "Multifoliate rose" (imaged in cathedral windows as in Dante's *Paradiso*)—and it is just such a "final meeting" that Eliot's speaker recoils from.

In Part III he again describes the "cactus land" where he is subsisting and now wonders about "death's other kingdom"—other than the divine Kingdom first mentioned, this one (with no capital) evidently Hell, for in it, "Waking alone," he says, "Lips that would kiss / Form prayers to broken stone." This kingdom is no dream, but all too possible. Part IV then recalls him to life as one of "the hollow men," "the stuffed men."

> In this last of meeting places
> We grope together
> And avoid speech
> Gathered on this beach of the tumid river

The last line recalls the souls collecting before the river of death in Virgil and Dante, as well as Kipling's "broken men" waiting for ships from home.

Up to this point the poem oscillates between terror of a kingdom where the speaker will *be seen* and hope for a kingdom ("death's dream kingdom") where he will not be recognized but will be able to *see* "eyes [that] are / Sunlight on a broken column." To be able to see without being seen is the prayer of the poem's first four parts. By contrast with *The Waste Land*, this dreaded Other is no delusion (as there in "the third who walks always beside you") but a fearful reality. "The Hollow Men" reaches its climax in the last strophe of Part IV when the speaker, who has described himself as hollow but also "stuffed" like a scarecrow (the filling with straw mentioned three times in Part

I), reflects that hope exists for "empty men"—men who go without stuffing, presumably. Conrad, too, distinguished between stuffed men (like "the hairdresser's dummy" accountant or the papier maché Mephistopheles brickmaker) and the absolutely empty Kurtz. Eliot's strophe sees hope for such empty men:

> Sightless, unless
> The eyes reappear
> As the perpetual star
> Multifoliate rose
> Of death's twilight kingdom
> The hope only
> Of empty men.

These last two lines would read differently if they were made one line: "The hope only of empty men," as Eliot might have made them, given the irregular stanzas he was writing. With the line broken after "only," the ambiguity leans toward this hope as the sole hope of empty men, rather than as the hope "only of empty men." Even as the sole hope, it leaves the speaker in his limbo (for it may also be *merely* a hope), and the last part describes this limbo. We are taken back to a zany child's world with the singsong *"Here we go round the prickly pear"* stanza beginning the part and another singsong stanza, *"This is the way the world ends,"* at the end. The dance around the cactus "at 5 o'clock in the morning" (instead of a "mulberry bush early in the morning") emphasizes the plight of a sleepless man, who cannot think or pray. Framed by the hollow man's weirdly childish regression are four strophes describing seven conditions of paralysis between potentiality and fulfillment. The in-between states are divine ("Between the essence / And the descent") as well as human (between emotion and response, desire and spasm), and the refrains of the stanzas suggest that the "Shadow" separating power and act may be either God's will ("For thine is the Kingdom") or just the failures of "life," which "is very long." A shadow falls too between attempts to pray and weary resignation, the mind on its treadmill evidently losing all forward motion just as the prayer ("For thine is the . . .") almost wins out. "The Hollow Men" thus concludes in an aborted prayer which the speaker humorously turns into a chant on the ending of his world, not as a divine apocalypse but an entropic, expiring whimper.[34]

[87]

The poem reads as Eliot's last poetic effort to dispose of Christian belief "by rejection and elimination," as he said (in his essay on Pascal) the Christian thinker must proceed. No poem was published after it until his conversion two years later. Even after that turning, however, negations figured prominently—in the annual Ariel poems at Christmas as well as the more ambitious "Ash-Wednesday," which came out in parts between 1927 and 1930.

The first of the Christmas poems, "The Journey of the Magi," is a complaint lamenting the consequences of the wise men's journey to Bethlehem. Only their arrival at the Birth—"not a moment too soon / Finding the place; it was (you may say) satisfactory"—was as they had foreseen. Life since then, for the wise man remembering, has been only "Hard and bitter agony . . . like Death, our death." Instead of the promised fulfillment, the transformation of Jew and Gentile, the world goes on living "in the old dispensation." And those who have *seen* the arrival of the new are worse off for the disappointment. "I should be glad of another death" (the old man's last words) suggests the truth that those who most waited for the Messiah also (in many cases) were eager for His death, for mankind is incurably disappointed with receiving what it longs for. Of course the old man does not know that his premonitions of the crucifixion ("another death") will culminate in the death of Death, or that his wish is prophetic. And the ironic prophecy of the last line does reverse *The Waste Land*'s "He who was living is now dead," since that was spoken *after* the Resurrection by a voice merely longing for peace, not rebirth.

The next Ariel poem, "A Song for Simeon" (1928), varies the Prayer Book song by being a song *for* rather than *of* Simeon, thus emphasizing Eliot's personal tribute, his praise, for one like himself who saw "the salvation promised for all the nations to see" and asked then to be allowed to "depart in peace." The negative thrust is diminished, as compared with the magi's memory, but still retains their *memento mori:*

> Now at this birth season of decease,
> Let the Infant, the still unspeaking and unspoken Word,
> Grant Israel's consolation
> To one who has eighty years and no to-morrow.

The three negatives here resound in the next strophe in Simeon's not-to-be completed vision of the risen Messiah:

> Not for me the martyrdom, the ecstasy of thought and prayer,
> Not for me the ultimate vision.

Given that the poem is "for" Simeon, isn't Eliot suggesting that the saint's vision is not for him as well?

The next Ariel poem, "Animula" (1929), is a little autobiography, imitating Dante's lovely lines on the emergent soul in *Purgatorio,* XVI, but ending very differently: "Pray for us now and at the hour of our birth"—of our efforts to be reborn, as well as the hour when the infant "issues from the hand of God." Through all their negations the first three Ariel poems express with ruthless sincerity the desert places of a newly discovered spiritual country, "a temperate valley . . . smelling of vegetation," unlike *The Waste Land* and the land of "The Hollow Men," but still a country dying into life.

Only in 1930, the Christmas after publishing "Ash-Wednesday," did Eliot achieve his first exuberant release into poetic vision of birth without agony, an emptiness completely filled. Finding in Shakespeare's *Pericles* the adequate symbol for Christmas—a lost child recovered—he sings in "Marina" of an incorruptible gift in the possession of which all negatives fail. All forms of living death "Are become unsubstantial . . . / By this grace dissolved in place." Even the invisible, incalculable unknown, groped for in questions that have no answers, has a "face":

> What is this face, less clear and clearer
> The pulse in the arm, less strong and stronger—
> Given or lent? more distant than stars and nearer than the eye
>
> Whispers and small laughter between leaves and hurrying feet
> Under sleep, where all the waters meet.

The speaker of these lines is identified only through the visionary Marina named in the title, as if to say that the vision gives him his identity. Like Pericles, the commander of ships and their construction, the speaker visualizes his own life as like those ships—wondrously constructed and renewed by the work of another agency, known in the moment of discovering a lost part of himself. Imagery from the New England coastal waters recurs here, not to be rejected as a distracting temptation, the way it appeared in "Ash-Wednesday," VI, but now as restored in a new way, as part of a fresh vision. Thus "Marina" can be read as the end point in a series of ascents, beginning with "Ash-

Wednesday" and "The Journey of the Magi," each poem recording an "in-between time"—here between dream and waking, whereas in the earlier poems the midway conditions were between birth and death, between the Old and the New Dispensations, or between hope and expectation. In the earlier "Ariel" poems the midway time was experienced as a deprivation, a denial to the speaker separated from the time of fulfillment, but in "Marina" the moment recorded is a passageway into fulfillment.

"Marina" is the last poem Eliot finished before writing *Four Quartets*. To fully understand the new via negativa traced in that finest of all his poems, however, we must step back to "Ash-Wednesday"; for there he translated into poetry all that could be said of his "way" until 1935.

Elisabeth Schneider comments concerning "Ash-Wednesday" that dating "from the time of his formal admission into the Church . . . a new and frankly personal tone enters into Eliot's poetry, and with the new tone comes once more a new style."[35] I have urged that we can find this intimate tone and style already in the first and last parts of *The Waste Land*. Also in "The Hollow Men," the broken prayers and fears of a new challenge to the spirit ring with unquestionable authority as a confession. But I am glad to have Schneider's confirmation of my sense that in "Ash-Wednesday" the last traces of "dissembling" and "doing" of voices are given up in favor of a voice that comes directly as the poet's own. (Perhaps he merely saves the voices for the theater, for which he had begun to write in 1925, with the unfinished "Sweeney Agonistes.") To say that Eliot's voice comes to us directly is not, of course, to forget his assertion in 1919 that the "man who suffers and the mind which creates" are separate, though it calls in doubt that they are "completely separate" to the extent that they were, for instance in "Prufrock." Also these observations must challenge those like I. A. Richards who would argue that the man who suffered is of no concern to the critic.

The poem's status is "only" that of a poem. It is not an actual confession any more than an actual confession is a work of art. Yet the power of the confessional poem derives from its authenticity, that is from a true correspondence between the poet's condition of being and the words of the poem at the time of its writing. As Eliot said in his 1929 essay on Dante—in answer to Richards—we would not trust a poet who could, say, write Lucretius's *De Rerum Natura* for exercise after completing *The Divine Comedy*. We have Eliot's word for it that *The Waste Land* was already confessional, written in a state of "doubt, uncertainty, futility" for "relief of a personal ... grouse against life."[36] Schneider makes the important point that "Ash-Wednesday" initiates a new vision by associating its personal revelations with the *ritual* of confession. It associates its vision, in fact, with "the negative way" of the Christian mystics rather than with the private idiosyncratic "way" Eliot had heretofore followed. The year after finishing "Ash-Wednesday," he wrote of Pascal: "His despair, his disillusion, are ... no illustration of personal weakness; they are perfectly objective, because they are essential moments in the progress of the intellectual soul; and for the type of Pascal they are the analogue of the drought, the dark night, which is an essential stage in the progress of the Christian mystic."[37] Eliot could not have applied those points to himself before writing "Ash-Wednesday."

Begun near the first Ash-Wednesday (1927) after his entry into the Church and finished three years later, the six parts of "Ash-Wednesday" reflect in several moods upon the step he has taken. The first two stanzas are variations on the theme of conversion (which is the focus of the Mass for Ash-Wednesday) and on the Mass's epistle from the prophet Joel (2:12–29), which Eliot uses also elsewhere in the poem: "Turn ye even to me, saith the Lord ..." But Eliot characteristically casts his opening in the form of negations, praying that he will *not* turn—not be converted—"again":

> Because I do not hope to turn again
> Because I do not hope
> Because I do not hope to turn
> Desiring this man's gift and that man's scope
> I no longer strive to strive towards such things
>
> . . . . .
>
> Because I do not hope to know again
> The infirm glory of the positive hour
> Because I do not think
> Because I know I shall not know
> The one veritable transitory power
> Because I cannot drink
> There, where trees flower, and springs flow, for there is
>   nothing again

Renouncing any further step he might, in later conditions, take into another "way," he also here asserts that neither hope, nor thought, nor knowledge, nor sensuous thirst for an earthly paradise can divert him again, "for there is nothing again." The passage ends in a double meaning: nothingness will return in all earthly things; but also no such "transitory power" as he once hoped for (and perhaps possessed fleetingly) can be had again.

> Because I know that time is always time
> And place is always and only place
> And what is actual is actual only for one time
> And only for one place
> I rejoice that things are as they are and
> I renounce the blessèd face

Ash-Wednesday reflections on the perishable "dust" that is forsaken for eternal treasures (as the day's Gospel from Matthew 6:16–21 tells us) "where neither moth nor rust consume them," in Part I leads Eliot to honest recognition of negative states not wholly in tune with joyful divestments: "I rejoice, having to construct something / Upon which to rejoice."

The poem is in fact such a construction. "These matters that with myself I too much discuss" must be forgotten precisely "Because I do not hope to turn again." The poem contains its own self-reflexive apology: "Let these words answer / For what is done, not to be done again." The "blessèd face" he has renounced is evidently a closer, clearer vision of God than he has been allowed—a reading that makes sense when we recall that two years after publishing this Part in 1928, he wrote in "Marina" (1930) of having glimpsed such a face, "more distant than the stars and nearer than the eye." There are two Ladies in "Ash-Wednesday," the Virgin to whom he prays at the end of Parts I and IV (echoing the "Hail Mary" and then the "Hail Holy Queen") and a more mysterious Lady who appears in Parts II, IV, and VI, but I do not find any secret lover—or even Eliot's wife—as many readers do.

This mystery Lady has usually been taken as inspired by Dante's Matilda in Cantos XXVIII and XXIX, and this seems valid. In both poems the Lady comes to the poet at a moment when he feels abandoned (Dante has just been abandoned by Virgil) and leads him to a garden where he will eventually see "the blessèd face"—of Beatrice and of Christ reflected in her eyes. As in Dante, Eliot's Lady of the Garden represents original goodness in Eden, before the Fall, and also represents silence, contemplation, and relief for the exhausted spirit. To her, in Part II of "Ash-Wednesday," Eliot shows his decimated soul. Three white leopards have "fed to satiety" on his legs, heart, and liver (that is, all his lusts have been consumed by the beast of deceit in Dante); and his dry bones sing to the Lady, longing for "forgetfulness" so that he may be "concentrated in purpose." The Lady is a perfect consoler because she is at once "Calm and distressed / Torn and most whole / ... / Exhausted and life-giving / Worried reposeful." She shows him the Garden that is the "End of the endless / Journey to no end"—Eliot's most succinct summary of the negative way he has turned away from, with its "end" in a new way. Now the desert derided before is a "blessing of sand," and the picked bones of his spirit rejoice "In the quiet of the desert."

Part III has been variously interpreted, but I think one fresh insight might be added. In the month Eliot died, the London *Times* published a note by K. Hazareesing recalling a conversation with Eliot in which Eliot "wondered if, in writing 'Ash-Wednesday,' he had not been unconsciously influenced by some aspect of Indian philosophy."[38] The suggestion is not pursued, but I am persuaded that the three stairs which constitute the third movement of the poem are related to the three stairs imaged in the Buddhist *Way of Purification* (*Visuddhimagga*) by Buddhaghosa, whom Eliot studied in 1912-13 with Charles Lanman. We shall see again in *Four Quartets* that Eliot drew effectively from early Buddhist texts in support of Christian experience. In "Ash-Wednesday" the difficulty of understanding why Eliot uses only three steps, rather than the ten of the Christian mystics, can be solved if we remember Nāgārjuna's and Buddhaghosa's teaching about the saint (called the *arhat*) who has achieved the complete detachment that leads to perfect release, or *Nirvāna*. The four stages leading to arhatship require a passage up three steps: first the step of devotion and intellectual discipline (taken as already achieved and not mentioned in "Ash-Wednesday"); second the step of returning once to repeat the cycle of earthly life; and third the step on which he frees himself from "the lower bonds" of belief in a permanent self, of doubt, and reliance on mere morality and rituals, while also freeing himself from sensual passions. This third step gives the Buddhist arhat access to the highest possibility of man, which is freedom from death, for he is now free from even the desire for existence. Such negativity, while it was congenial to the poet of *The Waste Land,* has clearly now been modified by his vision of the Lady's Garden. Part II of the poem therefore ends with an undecidability as to the ultimate number of stairs the climber will finally pass.

Reading Part III in this light, the lines correspond surprisingly to the Buddhist teaching. On "the second stair"

> I turned and saw below
> The same shape twisted on the banister
>
> . . . . .
>
> Struggling with the devil of the stairs who wears
> The deceitful face of hope and of despair.

And "At the second turning of the second stair / I left them twisting, turning below; / . . . the stair was dark, / Damp, jaggèd, like an old man's mouth drivelling, beyond repair." The second stair thus shows the climber his own earlier life, repetitively grappling with disordered passion. (The manuscript originally read "My own shape" instead of "The same shape," the change suggesting a dim, recurring nightmare.) As he looks down from the second stair on "the devil of the stairs," he recognizes its deceits, but now (at the second turning) he feels a generalized disgust accompanied by a feeling of terror. Then "At the first turning of the third stair / Was a slotted window bellied like the fig's fruit." His mind finds relief in a pastoral scene where he glimpses a "broadbacked figure drest in blue and green" who "Enchanted the maytime with an antique flute." This sight of a Pan-like reveler suggests all the "lower bonds" from which the climber is finally freeing himself. The relief is momentary—a distraction—and recognizing the inadequacy of such relief, he summons a new strength "beyond hope and despair."

The "antique flute" is mentioned in Eliot's Harvard Philosophy 12 Notebook—on the same page as the comments on reincarnations in lower forms of life as judgments for human misdeeds (apparently recalled when Eliot wrote "The Death of Saint Narcissus"). To avoid such regressions, the notes say, "Do not listen to flute or cymbals."[39] (Eliot would have read a similar remark on flute music as a dangerous distraction in Aristotle's *Politics*, VIII, 6.) Such distant memories, transmuted into symbols requiring no sources, enrich the scene visualized from the dark stairway of "Ash-Wednesday":

> Distraction, music of the flute, stops and steps of the mind over
> the third stair,
> Fading, fading; strength beyond hope and despair
> Climbing the third stair.

For the first time in all the stairway imagery of Eliot's poems, the stairway leads upward *after* a preliminary descent—into the penitential desert of Part II. The Augustinian idea, "Descend that ye may ascend," governs the imagery of this poem in a Part written in 1929, the same year as Simeon (in the "Song for Simeon") imagines those who will follow the Resurrection, "mounting the saints' stair"—unlike himself. Was Eliot in "Song for Simeon," as in "Ash-Wednesday," loath to associate his own ascent with the ten stairs of St. John of the Cross? It would seem so in his stopping at the third stair, whether or not that was a reflection of the "old dispensation." Schneider is surely right when she notes the ambiguity of the last lines of Part III of "Ash-Wednesday": "Lord, I am not worthy / but speak the word only." Eliot only speaks the words of absolute humility, for the poem is only words; but read in the expected way, he here admiringly remembers the Roman centurion of Matthew 8:5–8, who considers himself unworthy to have Christ enter his house and knows that He needs only to say the word and his dying daughter will be healed. The words also recall us to the Mass, for they are spoken by the congregation just before Communion.

I cannot agree with Schneider, however, that the speaker of "Ash-Wednesday" is "removed not only from [*The Waste Land*'s] humanism but from human relationships" because "emphasis has shifted toward the need for belief, toward ritual and dogma, thus toward the institutional."[40] The poem's whole burden reminds us that joining the Church was an acknowledgment of human relationship for the Coriolanus who had broken his communal ties in the years from 1915 to 1926. Part IV of the poem plainly identifies the Lady of the Garden with the congregation of the Church. When he appeals to her in Dante's words (or Arnaut Daniel's words) "Sovegna Vos"—"Remember"—he visualizes her as part of a community whom the Lady represents, a community whose power she restores in Part IV. He addresses her as one

> Who walked between the violet and the violet
>
> . . . . .
>
> Talking of trivial things
> In ignorance and in knowledge of eternal dolour
> Who moved among the others as they walked.
> Who then made strong the fountains and made fresh
>   the springs.

This appears to echo the Ash-Wednesday epistle: "Between the porch and the altar [the priests, the Lord's ministers, shall weep and shall say]: Spare thy people, O Lord . . . And the Lord will answer and say to His people: Behold I will send you corn and wine and oil, and you shall be filled with them." Certainly Part IV of the poem sings of a shared renewal, "restoring / With a new verse the ancient rhyme." Eliot thought of Dante's "ancient rhyme" as one of the great *humanist* documents. The Lady Matilda in the *Purgatorio* guided Dante to a vision of the Church as a chariot drawn by the whole body of prophets and evangelists. Eliot refers to the pageant as an example of Dante's "high dream" in his 1929 essay on Dante, and here in Part IV his Lady walks with "the years," inspiring an "unread vision in the higher dream / While jewelled unicorns draw by the gilded hearse." Grover Smith convincingly tracks these lines to a source in Conrad Aiken's *Senlin: A Biography* and notes that Eliot seems also to remember Blake's "Marriage hearse" in "London." In Part IV, Eliot celebrates the Lady of contemplation who has led him to the Church but also remembers that the Church has become a "gilded hearse" for those who make an idol of it.

The poem's next part probes more deeply into the impediments thrown in the way by acceptance of a creed without seeking "the word" (the unspoken word) and "the face" (the unseen face) behind it. Again negations point to the "néant" where word and face are to be sought after their loss "here" in the world.

> Where shall the word be found, where will the word
> Resound? Not here, there is not enough silence.
>
> . . . . .

> The right time and the right place are not here
> No place of grace for those who avoid the face
> No time to rejoice for those who walk among the noise and
>   deny the voice

Part V is a warning not only to those who end by accepting the Church without its inner reality (those "who chose and oppose thee") but also to those who look "here"—in this poem, perhaps, as well as in the noisy world—for the word and the face.

Part VI ends the poem with a final confession, first echoing the words that begin a *private* confession ("Bless me father [for I have sinned]") and then ending with the words of *public* confession spoken by the congregation at the beginning of the Mass: "[O Lord hear my prayer] And let my cry come unto Thee." The first reference is followed by an equally private recollection of what I take to be Eliot's tormenting memories of the world he has left behind in entering the Anglican community, for the third strophe recalls his American memories of Cape Ann and his Protestant tradition's encouragement of the rebellious spirit. He asks forgiveness, for "I do not wish to wish these things"—glimpsed through "the wide window towards the granite shore" that recalls the view from his family's house in Gloucester, Massachusetts. From that view, "The white sails still fly seaward, seaward flying / Unbroken wings," while (as Part I had said) his own eagle's wings are no longer to be stretched in rebellious flight. Haunted in a "dream-crossed twilight," he names "three dreams"—associated with the dreams of "The Hollow Men" and now further identified with the "empty forms between the ivory gates" that are unreal dreams, as well as the "higher dream" of the Christian vision contending with "the low dream" of everyday life (so named in the 1929 essay on Dante). If the last line of the poem, as I suggest, takes us back to the beginning of the Mass and the public confession at the foot of the altar (making the poem a meditation before Mass), "Ash-Wednesday" as a whole marks a beginning of that submission to the will of Another which Eliot first found a reality in Dante's line "la sua voluntade e nostra pace," and now translates into his own language. This is not merely poetry or metaphor, and now he does not "speak the word only"; for as the Dante essay had said the year before, "Our peace in His will" now "seems to me *literally true*."[41]

Grover Smith, following Leonard Unger's essay on the negative mysticism behind "Ash-Wednesday," cautions against overemphasizing it,[42] but I feel that we cannot emphasize it enough if we once understand it. Understanding it will be possible only after a deeper probing of the Christian via negativa and Eliot's culminating poetic view of it in *Four Quartets*. So far we have considered only his resistances to it and his gradual relinquishing of other negativities. We should remember that his reading notes from the years 1912–1914 at Harvard show that he knew even then the mystical writings of St. John of the Cross and their sources in Dionysius the Areopagite; they are mentioned on several of the cards he wrote then. But those cards were equally explicit on the pathologies of mysticism, and it was these pathological aspects that Eliot first treated in poetry, as we have seen. The turning point, as we have also seen, came in response to challenges from Richards, forcing Eliot to question "the unified sensibility" which he thought he had understood in the "metaphysical poetry" of the early seventeenth century. By 1925, as "The Hollow Men" revealed, he not only doubted that he had a grasp of Donne's "way" of unifying spirit and sense but also had lost his own belief in the high philosophical detachment he had espoused before then. The real turning point came in 1926 when he interrupted his arguments with Richards and others to concentrate on tracing the course of metaphysical poetry from the time of Dante to the twentieth century, a development which he presented as the Clark Lectures at Trinity College, Cambridge, some eleven months before his reception into the Church.

In these lectures he proposed a new approach to metaphysical poetry. Deploring "the diversion of human inquiry from ontology to psychology," beginning in the seventeenth century, he said that "Donne is in a sense a psychologist," and noted the consequences later: "Mankind suddenly retires inside its several skulls, until you hear Nietzsche ... declaring that 'nothing is inside, nothing is outside.' And the most brilliant of contemporary critics of criticism, Mr. I. A. Richards, declaring (after Kant and Descartes) that love is a spontaneous emotion bearing no relation to the object of affection." He notes that in Donne "the notions of the pseudo-Dionysius are revived sometimes telles quelles, as they are in the thought of the XV century Eckhart." Eliot now charges the whole Christian world, both Catholic and Protestant—*since* Dante—with the very spiritual diseases he had diagnosed in his poems against the Church and its saints written from 1915 to 1925. As the Clark Lectures proceed, he stresses the autohypnosis of Romantic thought and feeling that afflicts both philosophy and poetry throughout the Christian world—and not just from the time of Rousseau. The pathological condition, he says, was as evident in John Donne, St. Teresa, and St. John of the Cross as it became later. These three he describes in the Clark Lectures as "voluptuaries of religion, recklessly playing [their] parts . . . in the destruction of civilization." St. Teresa confused the passion for God with desire for a human lover, adumbrating the fleshy demoiselles of Rossetti. Here Eliot checks himself. A deeper study of mystical psychopathology would require him "to defend the memory of a great saint against calumny and degradation." Yet he includes St. Teresa with St. John and with Donne, calling them all "as much romanticists as Rousseau." He concludes: "Whether you seek the Absolute in marriage, adultery, or debauchery, it is all one—you are seeking in the wrong place."[43]

We cannot know how much of Eliot himself lay behind the images of seekers hunting the Absolute in the wrong place before "Ash-Wednesday." We do know that for him in 1926 the condition of beatitude he described as possible to civilization *before* the fourteenth century was not to be found *in* human relationships, though he increasingly saw that it could be glimpsed *through* human relationships. This Absolute, when he thought of it seriously before 1926, was closer to the Absolute of Aristotle and the Buddha's "emptiness" than it was to the human figure of Christ (who is not imaged as a flesh and blood man even in Dante). Four years after writing *The Waste Land,* Eliot agreed with Dante that the beatific vision could be—and could only be—glimpsed as some object wholly transcendent. All images for it—even that of Jesus as visible man—appeared to him soul-destroying and blasphemous.

We cannot presume to understand the change of heart that turned him from a devastating critic of every modern form of Christianity in 1926 to the penitent poet of "Ash-Wednesday," accepting his own insufficiencies as well as his fellow men's in a community of believers. We would be misled, however, if we held that he had been a sort of closet Christian, dreaming of sainthood, before that time. It was only after 1927 that he could speak of blasphemy as "a sign of Faith," a "product of partial belief" that is "as impossible to the complete atheist as to the perfect Christian."[44] Preoccupied with the subject, he wrote long passages on it not only in "Baudelaire" but in *After*

Strange Gods, where he distinguished "that first-rate blasphemy [which] is one of the rarest things in literature, for it requires both literary genius and profound faith, joined in a mind in a peculiar and unusual state of spiritual sickness." Here he said he was not defending blasphemy but "reproaching a world in which blasphemy is impossible." In such a world blasphemy "might now be taken rather as a symptom that the soul is still alive . . . for the perception of Good and Evil—whatever the choice we make—is the first requisite of spiritual life."[45] He had been making this point since 1928, when he wrote, "It is only the irreligious who are shocked by blasphemy . . . Imagine Mr. Shaw blaspheming! "[46]

Despite such convincing, if indirect, comments on his own blasphemous poems before 1925, the critical years reviewed here—between 1922 and 1930—reveal to us a poet continually dissatisfied with "the gilded hearse" of pageantry which even in Dante's vision of the Church, perhaps, seemed inadequate. "Ash-Wednesday" expresses impatience with all such images—even if they may be the poet's only "way." After "Ash-Wednesday," Eliot continued to experiment with new "ways" to express the via negativa he had by then found, you might say, satisfactory. The fullest poetical expression of it appeared in *Four Quartets,* which came closer than any other poem he wrote to meeting the goal he set himself in 1933, when he said, "I have long aimed, in writing poetry, to write poetry . . . so transparent that we should not see the poetry, but that which we are meant to see through the poetry . . . To get *beyond poetry,* as Beethoven, in his later works strove to get *beyond music.*"[47] Within a few months of this remark, however, he entered a path leading away from the confessional mode of "Ash-Wednesday" toward a very different genre—the drama. In any other poet's life at the time, the twenty-five years Eliot devoted to the theater could only have been an affirmative way, toward reinvestment in the matter of human conflict and comedy. Perhaps only to one for whom "the negative [was] the more importunate," could writing plays have led to still further ways of exploring negativity, opening astonishing vistas for other writers, like Samuel Beckett and Harold Pinter.

Tereu, twit, twit, this metaphysical mime
That should have been
The most distinguished failure of all time
Proves quite the opposite.

5 The Stage as Still Point: Plays, 1935–1958

Eliot's unforeseen conquest of Shaftesbury Avenue and Broadway in the 1940s, like other surprising changes in his career as poet, began by way of Canterbury—the Canterbury of Christian England, which presented itself to him in 1935 with the call to write a play about St. Thomas Becket. Antecedents for the writing of this first of Eliot's finished plays can be found, of course, in his choruses for *The Rock,* a religious pageant; in his earlier experimental "Aristophanic melodrama," *Sweeney Agonistes* (dating from 1925 and never finished, though several times performed); as well as in the still earlier dramatic scenes—monologues and dialogues—set into the poems of 1917 and 1920, *The Waste Land,* and the Ariel poems. For him to pursue the genres of dramatic poetry may appear at first, however, a reversal of the line I have traced from his poetry of satire to his poems of contemplation. We might have expected him to pursue the via negativa foreshadowed in "Ash-Wednesday" and "Marina," poems in the confessional mode, expressing his own new life. But after the year he spent in America (1932–33), delivering lectures at Harvard and other universities, he began to move increasingly away from what he called the first and second "voices" of poetry toward the third, the fully dramatized voice, of the poet: the poet "saying, not what he would say in his own person, but only what he can say within the limits of one imaginary character addressing another imaginary character."[1]

He said of this juncture in his career, "It may be that from the beginning I aspired unconsciously to the theatre—or, unfriendly critics might say, to Shaftesbury Avenue and Broadway." Such unconscious aspiration seems evident in much of his early work. He had originally shied away from the first voice of poetry, that of "the poet talking to himself—or to nobody," probably because it had been overused in the poetry of the previous century; and the second voice, that of "the poet addressing an audience, whether large or small," tended toward the more ambitious forms of the third, fully dramatized voice.[2] While in America (appropriately) he had written, "I believe that the poet naturally prefers to write for as large and miscellaneous an audience as possible . . . I myself should like an audience which could neither read nor write. The most useful poetry, socially, would be one which would cut across all the present stratifications of public taste—stratifications which are perhaps a sign of social disintegration. The ideal medium for poetry, to my mind . . . is the theatre."[3]

Even in his earliest literary essays Eliot had been preoccupied with the theater, reviewing a broad range of ancient and modern plays from Greek tragedy and Japanese Noh plays to Elizabethan drama and recent musical comedy. The theater, he was to say often, answered a deep psychological need of human nature, both the nature of the poet and the nature of the audience. In "Tradition and the Individual Talent," he had spoken of the poet's need for a "continual self-surrender of himself as he is at the moment to something which is more valuable."[4] And this more valuable thing clearly is not only the enduring poem but the common experience of which, and to which, the poem speaks. As Eliot said, this common experience in art has always been most powerfully conveyed in the theater, where the poet and his audience meet in immediate union through the mediation of public action. "All poetry tends toward drama," Eliot has "C" say convincingly in his 1928 "Dialogue on Dramatic Poetry."[5] Thus even the first voice tends toward the third voice from the beginning of Eliot's career, because all poetry is "a continual self-sacrifice, a continual extinction of personality"[6]—of the private self as it transforms personal feeling into universally accessible experience. This is not to say that the drama is a "higher" form than the others. Eliot avoids the hierarchical taxonomy characteristic of some Romantic criticism (for instance of Victor Hugo's Preface to *Cromwell*), probably because, he said, different periods and different individuals respond best to different forms. For him, in a period when drama seemed at very low ebb, Dante's *Commedia* was the highest expression of poetic power, not because it was a poem but because it conveyed reaches of experience inaccessible even in the greatest of dramatists, Shakespeare. We might conjecture that if Shakespeare's plays (like Dante's poem) had dramatized "everything in the way of emotion, between depravity's despair and the beatific vision, that man is capable of experiencing,"[7] then Shakespeare's plays would have appealed to Eliot more than the *Commedia*—because of their dramatic form. But this is conjecture, important only in view of his long and intense dedication to the theater.

Granting that his long-standing respect for the theater loomed large among his reasons for turning playwright, we may find another motive—beyond the incentives offered by his director, E. Martin Browne (an avid proponent of religious drama), and the practical incentive of money. He knew that hope for financial gain had lured Henry James and Joseph Conrad away from their writing desks to their humiliating ventures in the dramatic genre. For a poet as ill-suited as Eliot was to face the footlights, such examples would have been more than cautionary if a new attitude toward his own writing had not persuaded him to breast the possibility of failure. This incentive came in the particular fitness of the stage to offer conditions for the kind of poetry he said in 1933 he had long aimed to write: a poetry "so transparent that we should not see the poetry, but that which we are meant to see through [it]," a poetry that would move "*beyond poetry,* as Beethoven, in his later works strove to get *beyond music.*"[8] That the stage was suitable to realization of this aim is not immediately clear, but we have a clue in his use of the image of the theater in *Four Quartets* to express the way toward union with God described by St. John of the Cross. Eliot's passage, pointing to the mystical dark night of the soul, comes in "East Coker," III:

> I said to my soul, be still, and let the dark come upon you
> Which shall be the darkness of God. As, in a theatre,
> The lights are extinguished, for the scene to be changed

With a hollow rumble of wings, with a movement of darkness
    on darkness,
And we know that the hills and the trees, the distant panorama
And the bold imposing façade are all being rolled away—

. . . . .

So the darkness shall be the light, and the stillness the dancing.

In this passage, the "movement of darkness on darkness" refers literally to the movement on a blackened stage within the stillness of a
blackened theater. Metaphorically, it refers to the movements of the
individual mind when, like stagehands, they are directed to change
scenes in front of the stillness of a deeper consciousness, preparing to
become one with "the darkness of God." The stage image includes
three negatives, together included in the darkness and stillness to
which the audience submits, all of which are enforced by expectation
of their opposites—light, sound, and motion. The contrast evoked, we
have come to recognize, is a controlling perception in *The Waste Land*
and the *Coriolan* fragments. In *The Waste Land* (as in several unpublished poems in the Berg Collection, especially "Silence"), the dark
center—whether "under this red rock" or at "the heart of light"—
brings fear and paralysis:

fear in a handful of dust

. . . . .

I could not
Speak, and my eyes failed, I was neither
Living nor dead, and I knew nothing,
Looking into the heart of light, the silence.

But by 1931–32, in the *Coriolan* fragments of a *dramatic* poem—the
dark, still center is a point toward which both the spectators at Coriolan's triumphal march and Coriolan himself converge in their longing,
the spectators not knowing who or what it is they are really waiting
for; Coriolan meanwhile knowing that it is not he: "At the still point
of the turning world. O hidden"; "May we not be / O hidden / Hidden in the stillness of noon, in the silent croaking night."

Thus by the time Eliot abandoned these fragments, he was searching for the new start that the conditions of the theater presented. He
summed it up in a little-noted essay on Gordon Craig written in 1955,

comparing the difference between stage plays and motion pictures in terms of the stillness and silence that distinguish the form of stage productions from the virtually perpetual movement and sound of the film as genre:

> I cannot but think that the development of the screen-play will prove to have influenced, imperceptibly perhaps but profoundly, the stage of our day and of tomorrow. Just as photography has influenced the art of portrait painting, in that the aim of the modern portrait painter is directed to what *the photographer cannot do,* so the people of the theatre—from author to actor—are likely to concentrate on what *the screen cannot do* . . . On the stage, you can present action as an interruption of stillness: on the screen, you can present stillness only as an interruption of action. On the screen the words, however important and however beautiful (as in a screen-play by William Shakespeare) can only complete the message conveyed by the picture: on the stage, accordingly, it should be permissible and acceptable that the picture—the total scene, the movement, posture, and gesture of each member of the cast—should be calculated with a view to completing the message conveyed by the words. Hence . . . every statement about the theatre . . . is limited by conditions of the critic's time and place. He cannot foresee changes to come in the world, or the relevance of such changes to the theatre.

This essay, read beside the passage from "East Coker" written more than fifteen years earlier, suggests the length of time Eliot had reflected upon stage action "as an interruption of stillness." Furthermore the essay, like the poem, takes the "empty" moment in the theater, before the action starts, as crucial to the dramatic experience:

> For a stage set is, to my mind, something on which the attention of the audience should be focused only when it is empty, or before the action starts. It should, certainly, be designed with a view to reinforcing the mood, the meaning of the play, though the ways in which it is to do so, the symbolism, abstraction or realism, elaboration or simplification . . . may be as various as the varieties of drama itself. But ordinarily, the set should only be the conscious centre of attention for the audience for a few seconds after the curtain is raised. After that, its impression should be unconsciously received.[9]

The stage set, "when it is empty, or before the action starts," resembles both the stillness of "the dark night of the soul" and the stillness out of which all art ideally proceeds.

It may be that Beckett and Pinter made even more than Eliot did of his insights in the essay on Gordon Craig, seeing the further implications for the stage of action as an interruption of the theater's stasis, its primal inertia, as compared consciously or unconsciously with its antitype in the motion picture. For Beckett, as for Eliot, this inertia has both cosmic and psychological associations, bringing actors and audience to experience life's mysterious invasions into an engulfing void. For Pinter, however, the stillness and silence out of which the dramatic action painfully asserts itself point rather toward the inverse ratio between experience and articulation. Of the "silences" indicated in the text of his *Homecoming*, for instance, Pinter says that a silence should simply mean that "something has happened to create the impossibility of anyone speaking for a certain amount of time—until they can recover from whatever happened before the silence."[10] Katherine Worth has noted this difference between Pinter and Eliot, discussing their dramatic language. On Pinter's possible debt to Eliot, she says, "It is in [Pinter's] techniques for getting both the inner and outer reality that he often comes remarkably close to Eliot . . . They meet in the middle . . . from opposite ends, Eliot arguing that intense feelings tend to express themselves in verse and using a near-prose verse as a ground to take flight from; Pinter starting with the idea that intense feeling makes for incoherence and using a sharply stylized prose."[11]

The importance of silence in the theater had been a subject for discussion and theory long before Eliot. Pinter's employment of silence, in fact, seems an extension of that of Yeats, the first to note that modern men and women are inarticulate in moments of powerful emotion, and therefore should be so in the theater: "When they are deeply moved, they look silently into the fireplace," Yeats said in "Discoveries." And in the 1920s and 30s, Jean-Jacques Bernard had carried this same view to elaboration in a new kind of theater, which he called "the theater of the unexpressed." As May Daniels has shown, Bernard's theory of silence in the theater—closer to Pinter's than Yeats's—could be compared to still another theory—to Maeterlinck's, which at first might seem to anticipate Eliot's. Maeterlinck used silence to express the incursion of invisible realities into an everyday, less real, world: "We speak only at those times when we are not living," he wrote.[12] But for Eliot, the everyday world is fully real, and language—better than silence—expresses *that* reality.

Often as he had used silence in such poems as *The Waste Land* and "The Hollow Men" to express aborted thought and feeling, for the stage Eliot demanded language that would produce a "continuous hour and a half of *intense* interest," and for this he wanted not only articulation but "verse rhythm." "Some writers," he said as early as 1919, "appear to believe that emotions gain in intensity through being inarticulate."[13] The power of even inchoate emotion to seek and find words is related to his view that there is an order in human things which we are called upon to find—a view quite contrary to that of Beckett and Pinter. Eliot connected his idea of language in the theater with this order: "the ideal towards which poetic drama should strive . . . [is] to give us some perception of an order in life, by imposing an order upon it."[14] The imposition would be an offense to the audience, of course, unless the order already existed in the nature of things, to be sought and found.

For this "order," negativity has a crucial part to play in the framing silence of the theater itself, that world out of which language and action both emerge. Thus a play reproduces the movement from silence to speech and from speech back to silence which had also served St. Augustine (in Book XI of the *Confessions*) as exemplum of human life. Eliot's "Little Gidding," V paraphrases Augustine: "Every phrase and every sentence is an end and a beginning"—an action breaking silence, initiating a movement again toward silence. And each of his plays follows the same "order," for

> Only by the form, the pattern,
> Can words or music reach
> The stillness, as a Chinese jar still
> Moves perpetually in its stillness.   ("Burnt Norton," V)

Invited to write choruses for a church pageant, *The Rock*, Eliot began shaping his idea of the theater as a "still point of the turning world." He was at one of those times of stasis from which he had often suffered, which he had learned to tolerate as affording moments of new insight. The *Coriolan* poems were at a standstill as he returned from his own "triumphal march" in America in 1933, his personal life also stymied as he faced the necessary separation from his wife. "I seemed to myself to have exhausted my meagre poetic gifts, and to have nothing more to say," he later recalled.[15] The inverse relation between heroism and holiness, which was to emerge in *Murder in the Cathedral,* was already implicit in the "Difficulties of a Statesman," as the last words haunt the consciousness of the baffled Coriolanus: "Resign Resign Resign." In Coriolanus and in Becket (as in Eliot's own life), a man at the crest of his public career feels compelled to choose between the acclamations of continuing celebrity and a terrifying submission to "the darkness of God." In both the dramatic poem and the poetic drama, adulation of the hero betokens hunger in his subjects for significance; and the subjects cannot be released into this significance until their official leader has resigned himself to apparent negations. The "true triumphal march is Christ's entry into Jerusalem," as B. Rajan phrases the point of the *Coriolan* poems.[16] In the poems, both the hero and his subjects long for a center of significance, in contrast to which the political occasion is a mockery. In the play, Becket endures all the temptations to illusory refuges, recognizing at last the real "center of the turning world." Thus the play about Becket consummates the tendencies in the *Coriolan* poems, finding in the theater a genre ideally suited to Eliot's preoccupying theme: the confrontations between public expediency and individual responsibility, between action and suffering, between the clamor of crowds and the silence of God.

Murder in the Cathedral opens—breaks the dark silence of the theater—with the choral clamor of women in the Archbishop's Hall. *They* are not actors, they declare. There is no danger for them. Nor are they sufferers seeking safety, for certainly "there is no safety in the Cathedral." So why are they there? They feel instinctively drawn, they say, "forced to bear witness."[17] Like all crowds, they move toward a spectacle half wittingly. Half knowledge moving toward knowledge, like the change from detached witness to the role of coadjutor, is a process that structures the whole play, finally uniting the chorus of women and the priests with Becket at the point where he surrenders (turns from "actor" to "patient") to the unavoidable assault of the king's henchmen. At that point Becket's paradoxical words in his first address to the women and priests will finally make sense:

> They know and do not know, what it is to act or suffer.
> They know and do not know, that acting is suffering
> And suffering is action. Neither does the agent suffer
> Nor the patient act. But both are fixed
> In an eternal action, an eternal patience
> To which all must consent that it may be willed.   (P. 17)

Those who act by surrendering to the will of God do and do not suffer; and those who suffer (or bear) the pain of submission both act and do not act. So paradoxically in the play the chief actor, Becket, learns how not to act; and the chief witnesses—forced to be patient and suffer—learn how to act, "That the pattern may subsist" which unites everyone with the will of God.

Into the wheeling of seasons (known of old to the working women of the chorus) and the wheeling of political fortunes (known too well by the priests), fear has come to break the usual round. Becket's return from seven years of exile, his "coming" in December, coincides with the season of Christ's coming. But as before, the world is not ready: "What peace can be found . . .?" asks the Third Priest (p. 13). And the Messenger answers: "this peace / Is nothing like an end, or like a beginning" (p. 14). The audience may remember Eliot's Magi, lamenting over the inconclusive and ominous "coming" they have witnessed.

This coming of Becket, too, is more like a death than a birth of harmony. As the Messenger says, Becket left France foretelling his own death. The chorus feels it: "a great fear is upon us . . . / A fear like birth and death" (p. 16). The action to which they felt drawn merely as witnesses begins to involve them. "O Thomas our Lord, . . . do you realise what it means / To the small folk drawn into the pattern of fate . . .?" (p. 16).

Hearing them, Becket observes how much they know even in their ignorance; also how much they act and suffer even in their seeming separation from the center of action. He reminds the officious priest, trying to silence the chorus, that unless they do identify themselves with the coming action and suffering, "the wheel" which is the pattern of God's knowing, will not "turn and still / Be forever still." Thus when Becket enters, the stillness and silence of the theater have been broken already by images of a wheel of seasons and political quarrels that the people of Canterbury wish to divert as senseless and even destructive. Identified as he is by his people with the center of the wheel, he draws them too into the center, searching again for the stillness. They will all share in the "act," and he says, "the substance of our first act / Will be shadows, and the strife with shadows" (p. 18). With them, he has only half-knowledge of this "substance." Immediately, as if admitted by his anticipation, the four tempters intrude. The first tempts him to renew "the good time past" in his youthful intimacy with the king; the second tempts him to take back his power as chancellor, resigned because it conflicted with his spiritual office; and the third, like the others anticipated by Becket, counsels him to join forces with the dissident barons against the king's tyranny. These three "shadows" are easily repelled, but the fourth Becket does not even recognize: the sudden temptation to seek martyrdom, the "enduring crown to be won" (p. 27).

Here the "still point" at which Becket stood is shaken, when for the first time he thinks of himself as one who may "rule from the tomb." This fourth tempter is right, then, for he echoes Becket's own earlier words: "You know and do not know . . ." He may be taunting Becket for his pose of superior wisdom, but as the archbishop's inner voice he is also speaking prophetic truth. Eliot saw the dual possibilities of this "temptation" in 1956—after twenty years of the play's performance—when he wrote to E. Martin Browne that the audience should here be able to wonder whether this tempter is "an evil angel or possibly a good angel. After all the fourth tempter is gradually leading Becket on to his sudden resolution and simplification of his difficulties."[18] Only a playwright thoroughly versed in "the negative way" could imagine a good angel appearing to Becket in the guise of a dangerous tempter. For this "shadow" plants in his mind the idea of martyrdom which is simultaneously to be resisted as suicide (insofar as he might will it himself) and grasped as an intuition of the "pattern" in store for him, insofar as God may will it. The dual interior action accounts for Becket's long silence after the last tempter has spoken. He is neither inarticulate (as Pinter might have it) nor possessed by an otherworldly vision. He is silently reaching that "sudden resolution and simplification of his difficulties" that we shall see occurring later in similar circumstances to Harry Monchensey, Celia Coplestone, Colby Simpkins, and Lord Claverton in Eliot's next four plays. It is a moment of what Keats would call "negative capability"—"when man is capable of being in uncertainties, Mysteries, doubts, without any irritable reaching after fact & reason"[19]—with the added positive disposition of "consent[ing] that it may be willed," whatever "it" may be (as Becket and the fourth tempter, who echoes him, both say). Just how uncertain Becket has cause to be must appear from the fourth tempter's joining in unison with the evil tempters (during Becket's silence) as they chant, "This man is obstinate, blind, intent / On self-destruction" (p. 28). The germ of resolution has sprung from the worst source, for "The last temptation is the greatest treason: / To do the right deed for the wrong reason" (p. 30). He will not destroy himself (as the chorus of women have just suggested in their terror). "I shall no longer act or suffer, to the sword's end," he says, meaning both that he will not serve the purposes of the sword, even as intentional martyr, and also that he will not act on his own volition until the sword has done its work. (Eliot believed in the intercession of the saints after their deaths, as the play indicates.)

As the scene ends, the chorus, priests, and tempters all surround Becket at their center, and the stage reverts to the still darkness of the theater before the beginning of the play. The scene thus ends in a negation such as could well be understood by an audience of Buddhists, with Becket standing neither for nor against the king's forces, and not even taking a position in the middle. He is, as Eliot says in "Burnt Norton," II, "Neither from nor towards . . . / But neither arrest nor movement. And do not call it fixity."

Twenty-three days later, on Christmas Morning, the stage lights again, and Becket delivers his sermon, which would be near the central sacrifice of the Mass, just as it precedes Becket's self-sacrifice in the play. The sermon describes the unique character of the Christmas Mass, the only Mass of the year that commemorates at once both Christ's birth and His death, thus teaching communicants to "mourn and rejoice at once and for the same reason" (p. 32). Through birth and death, Christ both surrendered His will and found it in the will of God. Therefore, says Becket, it is no "accident" that the day after Christmas should celebrate the feast of the first martyr, Stephen. "A martyrdom is always the design of God, for His love of men, to warn them and to lead them, to bring them back" (p. 33). In this Interlude, Becket stands alone, "at the still point," reflecting on the peculiar "Peace" announced by the Nativity angel, which comes with perfect trust in this pattern. The absence of the chorus and priests during the Interlude suggests that they have merged with the audience, as Frances White Fry has noted.[20] Warned and instructed by the fourth tempter, Becket "knows and does not know" how closely his own life will imitate this patern: "because it is possible that in a short time you may have yet another martyr," he says, "I would have you keep in your hearts these words" (p. 34). Again the stage darkens to stillness and silence.

When the action begins again, the chorus have profited from the

Interlude: "The peace of this world is always uncertain unless men keep the peace of God," they say (p. 35). In their roles as housewives and farmers, they speak as before of the seasons and harvest, but now they see that "the world must be cleaned in the winter, or we shall have only / A sour spring . . . / Between Christmas and Easter what work shall be done?" (p. 35). They "know and do not know" that the work of redemption must be done, as it was once done at the Crucifixion. They feel the corruption spreading again, like a disease, from the knights' charges against Becket. It seems to activate a devolution of all creation, literally reversing the work of God: "Rings of light coiling downwards, descending / To the horror of the ape" (p. 42). The lines indeed reverse Emerson's vision of nature: "striving to be man, the worm / Mounts through all the spires of form."[21] Neither Becket nor his good angel, whom he called on to "hover over the swords' points" (p. 31), can stop the evil, and Becket's one comfort to his people is that there is peace in recognizing they can only wait:

> These things had to come . . .
> This is your share of the eternal burden,
> The perpetual glory. This is one moment,
> But know that another
> Shall pierce you with a sudden painful joy
> When the figure of God's purpose is made complete.   (P. 43)

As in Act I, Becket stands at the still point of the stage, the Archbishop's Hall, but hearing him the priests, burdened with their offices, cannot see what he sees—"the wink of heaven" and the "joyful consummation" just then revealed to Becket alone. They lay hold of him, dragging him offstage, and in the dark there comes the "hollow rumble of wings, with a movement of darkness on darkness" that Eliot later described in "East Coker," III. The "darkness of God," there precisely imaged as "in a theatre," is exactly the effect here as the "Dies Irae" is sung offstage—still in the dark—while the chorus onstage speaks of

> The white flat face of Death, God's silent servant
> And behind the face of Death the Judgement
> And behind the Judgement the Void,

. . . . .

Emptiness, absence, separation from God;
The horror of the effortless journey, to the empty land
Which is no land, only emptiness, absence, the Void.   (P. 44)

The lights return, and Becket is once more the center of presence, but now he is struggling against his own priests:

Unbar the doors! . . .
I will not have the house of prayer, the church of Christ,
The sanctuary, turned into a fortress.

When he says, "We have fought the beast / And have conquered," he refers not only to the knights whose arguments have been justly answered but also to his own temptations and to the failures of his people to understand exactly what is occurring. His last words, after the drunken knights have broken in and are about to kill him, identify him as one with Christ and the saints in the regenerative work by which all accept this evil so that all may transcend it. The power of God to turn evil to good is not immediately apparent to the chorus as they chant, trying to avert the tragedy, "Clear the air! clean the sky! wash the wind!" (p. 47). They seem to have momentarily forgotten that "the world must be cleaned in the winter" (p. 35) or spring will fail; but more important, as Becket foresaw, they must undergo this purging experience with him. There is no scapegoat to send off the evil from them. They must feel themselves "defiled with blood" in the "instant eternity of evil and wrong": "it is not the city that is defiled, / But the world that is wholly foul" (p. 48).

Only King Henry's henchmen believe themselves exempt from the evil. They are the innocent scapegoats, they suggest, to be sent away into exile so that the nation may recover from their necessary unpleasantness, which in fact (they say) was a suicide. The body of Becket, at first the center of a wheel formed by the knights' swords (as staged by Eliot and Browne), remains at the center while the priests speak, gradually coming to consciousness that the church, like the people, is no longer defiled but consecrated by this action. New Year's Day is near, and the "Te Deum"—traditional for that day—sounds offstage, paraphrased by the chorus, whose spiritual cause has been won by

Becket's unmoving act. In keeping with Eliot's idea of the theater, the chorus here speaks of a darkness which the audience may see as their own in contrast to the stage lights: "the darkness declares the glory of light" (p. 53). Ideally the play should end here not with a curtain but with the darkening of the stage, as the chorus acknowledge their union with "the agony of the saints" and call upon Blessed Thomas to help them in the world to which the house lights then return the audience. Of course the play was originally staged in a church.

It is a bold venture for "this metaphysical mime" Eliot (as the mysterious "Saggitarius" called him), and Eliot was under no illusions as to the play's effectiveness in the theater, as opposed to the church.

WITH THE PLAY about Becket, Eliot was (perhaps consciously) recapitulating the phylogeny of all drama, as Aristotle described it in the *Poetics*. Greek drama, says Aristotle, advanced through the differentiation of characters (or "actors") from the chorus who sang in praise of a god at festivals, the god gradually yielding place as the drama developed to focus on a hero, who then became the chief actor. Aeschylus introduced a second actor, thus making conflict possible. Eliot's recognition in "Poetry and Drama" that *Murder in the Cathedral* lacks drama, because it focuses on Becket's inner conflict and the chorus's responses to it, suggests more than one parallel between the play and Aeschylus's *Prometheus Bound,* where the incipient "second actor"—Zeus—is absent. Prometheus's ordeal unfolds entirely in reaction to the emissaries of the invisible Zeus, just as Eliot's Becket responds entirely to King Henry II, the tyrant who never appears in the play. And as Prometheus dimly forecasts his victory over the tyrant from the beginning of the play, thus eliminating the major conflict, so Becket's triumph is intuitively foreseen and foreknown by both himself and the audience. Only the chorus of minor figures—representing natural beings and forces longing for divine guidance—progresses from ignorance to knowledge in both plays. Prometheus foretells that a savior, Heracles, will appear long after the play's action is done, to end the agony of the world; and Becket foretells that the savior who has come, Christ, will be known again through Becket's agony and death at Canterbury.

Thus the main weaknesses of *Murder in the Cathedral*, dramatically speaking, were strengths insofar as they led Eliot back to the origins of all drama, and to its generative impulses in religious ritual. From that beginning he could allow the demands of drama, as opposed to ritual, to guide his craft. The absent enemy in Becket's play is fully dramatized in Eliot's second play, *The Family Reunion,* thus making possible a radical change in the hero, whose conflict is fully presented on stage. In *The Family Reunion,* the chief character, Harry, Lord Monchensey, confronts and defeats (or rather transforms) the adversary: his mother.

Eliot's choice of an aristocratic family (here and in his two last plays) struck many critics as evidence of his missing the current of the times. "None of [Eliot's four plays] after *Murder in the Cathedral* comes near that work in power or in 'relevance,'" says Tom F. Driver. "If this generation cared little for religion, it cared less for polite society."[22] But was it the current Eliot missed or only a tide? The men and women in serious drama must represent their whole society— England, in Eliot's plays, his chosen land. And the most representative are those whose roots are deepest. As in ancient drama, the roots are diseased, however. Democratic tragedy cannot show root rot of this nature without suggesting that the whole of mankind is rotten; therefore the rootless must be the survivors. In Tennessee Williams's *A Streetcar Named 'Desire,'* for instance, it is the as yet unrooted Kowalskis who will carry on. In Arthur Miller's *Death of a Salesman* it is the rootless Biff who will inherit the earth. But in Eliot's social philosophy, the nation with the deepest roots will have the better story to tell. An "old house," however blighted, keeps better records; its inhabitants "listen" more attentively, and they hear more than is spoken at any given time. Everything and everyone counts and is counted, for better or worse. As it was in the Argos of Aeschylus, so it is in the Monchenseys' England, as the chorus of aunts and uncles say:

> In an old house there is always listening, and more is heard than is spoken.
> And what is spoken remains in the room, waiting for the future to hear it.
> And whatever happens began in the past, and presses hard on the future.
> The agony in the curtained bedroom, whether of birth or of dying,
> Gathers in to itself all the voices of the past, and projects them into the future.

> . . . . . .
>   all are recorded.
> There is no avoiding these things
> And we know nothing of exorcism
> And whether in Argos or England
> There are certain inflexible laws
> Unalterable . . .[23]

In an "old house," however, the family prefer to listen and do nothing: "There is nothing to do about anything, / And now it is nearly time for the news / We must listen to the weather report / And the international catastrophes" (p. 101).

Perhaps Eliot had to show in one play at least the complete negativity to which an "old house" had come—a vision of the waste land with its maimed king. The lord surveying *The Family Reunion*'s waste land is just such a maimed hero, named for all the dear Harrys of British history. Harry, Lord Monchensey, says, "I am the old house / With the noxious smell and the sorrow before morning, / In which all past is present" (p. 66). He has inherited whatever is good or evil in the tradition, and its amassed evils have fallen on him with a crushing weight. The curse is no simple crossing of a god's will—incest or murder breeding further bloodshed and incest as in the *Oresteia,* which Eliot frames behind *The Family Reunion.* The curse contaminating its thirty-five-year-old lord derives from a subtler compound. Three women have struggled for possession of him—his mother, Amy; her sister, Agatha (whose child might have been the Monchensey heir if she had met his father in time); and his nameless wife, "a restless shivering painted shadow," who "only wanted to keep him to herself" (p. 62), initiating his alienation from the family. But part of the suffering he experiences—the great complication of Christian tragedy—is his intuition of some ineffable happiness or reality that has been lost—a hint of which Agatha found momentarily with his father. In Harry's youth Agatha somehow conveyed this joy or grace to him, first by saving his life—preventing (for love of the unborn child) his father from murdering his mother—and later by maintaining a loving presence in his life. So the curse is a compound of sin and grace, the two struggling in him for mastery. Knowing nothing of events before his birth, Harry believes the alienation from grace began with his own marriage, culminating in his murdering his wife (as he thinks) by pushing her overboard during an Atlantic voyage. Returning home to find a refuge, he discovers that the curse afflicts him even more virulently there. Why? he demands to know.

As the curtain rises on the drawing room of "the old house," the center which might be the "still point" of happiness is occupied by the mother, whose stalled presence focuses that moment of arrest which Eliot saw as the beginning of stage action. A maid is the first to act, entering to close the curtains over the windows backstage, as if to undo the work of the stage curtain disclosing the scene. Amy's first words stop her with a commanding double negative: "Not yet! ... / Put on the lights. But leave the curtains undrawn" (p. 57). "Undrawn" may suggest here that the curtains be closed to the audience (where darkness holds) and open only to the sky where there is still light. (The ambiguity of "undrawn" is emphasized later when the chorus speaks of their worries that the curtains may be "drawn"—now meaning opened—to expose the family to public view; p. 74.) Amy wants the light but fears exposure: "I sit in the house from October to June" (p. 57). The month is March, and a typescript at Harvard specifies the "Vernal Equinox" in Eliot's hand, though he decided perhaps to save that marker for the "midwinter spring" of "Little Gidding," I—the season "between melting and freezing," when the dumb spirit stirs "in the dark time of the year." The ambivalence between desiring light and dreading exposure that stirs Amy is repeated when Harry enters after eight years away: "How can you sit in this blaze of light for all the world to look at? / ... / Do you like to be stared at by eyes through a window?" It is the family's nothingness that he cannot bear to see exposed: "If you knew how you looked ...!" He calls them "people to whom nothing has ever happened" (pp. 63, 65). Mother and son are both claustrophobic and agoraphobic—a condition that Eliot might say could be conveyed best to an audience in a theater.

What saves Harry is the Eumenides—the Furies borrowed from Aeschylus's *Oresteia,* who are different in Eliot's play in that they intend only good, though when Harry is driven back home by them, he sees them as clawed and terrifying. Nevill Coghill considers them a failure because they have no voices (and indeed Eliot said, "They are never right" in the productions he saw),[24] yet it is essential that they be silent and utterly mysterious. For Harry's main object in the play is to interpret as best he can a force that drives him first to seek refuge in the past—in order to understand it—and then to redirect the future—his family's as well as his own.

The problem of representing these "bright angels" should probably be solved with lighting effects, first terrifying and then brightly beckoning; for it is on their silent, so to say negative, presence that the action turns when they appear. They are first visible in Part I, scene 2, when they interrupt Harry's idyllic "moment . . . in sunlight" with Mary. He thinks he might stay with her at Wishwood, resuming the place that Amy has prepared for him: but if he did stay, the old self—molded to his mother's will—could at best keep the clock of the old house from stopping in the dark (Amy's metaphor for her all-pervasive fear). He tells Mary that "it seemed as if I had been always here" (p. 82). Her keen perception of his "terrified spirit / Compelled to be reborn" has insidiously given him the wrong signal even in its truth. He is weaker than Mary knows and would lapse, as his father did, into being run by "the clock" of the contaminated old house, with Mary "saving" him from his guiding spirits. "If you will depend on me," she says ominously, "it will be all right" (p. 83). At just this point the Eumenides become visible to Harry for the first time, and Mary (seeing them, as we know later) closes the curtains over them. Coghill and Helen Gardner say she either pretends not to see them or does not,[25] but in fact her words—"Look at me" and "Harry! there is no one here"—can only be interpreted to mean no one *here,* in her presence. Harry rightly concludes that she is "obtuse," that he "must face them [the Eumenides] . . . must fight them" (p. 84), as Becket fought the fourth tempter.

Not until Harry has penetrated to the deepest cause of his madness—the general contamination of his "house"—can he be "reborn" as Mary sees that he may be. She cannot know the real meaning of the terrifying spirits because she came to the house after the curse had possessed it. Having decided to "speak to them," Harry "tears apart the curtains: but the embrasure is empty," as the stage directions tell (p. 84). Scene 2 of the play ends where scene 1 began, first Amy but now Harry commanding that the curtains be opened. To Amy they meant a screen against light, and to Harry now a facing of the tormenting forces of darkness. The chorus, about to enter, will demand that the curtains be closed again and will express their fear of a future "long since settled," whose "beak and claws" have "torn / The roof from the house, or perhaps it was never there" (pp. 87–88). Thus empty darkness comes like the "movement of darkness on darkness," as the audience should feel its own, repeated in Eliot's analogy of the theater for "the darkness of God" in "East Coker," III, written the same year.

We have already seen that in *The Family Reunion* Eliot reverses the image of the stage as "still point," compared with what it was in *Murder in the Cathedral*. There, the place was Canterbury and the main figure a saint—both centers of a sacred "wheel" or pattern. Here, the "still point" (which is at Wishwood or anywhere) has been usurped by Amy, so the wheel becomes a "burning wheel," like the "wheel of fire" on which King Lear is racked—a wheel of senseless repetition. It must be stopped so that the true center may be found, both for the "old house" and for its occupants. The forward motion of *The Family Reunion* is not (as in Canterbury) a matter of keeping the center but of finding it and restoring human motivation.

When the Eumenides appear again, Harry has followed them into the darkness, as it were, pursuing the question of Oedipus (rather than Orestes): "Who were my parents?" (p. 104). He knows what was wrong with his mother, describing it to Dr. Warburton early in the play:

> When we were children, before we went to school,
> The rule of conduct was simply pleasing mother;
>
> . . . . .
>
> And whatever made her happy was what ·as virtuous—
> Though never very happy, I remember. That was why
> We all felt like failures, before we had begun.   (Pp. 89–90)

He does not know, however, what was wrong with his father. At his demands to know more about him, Warburton unwittingly hints at a "scandal" but steers the conversation to focus on Amy's weak heart, the danger that she will die if Harry goes on worrying her with his wild behavior instead of settling down to the role she has prepared for him at Wishwood. At this point Harry, frustrated in his desire to understand his father and be done with all the talk about his mother, feels all too willing to risk his mother's "health." But he is interrupted by a comic intrusion, which is one of Eliot's best pieces of stage business. A police sergeant, Winchell, arrives to announce that Harry's younger brother John has had an accident. Harry, just apprised by Warburton that he may cause his mother's death as he thinks he has caused his wife's, imagines that the policeman is another spirit (like the Eumenides), who intends to madden him with guilt, now for his mother's danger. If Winchell is "real"—that is, not a spirit—Harry tells Warburton, then nothing can happen to his brothers—nothing ever happens to such people in the ordinary world, as the chorus has indicated—so they can ignore him and pursue the question of his father. If Winchell is a spirit, then Harry must face him, for his brothers' sake as well as his own. The scene stresses the extent to which Harry sees everyday accidents in the family as insignificant compared to the "monstrous aberration" of their spiritual condition. The comedy appears in Winchell's confusion, mixing up Amy's birthday (which everyone has gathered to celebrate) first with Harry's—a telling mistake—and then with his own mother's. Poor Warburton begs them both to forget their absurdities so he can learn what accident Winchell has come to report. But Winchell tries to recover his balance with seeming irrelevance by asking, "How is her Ladyship?" Harry, interpreting this question as an insinuation that he is about to murder his mother as he has murdered his wife, shouts, "I'm not afraid of you . . . Well, do you want me to produce her for you?" As Winchell demurs, Harry adds, "You mean you think I can't" (Part II, scene 1).

Raymond Williams calls the policeman "a weary caprice," a distraction,[26] yet the scene serves two vital purposes, in addition to varying the pace and tone of the play. First it shows us Harry's desperation not to be interrupted in his inquiry after his father, and secondly it reveals his fear of what his hatred for his mother may do, repeating the cycle of his agony with his wife. (The resemblance to Hamlet's "mad scene" with his mother is striking, and Eliot perhaps improves on it by making Harry's reasons for fearing that he will murder his mother much clearer.) Furthermore it delays, thereby increasing suspense over, the complication of John's accident, calling attention to the part that John will eventually be able to fill when Harry resigns as master of Wishwood. Though John never appears, we must care enough about him to be sure that the "old house" can stand and be renewed when it has been purged through Harry's renunciation, his realigning of "the wheel." Harry is still half crazed when he learns that John has been knocked unconscious in a car crash (not John's fault, as the youngest brother Arthur's parallel accident is *his* fault, we later learn), and Harry says with a kind of judgment that is not without generosity: "If [John] was ever really conscious, / I should be glad for him to have a breathing spell" (p. 96). John will need to rethink the whole family situation, as Harry is in the process of doing.

Both accidents, John's and Arthur's, give us a chance to see the relation between the trivial and the monstrous in this accursed family. Harry knows, as the chorus of his aunts and uncles dimly perceived, that his family are "Making small things important, so that everything / May be unimportant" (p. 98). They are in effect making positives out of nothing, in order that the "real" may be negated. This crucial perception of negation relates in turn to the central problem of Harry's own life—the dysfunctions (also expressed as a negation) which he says, "I cannot put in order":

> I was like that [making something out of nothing], so long as I
>   could think
> Even of my own life as an isolated ruin,
> A casual bit of waste in an orderly universe.
> But it begins to seem just part of some huge disaster,
> Some monstrous mistake and aberration
> Of all men, of the world, which I cannot put in order." (P. 98)

Thus enabled to distinguish "the real" through perception of "the unreal" at Wishwood, he beings to be able to see his mother not as the menacing presence he remembered but rather as dependent upon him: "I shall make you lie down," he tells her with sudden mastery, answering her remark, "You looked like your father" (when he spoke of John as needing a breathing spell). Indeed he then puts her to bed; and when he returns to the stage, he reports that she fell asleep at once, looking "as she must have looked when she was a child" (pp. 97–98).

After his admonitions to the chorus of aunts and uncles, however, Agatha sees a new menace in Harry's hint of a prideful negativity and detachment. Using yet another negation, she says that "we cannot rest in being / The impatient spectators of malice or stupidity" (p. 99). The warning (as the metaphor suggests) extends to the audience, who should be doubly alert at the play's self-reflexive marker. Other explicit analogies between the Wishwood family's behavior and the role-playing of actors also signal how the audience is to "act" as witnesses. We should not be like the chorus who felt like "amateur actors who have not been assigned their parts / . . . dressed for a different play, or having rehearsed the wrong parts" (pp. 62–63). We should identify with Harry, "Playing a part that had been imposed upon me," as he says referring to Amy's plan for him ten years earlier (p. 106). Harry is both rejecting an imposed part and searching for his true rule, as by implication "every man" should do, helping relatives to overcome their "amateur" status—to dress for "the play" where they belong, and to know their right parts. In *The Family Reunion* this can be achieved only when Harry discovers "the play" that occurred before the curtain rose.

When he willed his wife's death, without actually causing it, he found momentary peace, but it was only "reversing the senseless direction / For a momentary rest on the burning wheel / That cloudless night in the mid-Atlantic / When I pushed her over" (p. 66). (We know from the newspaper reports and his servant's recollection that it was cloudless only for Harry.)

After the diversions created by the accidents of John and Arthur, the chorus departs to distract itself with the radio, leaving Agatha alone with Harry to probe the meaning of his decision to abandon Wishwood. He seizes the chance to quiz her on Warburton's hint that he must not ask Agatha about a "scandal" (p. 91). From her he learns the truth: that his father "might have lived . . . not neglecting public duties" if he had not been weak with the "diffidence of a solitary man" and resigned himself to his wife's "power"(pp. 103–104).

Into the vacuum of his life Agatha then came, experiencing with him "a present moment of pointed light" toward which they stretched their hands as to a fire. (We recognize the image from *Murder in the Cathedral*: St. Peter's reaching toward the flames in his desertion of Christ.) But Agatha's guilty love has been expiated first by her saving Amy's life and her child Harry's, then by years of fighting for "dispossession," which have left her life in order—an order whose "deeper organisation" Harry's question "disturbs" (p. 103). That order resembles the terrible "repetition" in which Harry has been moving for the past year—a hideous state of negation leading to his present feeling of being

In and out, in an endless drift
Of shrieking forms in a circular desert

. . . . .

Until the chain broke, and I was left
Under the single eye above the desert.   (P. 107)

This account is a variation on "the burning wheel" in an "over-crowded desert" he had already described in scene one, the only new element being "the single eye," which he has apparently remembered through Agatha's parallel account of her life after she left Harry's father:

I was only my own feet walking
Away, down a concrete corridor

. . . . .

I was only the feet, and the eye
Seeing the feet: the unwinking eye.   (P. 107)

For in this scene, guided by Agatha's kindred experience, Harry discovers the "eye" (which is also an "I" in Agatha's phrasing) that he seemed to have lost: "That was the second hell of not being there, / The degradation of being parted from my self, / From the self which persisted only as an eye, seeing" (p. 102). In glad recognition, Harry now sees that the "eye" (or "I") in Agatha's vision was always there in his own, capable of breaking "the chain," clearing the crowds: "the desert is cleared, under the judicial sun / Of the final eye, and the awful evacuation / Cleanses" (p. 107). In giving him the experience of authentic selfhood, Agatha has removed his dread of the "final eye."

The poetry in this scene has not been sufficiently admired for its illumination of Harry's emergence from "insanity" into the clear recognition of his readiness for joy, or grace. He has been pursuing "a story of . . . crime and punishment," but he has found instead a case of "sin and expiation," as Agatha reveals (p. 105). The ensuing "evacuation" of the deceiving "shadows" allows him to see Agatha as one with him in their longing for a purifying love. Wanting him to be born, at the cost of her guilty union with his father, she had thought "the little door" into "the rose-garden" of happiness was closed to her. Instead, Harry says, "O my dear . . . I ran to meet you in the rose-garden," for "what did not happen" (her wanting him as her own child) "is as true as what did happen." He *is* her child in a way they have only now understood. Almost at once the Eumenides appear to them, and Harry speaks to them for the first time as real, not as figments of his diseased brain: "Now I see at last that I am following you, / And I know that there can be only one itinerary / And one destination. Let us lose no time. I will follow" (p. 108). Ideally, the spirits should be seen as light through the closed curtains, still in the window when Agatha goes to open them, unlike Mary, who had closed the spirits out. Agatha stands in the window to say:

> O my child, my curse,
> You shall be fulfilled:
> The knot shall be unknotted
> And the crooked made straight.

According to Eliot's stage directions, the spirits have departed when Agatha says these words: "She steps into the place which the Eumenides had occupied." It is a moment of new danger (a "curse . . . shall be fulfilled"?), emphasized all the more because Amy enters to hear Agatha say to Harry, "You must go," justifying Amy's charge that Agatha has long intended to destroy her plan for Wishwood. She has not heard Agatha's claim of Harry as her "child," which may be spiritually benign but is fraught with possible conflict, for Agatha as well as for Amy. Eliot's instinct was assured when he wrote the following scene between Amy and Agatha as a cat fight that turns into the mauling of tigresses, bringing into the open for the first time the thirty-five-year enmity between the sisters. Till now we have seen nothing of Amy's side of the hidden history—her "humiliation, / . . . the chilly pretences in the silent bedroom, / Forcing sons upon an unwilling father" (p. 112) and her accurate thrust: "You who took my husband, now you take my son" (p. 113). Improperly acted, the scene shows Amy as all villainy; but just as Eliot came to see Harry as a more fully realized character than he feared he had made him, he also came to see Amy as deeper than he expected. Paul Scofield "redeemed" Harry for the first time in 1956 by playing him as a truly *"haunted man,"* Eliot said, and wrote at about the same time, "I consider the role of Amy in this play of equal importance with the role of Harry: in fact as I have come in retrospect to understand the play better than I did when I wrote it, I now find that [it] is not so much the comedy of Harry as the tragedy of his mother."[27] Harry's "comedy" lies in his recovery of sanity, his resignation of his title to John to devote himself (like Charles, Vicomte de Foucauld) to prayer and service.[28] His departure from Wishwood precipitates Amy's death in the final scene of the play, but she has been loosening her hold almost imperceptibly since Harry's tormented return to Wishwood, deferring to him more and more, as we saw. "Now it's for you to manage," she has said (p. 65). And defending his callous affronts to the family, she has admitted, "I do not know very much: / . . . I am coming to think / How little I have ever known" (p. 96). When Harry announces his departure, she says more with resignation than menace, "If you go now, I shall never see you again" (p. 116). There is even a note of penitence:

> I only just begin to apprehend the truth
> About things too late to mend: and that is to be old.
> Nevertheless, I am glad if I can come to know them.
> I always wanted too much for my children,
> More than life can give. And now I am punished for it.   (P. 117)

Feeling ill, she retires, and Harry's "nice" uncle Charles senses the cataclysmic change in the house, the moving of the center away from Amy and Harry in an unknown direction. It is as if "the earth should open up / Right to the centre"—a center restored, as the metaphoric structure of the play has suggested. At this point the pace and tone briefly turn comic again. Harry's servant Downing comes back for Harry's cigarette case, affording Mary a chance to disclose that she *has* seen the Eumenides and still fears that they will destroy Harry. Downing reveals that he is more guardian angel (or the god Mercury) than chauffeur; he saw the Eumenides long before Harry saw them and has gotten "Used to them" (p. 119). Now that Harry is following these "bright angels" (p. 111), Downing knows that "he won't want me long, and he won't want anybody" (p. 118).

Amy chose to leave the stage with the help of "the stupidest" and "most malicious" of her relatives, Gerald and Violet, but in the moment of her death it is to Agatha (her old enemy) and Mary (whom Agatha is taking away from Wishwood) that she calls for help, announcing that her "clock"—which has been the cursed clock of Wishwood—"has stopped in the dark." Thus "Everything tends towards reconciliation," as Harry foresaw (p. 105), and Amy finally glimpses the "meaning" in death that she had earlier said scornfully only Agatha could see (p. 59). When Mary and Agatha return from the deathbed, the stage darkens; the chorus of relatives complain: "We have lost our way in the dark," but "we must adjust ourselves to the moment: we must do the right thing," and the long-awaited birthday cake is brought in by the dutiful Denman. The play resumes the static, ritual character of the "family reunion" in its opening scene. Mary had said that "the moment of birth / Is when we have knowledge of death" (p. 82), and Agatha had spoken of the "birth" in which sin struggles to consciousness before expiation (p. 105). She and Mary appropriately therefore celebrate the ritual of blowing out the birthday candles, leaving the stage and audience finally in total darkness at Agatha's last word, "peace." It is just such an effect as Eliot said only the stage can achieve: "present action as an interruption of stillness," the "total scene, the movement, posture and gesture of each member of the cast . . . calculated with a view to completing the message conveyed by the words."[29]

This is a celebration of stillness that can, of course, be aped by stagnation, as Samuel Beckett may have done in *Endgame*, where he not only has Hamm seem to parody several of Eliot's lines (as when he says to Clov, "The end is in the beginning and yet you go on") but also has Hamm (like Amy) fixed and tyrannical until Clov (ambiguously his son) refuses to serve him and prepares to take off for unknown places, presumably allowing Hamm to die. Even the clock is there to measure out Hamm's life, as it had been—comically, in fact—at the end of *Sweeney Agonistes,* where both the world and the year of the play end as to the sound of Father Time's alarm clock going off, and the curtain falls. Such knowing humor was possible only after the "metaphysical mime" (as Eliot was to be called) had explored the tragic limits of human existence.

BY NOW it is apparent that Eliot had more to say for the virtues of stillness than for those of action in general and that this could be a disabling preference in the genre of drama, whose very word derives from the Greek *dran,* meaning "to act." Martin Browne notes repeatedly in his book on the plays that Eliot was troubled as well as fascinated by every play's tendency to revert to inaction—unintentionally. There is justice as well as irony in the fact that his experiments with drama were forced to a halt in 1939 by the terrible public drama of the second World War and the closing of London theaters, which cut short the run of *The Family Reunion,* imposing on Eliot the relatively inactive span of years he devoted to the completion of *Four Quartets.* Indeed the war inspired the long, dark meditation on time and history that summed up his personal as well as communal experience. Soon after the war, as if celebrating the renewal of public harmony, he wrote the first of three comedies, all dramatizing the brightening of the social world and also his own long recovery from personal tragedy.

The Cocktail Party may have some relation to that tragedy. It has for its theme the return of a dead wife, Lavinia Chamberlayne, to a husband (Edward) whose life he thinks she has ruined. Lavinia's restoration to him, through the agency of a mysterious therapist hired by both of them, ends in reconciliation and happiness. It suggests not only a return of the "dead wife" motif—and even the "dead mother" motif—in *The Family Reunion* (for Lavinia shares characteristics with both figures), but also suggests a tribute to Eliot's own wife Vivien, who died unreconciled and still hospitalized the year before he began *The Cocktail Party* in 1948. At any rate, "the man who suffers" and "the mind that creates" are sufficiently close and sufficiently separate to achieve in the play that ring of authenticity necessary to all art, as Eliot had intimated from his first essays on.

Helen Gardner's brilliant discussion of the comedies, beginning with this play, notes how much Eliot added to the plots of the Greek plays he continued to use a substructures for his themes. She comments on the techniques he borrowed from English high comedy, from Shakespeare, Dryden, and Restoration comedy all the way through Oscar Wilde and Noel Coward—the tangled love matches, the excursions of well-to-do men and women into disreputable affairs, and the comic confusions and coincidences that have marked all "high comedy" from the time of Plautus.[30] The new comic manner of *The Cocktail Party* is, as Gardner says, the means he found "to embody in works of art problems he had resolved and conclusions he had arrived at" in the previous twenty-five years. The last plays are didactic in ways that only good comedy can be didactic—that is, they present affirmations with which a seasoned mind has become comfortable. But the comedies also dramatize—in soluble form so to speak—the insoluble questions Eliot had pondered in *Four Quartets.*

In *The Cocktail Party* the moments of arrest that we have learned to expect in Eliot's plays occur even more prominently—in mid-action—than they did in the two earlier plays, illuminating a central abyss in the lives of three people who (unlike Becket and Harry Monchensey) have been responsible for creating the void into which they are compelled to look. The case of "sin and expiation" that Agatha described in *The Family Reunion* was chiefly deployed in retrospective response to things that happened before the play began. The case also had its conclusion in Harry's uncertain career after the last curtain. By presenting on stage the deeds by which the characters of *The Cocktail Party* most dramatically affect one another in their histories, Eliot's new play gained immensely in power.

Feeling as he did that all works within an author's art (and in his whole tradition) should speak to one another, he intended that even in the title the audience should recognize a link with the play that went before. "A cocktail party of guests whom the host didn't want, corresponds very well to a family reunion from which part of the family was absent," he wrote to Browne.[31] But here the guests whom the deserted host, Edward, has to entertain, and the mysterious "unidentified guest" who helps restore peace to the joyless household, begin and finish their work before the audience's eyes. The first act opens with a resounding negative, like *The Family Reunion*—Alex's "You've missed the point completely, Julia: / There *were* no tigers," suggesting that the play has to do with human violence alone. The bantering chatter gradually gives way to the stark discovery that the hostess has left her husband, possibly forever, and that the host is lying to cover for her absence. His tension increases as the guests' annoying trivia—and the still more annoying remarks of Celia, with her now repellent claim upon him as his lover—expose the raw nerves beneath his composure. When the mysterious unidentified guest, after a long sequence of comic negatives expressing his detachment and ignorance of everything agitating the others, makes a move to leave with the others, Edward—in terror of solitude—clutches at him:

> Don't go yet.
> I very much want to talk to somebody;
> And it's easier to talk to a person you don't know.
> The fact is, that Lavinia has left me. (P. 131)

The guest (showing his kinship to the wife-rescuer Heracles in the *Alcestis*) begins to drink gin heavily at this point but also recommends the relaxing potion to Edward, beginning his rescue of the husband as well as the wife. The comic dialogue resembles a psychoanalyst's first interview with a patient in all except this analyst's probing beneath the issues of marital infidelity to a core of absolute emptiness below the reasons Edward recognizes for his desperation. The unidentified guest says to Edward:

> I knew that all you wanted was the luxury
> Of an intimate disclosure to a stranger.
> Let me, therefore, remain the stranger.
> But let me tell you, that to approach the stranger
> Is to invite the unexpected, release a new force,
> Or let the genie out of the bottle.　　　　　(P. 133)

To this spirit Edward has voluntarily released from its bottle, Edward shows only his accessible self, so the stranger's next move is to show him that he (Edward) is a stranger to himself:

> 　　　　　　　　　　Who are you now?
> You don't know any more than I do,
> But rather less. You are nothing but a set
> Of obsolete responses. The one thing to do
> Is to do nothing. Wait.　　　　　(P. 135).

This counsel is familiar—from the "wait without hope" passage in "East Coker," III to which I have already closely related the plays, a passage ending, "So the darkness shall be the light, and the stillness the dancing." But Edward is not ready to wait:

> I *must* get [Lavinia] back, to find out what has happened
> During the five years that we've been married.
> I must find out who she is, to find out who I am.
> And what is the use of all your analysis
> If I am to remain always lost in the dark?　　　　　(P. 136)

The guest obviously sees Edward following the right track, and he promises to "bring her back" if Edward will ask her no questions about where she has been. As Robert Heilman has shown,[32] Eliot deliberately dropped a clue here to the parallel with Euripides' *Alcestis,* but I think Eliot deepens the point. Edward must not only remain ignorant of the realm of "death" into which his wife (like Alcestis) has chosen to descend, but he must also not violate the mysteries of her own inner crisis through clumsily demanding an account of her desertion. He must learn that she, too, is a stranger.

Edward's desperate concentration on getting his wife back is thwarted by the same sort of comic interruptions we saw in *The Family Reunion* when Harry was interrupted by the policeman while pursuing the question of his father's scandal; only here the intrusion of Peter, the young novelist in love with Edward's mistress Celia, complicates the plot by introducing a parallel intrigue. Peter wants to know why Celia has disappeared just as Edward wants to know about his wife's disappearance. And we watch Edward's irritated reactions to this younger version of himself, becoming only gradually aware that Lavinia and Celia are two halves of a single force in Edward's life, both being women who will die in some sense in order to free both themselves and Edward from the "death" to which their meaningless lives have doomed them all. Edward's impatient promise, that he will bring Celia back to Peter, who has only to do nothing and to wait, comically echoes the unidentified guest's advice to *him*. His promise is fulfilled too soon, however, for just as Peter goes away, leaving Edward to his desired solitude, Celia does come back—to remind him of their plan to marry once Lavinia can be got out of the way. Her honest claim on him reveals the depth of his vacancy, and the humor of the first scene fades as this second one juxtaposes Edward's dawning self-knowledge (already advanced in the exchange with the mysterious guest) against Celia's terrible recognition that the self he is exposing is also exposing her use of him to fill a place he could never fill in her life. There are now three disappearing partners revealed in all these negatives, the third being the absent lover Celia has never found, whom she will follow literally into death, by contrast to Lavinia's and Edward's metaphoric journeys into the death of self to find each other.

The journeys that all three must follow are supremely dramatized in Act II. Leading up to it is the scene where Lavinia, according to promise, has been restored at least physically to Edward by the mysterious stranger, a scene in which the couple vent all their long suppressed grudges against each other to the point where Edward sees that he was wrong both to want Lavinia back and to wish to face his own inner torment with open eyes. "Hell is oneself," he cries (a perception that Eliot deliberately posed against Sartre's nihilism in *No Exit,* where Hell is "other people").[33] "In a moment, at your touch, there is nothing but ruin," Edward charges (p. 101). The curtain between Act I and Act II closes on Edward's vision of stasis and darkness as Lavinia—with fitting and brutal irony—sends him "downstairs" to have her luggage brought back home. Thus, when the curtain rises on Act II, Edward's resorting to a doctor in search of a cure is easily understood, and the mystery turns comic again when the doctor proves to be the uninvited guest—Sir Henry Harcourt-Reilly—curer of minds and souls. The long act in one scene is Eliot's best theatrical achievement. As Browne noted of the play in general, here especially the poetry is luminescent in revealing character; the characters act out their finest shades of feeling and meaning. Words and action, with the visual stage images that express them, fit one another seamlessly.

The scene is structured on the model we have studied, beginning with a still center—Sir Henry alone at his desk—progressing to crises of hectic conflict, and ending with a return to stillness as Celia departs for her journey and Sir Henry, with his fellow "Guardians," conducts a ritual ceremony of benediction on the resolutions arrived at. The moments of highest excitement result from Reilly's plan to have Edward and Lavinia confront each other by surprise, each having been independently driven to seek him out. Edward arrives first and tries to steer the consultation in the direction of Freudian analysis, only to be put down by Reilly:

> You see, your memories of childhood—
> I mean, in your present state of mind—
> Would be largely fictitious; and as for your dreams,
> You would produce amazing dreams, to oblige me.
> I could make you dream any kind of dream I suggested,
> And it would only go to flatter your vanity
> With the temporary stimulus of feeling interesting.
>
> (Pp. 174–175)

Reilly deliberately activates the deepest negations, or sense of nothingness, his patients have yet encountered in themselves. He asks whether it would have been better not to have brought Lavinia back. "I don't know," Edward replies, and the state of unknowing is symptomatic of both the disease and the cure. As the interview proceeds, Edward admits first that his wife's very strength of will (which maddened him before) was something he needed: "Without her, it was vacancy." But at first he cannot recognize this void as the possible ground of love. She has both "made me incapable / Of having any existence of my own" and "made the world a place I cannot live in / Except on her terms" (p. 175). So, he thinks, he must face his Hell of being alone and demands that Reilly send him to his "sanatorium" (one of several houses of prayer, as we learn later). Reilly momentarily wonders if Edward's case is parallel to Celia's when he says, "The single patient / Who is ill by himself, is rather the exception" (p. 177). To test Edward's power to be cured in solitude, Reilly then brings Lavinia into the room. It becomes evident that their "unknowing" and the "nothingness" they describe in themselves are not yet the "innocence" that Julia describes in Celia as her protection against horror (p. 193). Edward and Lavinia have surrounded themselves with a tissue of lies, concealing their love affairs and blaming each other for their ills. But Reilly perceives what is often missed in the play—that Edward and Lavinia need each other and therefore could not bear the regimen of total solitude that is the cure in Reilly's special "sanatorium." He says "you are both too ill" for such a cure. Though their need for each other is malignant in its present form, being evidence of their sickness, Reilly steers them to seeing that the malignancies are signs of a deeper bond that can be the grounds for their cure.

Critics often say that their "sickness" is connected with Eliot's indictment of marriage in general, that if they were "well" they would be as independent as Celia. But this is to overlook Reilly's assurance that their "way" is as good as hers. "Neither way is better," he will tell Celia later (p. 190).

> Each way means loneliness—and communion.
> Both ways avoid the final desolation
> Of solitude in the phantasmal world
> Of imagination, shuffling memories and desires.　　　(P. 191)

Edward and Lavinia, forced to make their accusations before a surrogate for "the judicial sun / Of the final eye" (as Harry had called it in *The Family Reunion*), admit to each other that Edward "is incapable of loving" while Lavinia is one whom "no man can love." When Lavinia then groans, "What we have in common / Might be just enough to make us loathe one another," Reilly corrects her: "See it rather as the bond which holds you together. / While still in a state of unenlightenment." To understand each other, he says, "you have only to reverse the propositions / And put them together" (p. 182)—each has only to see that both are unloved and unlovable *as they are,* and that even this proposition can be reversed. They have to be *shown* what Celia later perceives unaided about herself and all humanity when she says, "Are we all in fact unloving and unlovable? / Then one *is* alone, and if one is alone / Then lover and beloved are both equally unreal" (p. 188). The repeating negatives in Celia's context can be heard backward, as echoes of Edward's and Lavinia's, in such a way as to affirm that one is "really" never alone except when failing to love and to know that one is lovable.

The Cocktail Party makes clear that Lavinia and Edward have become "real" by the end of the play, not only in their freely given attentions to each other at the last cocktail party but in their expectation of a child after the years of "unreality" which the play has ended.[34] Even the best of marriages will remain a union where "Two people who know they do not understand each other" breed "children whom they do not understand / And who will never understand them," Reilly tells Celia (p. 189), but a man and woman for whom married love is the "way" to happiness should not be deterred by that. In the middle of Act II Eliot dramatizes the "stillness" from which action springs in the theater when Lavinia sees the choice before her as true marriage or nothingness. She asks, "Then what can we do / When we can go neither back nor forward? Edward!" And Reilly remarks on her calling to Edward for the first time, signaling her movement from stagnation to stillness and waiting. "You have answered your own question, / Though you do not know the meaning of what you have said," he observes (p. 182).

Edward finishes the movement using her name in a new way too: "Lavinia, we must make the best of a bad job"—a phrase that Reilly says now, as at other points in the play he suggests, is "all any of us make of it— / Except of course, the saints." Edward and Lavinia have made their choice (not had it thrust upon them, as D. W. Harding argues),[35] and the Christian "peace" that passes all understanding can be echoed along with the Buddha's last words of benediction as Edward and Lavinia leave Reilly's office. He says, "Go in peace. And work out your salvation with diligence" (p. 183). After they leave, he lies down on the psychiatrist's couch, comically suggesting both the healer's own need for cure and the Buddha's death scene—a perfect moment of arrest in mid-act.

Celia's entrance at this point begins the clarification of her desolation and longing which had emerged during Edward's rejection of her in Act I. It is the absolute absence of God she has experienced—not as a sense of misconduct in her adultery (for she wasn't "taking anything away" that Lavinia wanted; p. 187) but as a sense "of emptiness, of failure / Towards someone, or something, outside of myself" (p. 188). The only word she can find for her condition is "a sense of sin," but she has "always been taught to disbelieve in sin" as "either bad form" or as "psychological" (p. 187), rather than as the loss of the presence of God. Eliot here epitomizes both his own experience of growing up in America and his whole culture's main modern outlook, as was evident from his comments on his own "puritan" background and from Van Wyck Brooks's reaction against this theme in Eliot's work. The famous Puritan sense of sin, Eliot believed, was not that at all. As early as 1924, he had made a note saying, "there are only two things—Puritanism and Catholicism. You are one or the other. You either believe in the reality of Sin, or you don't. *That* is *the* important moral distinction—not whether you are good or bad. Puritanism does not believe in Sin: it merely believes that certain things must not be done."[36] That Van Wyck Brooks assented to Eliot's view of himself as out of step with American tradition in the concept of sin presented here is spelled out in the last volume of Brooks's study of American culture, *The Confident Years.*[37] What the Puritans had lost, as Eliot dramatizes in this central act of *The Cocktail Party,* is the experience of a broken relationship with God which may not even be connected with any breach in human relationships. Morality "is a means not an end," as he said.[38] Celia wishes to "atone" not for anything she has done to Edward or Lavinia but for having substituted what proved to be an unreal love for a true one, and it is her longing for the ultimate source of love which Reilly begins to suspect may be the longing of the saints.

To be sure of this, he probes her feelings about the human lover she has lost (as he had with Edward, there learning that it was Lavinia he clearly wanted). Celia describes her search for a being who "perhaps is not anywhere." Unlike them, she *has* been in love—with Edward—

and has found that "the ecstasy is real," that "the intensity of loving" exalted both herself and Edward until she found herself feeling that it alone was real and that the two of them "may have no reality" (p. 189). When Edward "ditched" her, he seemed to her like a child, lost with her in a forest, "wanting to go home" (which of course is what Reilly has helped him to do). Celia's negatives, compared with Edward's and Lavinia's, point to the certain loss of "something" unknown: "I think I really had a vision of something / Though I don't know what it is. I don't want to forget it." If there is no other way than what she has found, then she is "hopeless." There *is* another way, says Reilly, but that too is "unknown." It "cannot be described" and she will have to "journey blind," assured only that "the way leads towards possession / Of what you have sought for in the wrong place" (p. 190).[39] If Edward's condition was, as Edward said, like being in Hell, Celia's is like a Purgatory where the goal is always in view. Further echoes from Dante appear not only in the forest imagery but in the account of Celia's journey as "the way" in which she will be "transhumanised"—from purgatorial to paradisal illumination (p. 193), the word borrowed by Julia from the *Paradiso* (I, 70–71) after Celia has left Reilly's office.

Reilly here concludes that Celia "will go to the sanatorium," and we feel precisely what Celia feels, that this is "an anti-climax." The intensity of the long scene, with its excited interchanges between the three distraught patients and their analyst, winds down from a crest of poetic rhythms to a series of quiet negatives, ending when Celia says, "I don't know in the least what I am doing / Or why I am doing it. There is nothing else to do: / That is the only reason." Having grounded herself, she simply asks what she will need to take with her and what she is to pay. "Nothing," says Reilly. She will have "no expenses," and as to his own cost, "there is no fee" for a case like hers (pp. 191–192). Her renunciation thus is answered by his own submission on a plane of values where they perfectly meet. As she goes, he repeats the Christian-Buddhist words of parting he spoke to Edward and Lavinia but adds the words "my daughter," echoing not only a priestly blessing but Eliot's crucial poem "Marina." There, too, an older man (Pericles) discovers new life in the restoration of a recovered child.

The theme of a woman recovered from supposed death by a rescue that appears miraculous is dramatized in both *The Cocktail Party* and "Marina" through a crisscrossing of pagan and Christian plots, bringing us to consideration of another deliberate use of negativity. I have been speaking so far of the way plot and character in the plays plumb toward centers of stillness and void in the search for honesty, reality, and finally grace. Eliot often spoke also of the way poetry, whether dramatic or nondramatic, could use an overlay effect of negation and/or affirmation to reveal unexpected meanings. In a letter to Michael Sadleir about "Marina," for instance, he said: "I intend a crisscross between Pericles finding alive, and Hercules finding dead [their children]—the two extremes of the recognition scene."[40] The crisscross effect causes a shock of recognition which, in the plays too, arises from the parallel, with contrasts, between a "pagan" and a Christian plot. We have seen how Eliot's Eumenides reverse the function of Aeschylus's Eumenides as these spirits are seen haunting a man for the part he must play in redressing his parents'—and his wife's—wrongs. What Harry Monchensey thought were demonic spirits (like the Furies in Aeschylus) are purely beneficent; for in Christian terms, a man seeking the truth in good faith cannot be divided against himself, as in Greek drama the conflict among the gods themselves tore men apart. The ancient gods, divided among themselves, thus bore more responsibility for violence than their human victims. In *The Cocktail Party,* the crisscross of Euripides' *Alcestis* with Eliot's own plot at first seems to stress the more benign or romantic nature of the ancient sources. The *Alcestis* is a romance in Greek terms, allowing the mortal Heracles to undo the jealousy of Artemis (who demanded the death of Admetus) and the cool comfort of Apollo (who suggests that Alcestis may die in place of her husband). The *Alcestis* is more "positive" than *The Cocktail Party* in that both the husband condemned to death and the wife who dies for him are admirable from the start. Through Eliot's crisscross, therefore, we first perceive how contemptible their modern counterparts, Edward and Lavinia, are. At the outset, Eliot focuses on the question: is not their death in life a far worse condition than physical death—a question answered both by their mutual transformations (becoming alive to each other) and by Celia's choice of a life leading to physical death along a "way" ensuring possession of a love and life that cannot be taken from her. Enjoyment of the plays does not depend on awareness of the crisscross of ancient and modern situations, but one's pleasure is deepened by the effect.

Pursuing the point, we may profitably connect what Eliot said in *The Idea of a Christian Society* about negation and affirmation in the "pagan" elements of our society. A society, he said,

> has not ceased to be Christian until it has become positively something else. It is my contention that we have today [in English-speaking countries] a culture which is mainly negative, but which, so far as it is positive, is still Christian. I do not think that it can remain negative, because a negative culture has ceased to be efficient in a world where economic as well as spiritual forces are proving the efficiency of cultures which, even when pagan, are positive [that is, have clearly enunciated aims or goals]; and I believe that the choice before us is between the formation of a new Christian culture, and the acceptance of a pagan one.[41]

In this context too, by comparison with the pagan society of Euripides' *Alcestis,* the social world of *The Cocktail Party* is "negative." The marital bond is celebrated by Euripides as inviolable for the hero and heroine; and their devotion to the gods and to their children, as well as to their guests—invited and uninvited—is central to the action. By contrast, in the world of Eliot's play, the bonds tying the married to each other and both to anyone beyond themselves have frayed to almost nothing. People cannot even be true to their lovers. Children are never mentioned, nor is Christian faith, though at the end of the play both are implicit.[42] Eliot is thus using negatives, through character and plot, in two structural ways: (1) through what the characters fail to be and do, and (2) through what they seek to be and do without being able to speak of it, for an audience who themselves cannot speak of these things easily or hear them spoken.

Eliot uses some characters, however, who are *more* than they appear to be—as a way of suggesting that our world is "still Christian" and "positive" residually. This comes out in "the Guardians" and the cocktail party itself, a ritual survival in modern life, expressing the human need for sharing drink and food communally. It is only the cocktail party that can bring everyone together from their separate solitudes, so eventually there is something heroic about the ineffectual solicitude of Alex and the scatty Julia at the failed party when we see their transformation at the successful party beginning when the play ends. Sir Henry Harcourt-Reilly drinks a lot of gin in the first scene because he needs it and sees that Edward needs it. During the last scene Reilly is content with water. Eliot stressed the importance of such people in *The Idea of a Christian Society,* where he spoke of those who feel themselves "responsible for all other souls" as well as for their own.[43] Celia is the first (at the end of Act I) to intuit what Julia and Alex are up to, seeing Julia as a public manifestation of the "guardian" or "tougher self" whom Edward has just discovered in himself. (Underlying the personal "guardian" and the communal "Guardians" is the Pauline doctrine of "substitution," by which one person's action may voluntarily be offered for the sake of others, as Christ's was, all Christians thus taught to live for everyone's sake.) By implication Celia at this point begins to be one of the publicly committed, when she offers to drink with Edward "to the Guardians" and adds, "Give me [Julia's] spectacles" (p. 155).

The charge made by many reviewers of the play, that the "Guardians" are offensive intruders in the lives of others, is a false charge since they make no claim to understand what only God can know about the lives of others, and since they rely on the characters' own feelings, trusting that the love of God will appear in all "real love." As Eliot wrote to Geoffrey Faber about *The Cocktail Party,* "there are two primary propositions: (1) nobody understands you but God; (2) all real love is ultimately the love of God."[44] Beside this God, the peremptory gods in the *Alcestis* appear quite negative in the "crisscross" between the two plays.

A more serious charge, made by William Arrowsmith and many others,[45] is that the play goes flat in the last act through failing to dramatize the climactic revelation of Celia's martyrdom. Given that her loving sacrifice was fully foreshadowed, however, the main question is: how *does* the modern world become conscious of such a death, the death of a saint? The power of the play's final effect derives from the very inadequacy of Alex's words to describe what has happened to Celia, and the impossibility of an adequate response to it. What Eliot said in the Conclusion of *The Use of Poetry and the Use of Criticism* about the difficulties of modern poetry, relying as it does on what may be absent from the words, is nowhere better illustrated. Adequate reaction can be only tacit, and Celia's kind of death has enough precedents for its meaning to be as clear to the audience as to those on stage. There is nothing perverse in Reilly's recognizing a death undergone for others as "triumphant" or in his saying that Celia joyously chose the way that led to it. Since like her, Edward and Lavinia have also made the best choices in their lives, Reilly adds, "It is also right / That the Chamberlaynes should now be giving a party" (p. 211). Lavinia has been wishing that the party "was over," but left alone with her, Edward revives her flagging spirit; and when the doorbell rings, she is glad it has "begun"—the last word of the play, making the audience the guests, as it were, who have just rung the bell.

Audiences indeed responded to *The Cocktail Party* as if they had been admitted for the first time in large numbers to Eliot's world. The London satiric journalist who called himself Sagittarius called Eliot "a nightingale among the Sweeneys"—a "metaphysical mime / That should have been / The most distinguished failure of all time" but proved "quite the opposite."[46] And Leonard Lyons in his "Lyons Den" column caught the new spirit of fun with a conversation between two ladies purportedly overheard at a Berlin production of the play. The first lady said, "Rather obscure, don't you think?" The second: "Oh, I don't think so at all . . . Whoever knows religious philosophy, has read the medieval mystics, has an idea of the scholastics and has studied the Chinese philosophers should have no trouble understanding it." The first lady adds, "Only I'm not sure what Eliot meant when he had Celia say 'Good evening' in the second act."[47] Eliot would have enjoyed this, for he meant to give his audience problems to think about and was careful only that the poetry and the problems themselves should be clearly and immediately felt, as most people concluded they were.

HIS FOURTH PLAY, *The Confidential Clerk,* went even further in the direction of comedy than *The Cocktail Party.* This meant closer to normal human experience, which in turn meant closer to the amused and amusing didacticism we associate with all good-hearted mirth on the stage. The "mainly negative" values of our culture (as Eliot described them) seem to draw only wholesome laughter, not lacerating scorn. Folly is funny, and the love for God and one's fellow men is inspired by simple loneliness rather than a sense of sin. Many in Eliot's audiences, like David E. Jones,[48] felt that Eliot successfully fused his deepest message with the social mores portrayed on stage for the first time. Eliot's own words might have been interpreted thus when he explained why he was writing comedies: "People take tragedy seriously on the surface. They take comedy lightly on the surface but seriously underneath," he said in an interview.[49] Didn't this mean he had brought the superficial lives we lead ordinarily into fusion with the deeper truths ordinarily overlooked? Eliot seems to have been implicitly answering a charge (made eight days earlier) by New York's top drama critic, Walter Kerr, who said that *The Confidential Clerk* "gives off a curious double image, like a Sunday comic strip in which the colors have slipped." Kerr said, "The outline is light, the background is dark, and we have to look at both simultaneously—going just a shade cross-eyed in the process."[50]

While Eliot would not have wished his audience to go cross-eyed, he did often intend a crisscross effect as we have seen, and the effect in *The Confidential Clerk* derives as before both from his use of sources and from his reflection on the positive versus the negative elements in the society he is portraying. The underpattern of the play is a reworking of the *Ion* of Euripides with its comic tale of two parents' recovery of a lost child—a quest that involves them and the youth Ion in a web of coincidences, confused identities, and supposed infidelities. The *Ion* fathered a long history of comic plots, from Menander and Plautus, Shakespeare and Goldsmith, down to Oscar Wilde and the *Pinafore* of Gilbert and Sullivan. Onto this comic plot, however, Eliot grafts the serious plot of a young man's quest for God, a plot closer to *The Pilgrim's Progress* than to stage farce and one that incidentally introduces the tragic theme of a mother's deliberate pretense of being her illegitimate son's aunt, found in Kipling's "The Gardener." Kipling's "aunt" finds her son's grave among the war dead and realizes that she has deprived him of ever having a real parent. This serious plotting operates more subversively than any in the earlier plays of Eliot precisely because it appears to mesh hilariously with a comedy of errors until, as this play ends, the happiness of the reassembled family of Sir Claude Mulhammer (the counterpart of Euripides' Athenian nobleman) is called in question.

In Eliot's play the *Ion*'s complications are quadrupled somewhat in the way Shakespeare's *Comedy of Errors* doubled the twins of Plautus's *Manaechmi*. The son of Apollo, Ion, is multiplied by four to include (in Eliot's play) Colby (who feels himself to be no one's child but only a son of God) and also three illegitimate children: Sir Claude's dead child (whom he took to be Colby), his daughter Lucasta, and his wife, Lady Elizabeth's, lost son B. Kaghan. As a twist, Colby turns out to be the only legitimate child among the four, but his mother has told him she was his aunt so that he would be taken as the wealthy son of Sir Claude. Similarly Lady Elizabeth settles for having her new-found son, B. Kaghan, call her "aunt," since he can never bring himself to see her as his real mother (p. 283).

The "negative" elements added to the ancient plot are thus all from the modern cases of parents who consign their children to strangers to be reared. A passing allusion to *Pinafore*'s little Buttercup, who like Eliot's Mrs. Guzzard practiced "baby farming" and switched one child (Captain Corcoran) with another (Ralph Rackstraw) simply adds a comic note to what is otherwise the sad old custom of delegating parenthood, especially among the wealthy.

The two themes, ancient and modern, comic and serious, neatly cross in *The Confidential Clerk* through the argument against "make-believe worlds" that runs through the play. At first it appears delightful as Sir Claude benignly observes that his featherbrained wife has "always lived in a world of make-believe" and will therefore imagine that Colby is her son if she comes to think of him as "the kind of man that her son would have been" (p. 234). Only later do we see that this is exactly what Sir Claude himself has done, wrongly assuming that Colby was his the first time he saw him. But even before he finds out the truth, he admits that he has carried on his father's financial enterprise because he has treated it "as a kind of make-believe" which became real for him. To his father it *was* real (and to B. Kaghan the same occupation is real), but tormentedly Sir Claude recalls his father's knowledge as he died that Claude was only resentfully pretending to respect the business. Instead of letting life "impose its conditions upon him" (a phrase that runs through the play for all the characters), he should have followed his real passion—the art of pottery making—which he has instead relegated to a secret place in his life, divided off from the rest of his activities. He "escapes" to his collection of other artists' pottery, thinking of that world as "a pure one" while his life as financier is "only a shadow" (p. 236). We come to see that he has divided Colby off in the same way, secretly believing him to be his son but letting him grow up as a stranger.

Colby's feelings rebel from the start against such a splitting of life into ideal and actual, but at first he is persuaded that his own calling, to be a musician, must be abandoned because, like Sir Claude as a potter, he could never be first-rate. Only in Act II, when Lucasta visits Colby in his flat, does he stumble on the truth that what has kept him from inhabiting "the garden" of his calling to music is most of all his feeling so alone there. It has never become real to him because he cannot bring it out of the realm of his private wishes and into relation with the "world outside," where people need him and exist for him. "If I were religious, God would walk in my garden / And that would make the world outside it real" (p. 246). In a poetic duet where Colby and Lucasta excitedly finish each other's sentences, they reach the dual awareness that they each need another to understand them in order that they may be real to themselves.

Lucasta, too, has constructed a make-believe world, pretending to be a capricious nuisance to everyone in order to bring herself into the world where they are and expect to find her—the "guttersnipe" daughter of Sir Claude's worst youthful indiscretion. At her disclosure that she is his daughter, the plot combines the classic recognition scene with the reversal that Aristotle admired. Colby sees that he cannot love one he supposes now to be his sister, but she (not knowing Colby might be her brother) sees only his revulsion. The shock throws her into the "real world" she shares with B. Kaghan, the supposedly "vulgar young man" who loves her and lives unashamedly in the world of high-power finance where one "adopted from nowhere" is acceptable (p. 252).

Although Helen Gardner has found the play objectionable in assigning important parts to such "vulgar" and "banal" types as Kaghan and Eggerson,[51] Eliot needed these characters to show the negative and positive sides of modern life. They alone of the characters in the play refuse to erect a world of pretenses, and they effectively shock us by their flatness of speech as compared to the wit and lyricism of the other, mostly self-deceiving characters. To write witty lines for them would have been either to make them into posturers (like the comically uneducated folk in Shakespeare or Shaw) or to lose the contrast with upperclass figures in the play. Eliot evidently felt the risk of flatness worth taking, as he knew what he wanted when he refused to write lines for his Eumenides. In this very different case, he may have had in mind a point about the lower middle class he had made in *The Idea of a Christian Society:* "the society which is coming into existence, and which is advancing in every country whether 'democratic' or 'totalitarian,' is a lower middle class society: I should expect the culture of the twentieth century to belong to the lower middle class as that of the Victorian age belonged to the upper middle class or commercial aristocracy." He refuses to judge whether "this is either a good or a bad thing" but points out that so far no adequate provision has been made for such a new culture. It will depend on "what lower middle class Man does to himself, and what is done to him."[52]

Significantly enough, the retiring "confidential clerk" Eggerson is the only figure in the play who is conscious of the seasons, and there is surely a clue to the loss of comedy's traditional green world as the play begins. Eggerson comes to London to buy garden tools—"So as not to lose a moment at the end of the winter" (p. 217). He is also the only parent who has loved as well as lost a child (killed in the war). Though Gardner finds him "a crashing bore," the bare simplicity of his language, like the bald assertions of B. Kaghan, suggests a cultural emptiness in both their lives which seems fully intended. Kaghan's hunger for power in the financial world—to which he has every reason to belong, first as Lady Elizabeth's abandoned son and then as her newfound son—raises the issue of his parents' having left him to swim in the financial world both before and after he is identified. Eliot's anxieties over that world, expressed in the essay just quoted, would indicate that the Mulhammers, with the newly married Lucasta and B. Kaghan for heirs, will not face a world at the end of the play where everyone can "live happily ever after."[53]

The vacuum is also dramatized earlier in the play in the wistfulness of all the characters except Eggerson, creating what Walter Kerr saw as the comedy's "curious double image." The affirmative notes of comedy are recurrently negated—however lightly—by the loss, emptiness, and solitude felt by all the characters. Colby's search for the "other" who will meet him in his "garden" is expressed in the fine duet with Lucasta already mentioned and also in the terrible frankness of his words to Sir Claude and Lady Elizabeth, as they by turns try to claim him: he reminds Sir Claude that he is more a patron than the "father who was missing in the years of childhood. / Those years have gone forever. The empty years" (p. 239). And he tells Lady Elizabeth it is better not to know he is her son than "to know the fact and know it means nothing":

> At the time I was born, you might have been my mother,
> But you chose not to be. I don't blame you for that:
> God forbid! but we must take the consequences.
> At the time when I was born, your being my mother—
> If you are my mother—was a living fact.
> Now, it is a dead fact, and out of dead facts
> Nothing living can spring. (P. 262)

Lady Elizabeth's own childhood was arid and lonely because she had too many relatives, all "uncongenial" (p. 256). She wanted to believe that *she* was a foundling, and she humorously parallels Colby's inability to accept Sir Claude when she says she couldn't believe that her father could have been "an ordinary earl." Theological and psychological interpretations are equally valid, explaining why she allowed *her* child to be a foundling, thus passing on the disease and also the longing for its cure.

At the end of Act II, when three parents and three children have all discovered both their fits and misfits with one another, the comic vein sustained till then despite the negative currents almost breaks down. Sick of his own dilemma and the Mulhammers' confused claims on him, Colby loses his taste for consolation in music. Sir Claude experiences a kindred distaste for his ceramics, and Lady Elizabeth brings the second act curtain down with her blind sympathy for her self-deluding husband. "My poor Claude," she says, completely ignoring his real sorrow. They all go into the dark—a darkness which Martin Browne said was intentionally to be sighted in the sky behind the scene in Colby's flat. This scene, like the end of the play, seeks the stillness of the dark theater we have seen as implicitly part of Eliot's stage designs. At the final curtain, Colby leaves Sir Claude, who still cannot accept the fact. Here the curtain falls on his question—is Colby really someone else's son?—and Eggerson's nod that he is. All the ends of comedy are neatly tied; but the comic level slips out of fit with the serious, and the "double image" of affirmation and negation remains.

ELIOT'S LAST PLAY, *The Elder Statesman,* was also his last major poetic effort, as he evidently planned it to be. Crossing the plots of Sophocles' last testament—the *Oedipus at Colonus*—with the finest of medieval morality plays, *Everyman,* this finale of Eliot's completed the statement that he had long held before him as a standard for the work of major poets. It was, he said, no single work but the poet's work "as a whole, that is our criterion." And this could only be possible if that poet's whole work was felt "to be united by one significant, consistent, and developing personality."[54] For audiences, beginning in 1958, there was no question about the significance and consistency of the author's personality. There was, however, a question of whether that personality had developed. To many critics *The Elder Statesman* seemed the work of a tired laureate, "designed for the living dead,"[55] and even to admirers, its theme seemed an echo of his earlier plays. "These plays of masked actors in Savile Row costumes," Hugh Kenner wrote, each turned "on the establishment of someone's moral identity," discovered through reduction "to a nearly ritual simplicity of means."[56] And Carol H. Smith saw *all five plays* as employing the imagery of plays and players to dramatize the way men and women must rid themselves of false roles thrust upon them by others, "or assumed to protect ourselves from others, which must fall off before love can be freely offered or received."[57] It should be observed, however, that in his last play alone, Eliot's chief actor (like Shakespeare's Prospero) repudiates the idea of playing any role at all, thus saying farewell for the author to his craft. The "development" that is new in *The Elder Statesman* is presented as a supreme negation when Lord Claverton says to his daughter, "I've been freed from the self that pretends to be someone; / And in becoming no one, I begin to live" (p. 354).

The thought is all too easy to parody (as Beckett and Pinter may have done in *The Unnamable* and *The Caretaker*) or to reject out of hand as the antithesis of the assertions that modern man lives to prove. Yet in adding this new vision to what he had presented in earlier plays, Eliot put the finishing strokes on a portrayal of human existence that he would otherwise have left uncertain or undefined. He had not before presented on the stage the dying of an ordinary man who fully faces and understands what it is to become "no one" and to "begin to live" at that moment.

Lord Claverton, the elder statesman, retired Member of Parliament and director of companies, has lived sixty years without ever knowing that "awful daring of a moment's surrender" by which alone "we have existed / Which is not to be found in our obituaries"—*The Waste Land's* one directive for a "real" life. Claverton epitomizes all the empty elders, waiting for rain in a dry season, characterized in Eliot's earlier works: Gerontion, the Sibyl and Tiresias, Simeon, the Magi, and Amy in *The Family Reunion.* Among these, Lord Claverton is the only one for whom the healing rain actually falls. He sees both the birth of the promise and its completion. But in the plays Eliot wanted the audience to discover for itself the implicit Word within the universal words, and here again he structured his drama on a Greek fable, Sophocles' *Oedipus at Colonus.* As he wrote to Browne while *The Elder Statesman* was being performed:

> I should not like to think of Christian art as something contrasting with secular art and in competition with it . . . I am particularly concerned about drama, because I have always been most desirous to see ordinary plays *written* by Christians rather than plays of *overtly* Christian purpose. In the theatre I feel that one wants a Christian mentality to permeate the theatre, to affect it and to influence audiences who might be obdurate to plays of a directly religious appeal.[58]

By crisscrossing the religious vision of Sophocles with the Christian vision of *Everyman,* Eliot achieved this aim.

Sophocles' original begins with the terrible sight of Oedipus, former King of Thebes, filthy and in rags, a blind beggar led on stage by his daughter Antigone. He is seeking "a resting place" (and the first title of Eliot's play was *The Rest Cure*). In the *Oedipus at Colonus,* this place has been prophesied for him by the gods, a shelter from his enemies where he can end his days in peace. Instead, as he comes near the place of his death, Oedipus is revisited by the worst tormenters from his past: Creon, his former minister, his brother-in-law and uncle (by Oedipus's incestuous marriage to his own mother), who demands that he return to Thebes so that his grave may become a national shrine; then Polyneices, Oedipus's son, who has the same itch for power exhibited by Creon. The son wishes to be instated as king in succession to his father. Sophocles' focus of attention is the mysterious grace that will surround the death site of the hero, a world-renowned example of human endurance. "Because his sufferings were great, unmerited and untold," the gods themselves will sanctify this place forever. Finally Theseus, King of Athens, rescues Oedipus from his tormentors; and in return for his protection, Oedipus promises Athenians the benefits of his burial ground—the secret place near a hollow pear tree into which at the end of the play Oedipus disappears, led by "some attendant from the train of Heaven."[59]

Like Oedipus, Eliot's Lord Claverton has achieved his eminence through a marriage undertaken only for reasons of state. ("Would that I had never served the state that day!" says Oedipus; p. 110.) Like Oedipus, Claverton feels totally degraded by the loss of his honors and leans heavily upon his daughter, Monica. Like Oedipus, Claverton is visited by a tormenting son and former friend of his youth, Michael and Fred Culverwell (alias Federico Gomez). Also, whereas the daughter plays guide to her "blind" father through most of the play, at the end Claverton experiences a new spiritual power and might say with Oedipus, "See, now / I have become your guide, as you were mine!" (p. 159). Like Oedipus, Claverton knows when the moment of his death has come and goes to meet it with dignity and assurance.

These parallels are accompanied, however, by equally striking contrasts which in certain ways even negate the message of Sophocles. Most notably, from the beginning to the end of the play, Oedipus declares his innocence, even repudiating the guilt he had assumed in the *Oedipus Rex* as the temporary insanity of a horror-stricken man:

> how was I evil in myself?
> I had been wronged, I retaliated; even had I
> Known what I was doing, I went on. Went on.
> But those who wronged me knew, and ruined me.   (P. 96)

"It was God's pleasure" that he suffered all his calamities (p. 133), and it is the gods who must repair them through sanctifying his memory. The other major difference between the two plays is that although Oedipus proclaims, "one word / Frees us of all the weight and pain of life: / That word is love" (pp. 161–162), still he dies condemning his son and Creon for their meanness, avarice, and irreverence, prophesying retribution against them by an avenging justice. Thus in Sophocles' characterization there is virtually no *inner* development of the fallen statesman in the course of play. The case is very different in Eliot's.

We see Claverton at once as "a hollow man, who wears 'a public mask,' under which he fears there is no identity" (as Browne describes him).[60] At his doctor's orders he has resigned all his public offices, only to find that there is nothing left to preserve during his prescribed "rest cure." A subtle change occurs, however, when an unwelcome visitor, a "ghost" from his past, is announced. We wonder why the old man, threatened with a heart attack, admits him. Out of boredom?

No, he is too proud for that. We know only later that Claverton is haunted by the fear that nowhere in his past has he ever possessed a real self, and by admitting two intruders from his youth, he is conducting an inquiry into that self. He is a ghost interviewing ghosts. This means that through much of the play he presents an immobilized, unprepossessing figure, putting demands on the actor that could only be met (say) by the artistry of an Eric Porter, revealing impotent rage beneath cool rejoinders to his former Oxford companion; a snarl of jealousy disguised in overly civil answers to his daughter's lover; and the merest stirring of old embers as his early mistress (the revue star Maisie Montjoy) reminds him of the sensuous self he long ago suppressed in order to make a politic marriage.

Through the two *revenants,* Gomez and Maisie (as David E. Jones noted), Eliot constructs an Ibsenesque "revelation of the past embedded in the present."[61] But unlike Ibsen, Eliot is concerned with the exorcism of figures who are more like demons than ghosts. The New Testament parable of the house swept and garnished—empty and therefore all the more prey to demons than the house already unholy—is clearly suggested. Not only is Claverton "empty" but the three figures who come to assail him are "hollow" as well. Gomez, Maisie, and his son Michael all have motives of revenge in reawakening the past. The audience misses much of the pattern if we fail to see, however, that Claverton's incentives are even stronger than the intruders' as they burn away the brush concealing the contours of their common ground.

Gomez, now a Central American millionaire—and a widower like Claverton—recalls that he would never have committed forgery and been forced to leave England if Claverton hadn't cultivated extravagant tastes when Gomez was a penniless student. Despite his ill-gained wealth, Gomez is now a "broken man," whose crime in England condemned him to be forever (like Oedipus more than Claverton) a stranger both abroad and at home. (We should remember that in "The Hollow Men" Eliot had merged Shakespeare's and Conrad's "hollow men" with Kipling's "broken men"—the latter busted in England and homelessly living like unappeased ghosts in the colonies.) Gomez is nevertheless possessed by a potent devil with power to make Claverton writhe inwardly by insinuating that the idolized statesman is far worse off than he is. "We're both of us failures,"

Gomez says, "But even so, / I'd rather be my kind of failure than yours."

> The worst kind of failure, in my opinion,
> Is the man who has to keep on pretending to himself
> That he's a success—the man who in the morning
> Has to make up his face before he looks in the mirror.   (P. 312)

The scene has the power of Conrad's unforgettable scene in *Lord Jim* when the demonic Gentleman Brown, without precisely knowing Jim's story, probes into his past with sickening allusions to their common guilt, hitting the nerve he hardly knows is there, thus paralyzing his prey for the kill. Like Jim, Claverton finds no adequate way to exorcise the demon short of acknowledging even more (to himself) than Gomez is able to charge against him. It seems Eliot subtly suggests that Claverton is himself now like the body of the old man he ran over one moonlit night "without stopping," as Gomez reminds him. It did not help to learn at the inquest long ago that the old man (like himself being "run over" by Gomez) was already dead.

Mrs. Carghill, the widowed former actress Maisie, is possessed by another demon as she goads at wounds that can only open and bleed. Having loved neither of her two husbands, and retaining the memory of her affair with Claverton (paid off by his father) as her only experience of love, she hints exactly as Gomez does that she has been in Hell, the more explicitly in her case when she consciously echoes Isaiah 66 and Mark 9, while unconsciously recalling Francesca in Dante's *Inferno*, V:

> It's frightening to think that we're still together
> And more frightening to think that we may *always* be together.
> There's a phrase I seem to remember reading somewhere:
> *Where their fires are not quenched.* Do you know what I do?
> I read your letters every night.   (P. 325)

Claverton being no Paolo, Mrs. Carghill succeeds only in making him feel like Dante in Hell. She and Gomez reach out to him like self-damned souls seeking compassion and connection with the upper air. But it now appears that Claverton, unlike them, has not resigned himself to "death's dream kingdom," and failing to move him, they succeed all too well in latching onto each other as well as adopting Claverton's son Michael into their conspiracy of revenge.

In his scenes with Michael, the retired statesman sees his past return with redoubled force. Michael hurls back at him the failures of neglect and overindulgence that typified Claverton's hurried dealings with a child he never tried to understand. And Michael is also unwittingly reenacting "the sins of the father." He drives carelessly, relies on his father to get him out of scrapes, plays loosely (but less naively) with women, and finally resorts to the prospects held out for financial success to bring him happiness. Gomez and Mrs. Carghill carry Michael off in triumph to make for him such life as a "broken man" may salvage in Central America.

Claverton's motives in facing—refusing to escape from—all these intruders now become clear. "Those who flee from the past," he tells Michael, "will always lose the race" (p. 333). When Michael flees anyway, Claverton asks Monica, "Do I understand the meaning / Of the lesson I would teach?" And in words recalling Lear's last scene with Cordelia, he imagines himself "going to school" with Michael: "We'll sit side by side, at little desks / And suffer the same humiliations / At the hands of the same master" (pp. 337–338). Seeing her father face his "ghosts" for the first time and find himself at last a living person among them, Monica herself now changes from the officiously protective girl-about-town of the first act. She recalls not only Cordelia but Marina, Perdita, and Miranda, the daughter knowing her father for the first time as he is also ready to know himself. "She worshipped the part I played," he says to her fiancé, Charles. "How could I be sure that she would love the actor / If she saw him, off the stage, without his costume and make-up / And without his stage words?" (p. 341). At Monica's loving response, Claverton echoes Hawthorne's Dimmesdale (and also Pearl). Claverton includes his whole family in his elation, telling Charles and Monica that their souls "are safe" if they have one another to confess to. There is even a reminder of Roger Chillingworth when Claverton says of Gomez and Maisie, "It is through this meeting that I shall at last escape them" (p. 344). Like both *King Lear* and *The Scarlet Letter*, *The Elder Statesman* is a parable of redemption through self-discovery.

Claverton's newfound love radiates outward to his children (including Michael) and back again to him from Charles and Monica as he leaves the stage, drawn like Oedipus to the place of death, which Claverton has indicated will be "under the beech tree" (pp. 340, 355). Despite this almost explicit reminder of the Greek original, however, the last scenes clearly suggest that Eliot had the fifteenth-century morality play *Everyman* in mind; also the crisscross effect of the "negative" pagan and "positive" Christian themes that he spoke of in relation to "Marina."

A number of scholars have noted Eliot's continuing interest in *Everyman.* Some recall that he commented admiringly on the famous German revival, *Jederman,* by the Catholic verse dramatist Hugo von Hofmannsthal in 1911 and the earlier English production by William Poel in 1901.[62] In "Poetry and Drama," Eliot said he had used the verse patterns of *Everyman* while writing *Murder in the Cathedral* to avoid "archaism," and presumably the "neutral" verse measures would also have been appealing when he was trying to avoid other poetic mannerisms for plays set in modern life. But we might also recall that in his 1920 essay on Seneca, Eliot had said that the European popular drama "reached its highest point in *Everyman"* and that this play was more "refined . . . more *classical* in the profounder sense" than any Elizabethan drama. The later English theater, he said in this essay, suffered through "some fundamental release of restraint," from the gratification of tastes "always latent" and "now gratified by crime reports in the daily press."[63] Clearly Eliot was no devotee of Artaud's "theater of cruelty" either early or late in his career.

Everyman dramatizes the summons of Death to a man who may be eminent or lowly, a man who is compelled in the course of the play to call his past life in review and to discover the treacheries of Fellowship, Kinsmen, Wealth, and Good Deeds. Left hopeless when all these desert him, he composes his soul through Confession, who assures him of forgiveness and of life beyond the grave. After learning that angels will bear him up, Everyman's last good deed descends with him into the grave, and he speaks the words of Christ on the cross to his Father: "Into Thy hands I commend my spirit." In *The Elder Statesman,* it is Monica who speaks the equivalent of these words.

Claverton, like Oedipus meeting his welcome death near the pear tree, leaves the stage, going "too far to return to us," Monica says— "under the beech tree" (p. 355). Perhaps we are to remember Keats's "Ode to a Nightingale," for Keats hears the bird sing "In some melodious plot / Of beechen green, and shadows numberless," and he too, like Claverton, is "half in love with easeful death." It would not be beyond Eliot to remember also that the word "beech" is the source of "book" and to have us see an allusion to himself at this point, the old celebrity shriven and hallowed with a newly awakened love (pointedly declared in the play's dedication to his second wife), now retiring into the printed book that ends with this play. The last words spoken on-stage, returning the audience to stillness in a way that leaves no doubt where "easeful death" should lead, are Monica's words to Charles: "Now take me to my father."

Claverton's fullest expression of his ability to meet reality in himself and also to meet death is in his several speeches on giving up the role of actor. Finally he makes the still greater renunciation, referred to earlier, which is also unprecedented in the earlier plays: "freed from the self that pretends to be someone," he consents to be "no one," and in that moment, as he says, "I begin to live" (p. 354). One observes here that Eliot has in effect vicariously renounced "the third voice of poetry," never explicitly rejected before, the dramatic voice requiring a clearly objectified persona through which Eliot had spoken for over twenty years.

In Claverton's words he seemed even to renounce the first voice, "the voice of the poet talking to himself—or to nobody." After seeing *The Elder Statesman* through production, Eliot had less than seven years remaining, but he had written everything he wanted to write. The plays had explored the negative way, from void to the still point of the turning world, of "everyman"—the saints, the heirs of "old houses," and the children of the lower classes. There was but one other "way" he had left his audiences to understand, the one most essentially his own. This was the *poet's* "way" on which he had concentrated in *Four Quartets,* the work of all his career on which, he said, "I stand or fall."[64]

6 "At the Top of the Stair":
Four Quartets

Studying Eliot's whole career, one must use the phrase "negative way" in a broader sense than the usual Christian term would allow, but certainly one must first be clear what is generally understood in the Christian sense. James Johnson Sweeney, Raymond Preston, Louis Martz, and Leonard Unger in the forties wrote cogently on Eliot's preoccupation with the negative way in "Ash-Wednesday" and *Four Quartets,* the way recognizable through his allusions to St. John of the Cross and the fourteenth-century *Cloud of Unknowing.* Eliot had begun quoting St. John's sixteenth-century *Ascent of Mount Carmel* as early as the fiercely ironic epigraph to *Sweeney Agonistes,* circulated to friends in 1924–25. The epigraph, published in 1926, read: "Hence the soul cannot be possessed of the divine union, until it has divested itself of the love of created beings." Yet even Sweeney, Unger, and Martz, it seems to me, were confused about two of St. John's works—the *Ascent of Mount Carmel* and the *Dark Night of the Soul* (which is properly the fourth part of the *Ascent*)—in their otherwise excellent studies.[1] When St. John wrote of "the divine union" and its possession through the way of dispossession, he was describing a twofold path, one for beginners (whether religious or lay novices) and the other for experienced contemplatives. Only the latter "way" was the way of the "dark night of the soul," although both "ways" belong to the one *via negativa,* which St. John had found described in the earliest Christian writers, especially St. Augustine and the Pseudo-Dionysius the Areopagite (hereafter referred to as Dionysius). In Eliot's religious plays and poems, he sometimes treats one side of this twofold path and sometimes the other, as we shall see.

Both sides of the path demand a shift in our normal thought. Living in what Pitrim Sorokin called our "supersensate culture," we find it easier to think of the "ascent" to God as Shakespeare thought of it, by way of the great chain of being—straight up from lower beings to the highest. This "affirmative way" had always been acknowledged by the Christian saints as a valid means of recognizing God's handwriting in the universe, but St. John of the Cross (like others I shall mention) held that the *via affirmativa* was less effective than the *via negativa,* because God is *not* the highest in a hierarchical continuum. God is wholly *other* than any being we know by immediate perception or intuition. "For all things of earth and heaven, compared with God, are nothing."[2] Furthermore, God Himself is nothing, compared with everything we know. To begin "the way" toward union with God (different from intellectual recognition that He exists), the soul must actively seek a complete purgation, a way of pain and dispossession necessary because of the soul's propensity to mistake the love of creatures for the love of God. This purgation takes many forms and is excruciatingly painful, evidently leading not toward light but toward an abyss of darkness. God's light is "a ray of darkness to the understanding," St. John says, quoting Dionysius.[3] Such pain as the saints have borne on this negative way is not even permitted to any but those who can bear it.

> So powerful a purgation is the lot of but few souls, namely of those whom He intends to lift by contemplation to some degree of union; the more sublime that degree, the fiercer the purification . . . Each one suffers in proportion to his imperfections. This purgation is sometimes as fierce in its way as that of Purgatory, for one is meant to dispose the soul for a perfect union even here below, while the other is to enable it to see God hereafter.[4]

The "way of ignorance," as Eliot (following ancient tradition) called the negative way in "East Coker," III, initiates the soul seeking union with ultimate reality to two "nights": the dark night of sense and the dark night of the soul. Both are described in St. John's *Ascent of Mount Carmel,* the first night being for beginners, and the second for proficients. It is only the fourth part of the *Ascent* that is titled the *Dark Night of the Soul,* and it makes considerable difference in Eliot's poems to know which part of the negative way is in question. As one might guess, Eliot's play about St. Thomas Becket draws extensively from the second night, the night of the soul, intended for men and women experienced in perfecting their lives to conform to the will of God. But the poem Eliot began because its lines did not fit *Murder in the Cathedral,* that is "Burnt Norton," and the three Quartets that follow it, deal almost exclusively with the first night, the dark night of sense. Even Louis Martz has merged the two nights. Leonard Unger distinguishes them but reverses them when he says that "the active way of purgation is intended for proficients . . . counsel for the passive way, for beginners."[5] In the *Ascent of Mount Carmel* (I, i, 2–3), St. John points out that the beginner's way is *active.* The experienced contemplative is *passive* as divine love moves the soul toward union. Though Martz describes only the passive night of the soul as an ascent, both the active and inactive "nights" engage the soul in ascent as well as descent.

When Eliot speaks of "the one way" and "the other" in "Burnt Norton," III, he lays chief emphasis on the "night of sense" and mentions the "night of the soul" only briefly at the end of the passage. This is consistent with his differentiation between the way of most men and women and the way of the saints ("for most of us" there is only the trying) in "East Coker," V, and "The Dry Salvages," V, as also in *The Cocktail Party,* Act II. To an extraordinary degree, *Four Quartets* is structured throughout on the first night of the negative way. Many have noted that this "way" is succinctly conveyed in "Burnt Norton," III:

> Descend lower, descend only
> Into the world of perpetual solitude,
> World not world, but that which is not world.
> Internal darkness, deprivation
> And destitution of all property,
> Desiccation of the world of sense,
> Evacuation of the world of fancy,

Inoperancy of the world of spirit;
This is the one way, and the other
Is the same, not in movement
But abstention from movement . . .

But few, if any, have noted that "the other" way, the dark night of the soul—so quickly touched at the end of this passage—is hardly dealt with at all in *Four Quartets,* understandable since this is not the way of the poet, and *Four Quartets* is about the poet's experience rather than the saint's. The spiritual discipline described in the first eight lines just quoted, even though it includes "evacuation of the world of fancy" and "inoperancy of the world of spirit," is included by St. John in the first "dark night of sense," the "way" for meditants rather than for contemplatives (like Thomas Becket, Henry Monchensey, and Celia Coplestone in the plays). A poet who continues to practice his calling as poet may follow the purgative, negative way of meditation, and even write poems describing his experience, *after* the experience of course, since meditation in poetry is very different from spiritual medi-tation, at least in Eliot's view. When Eliot says that the night of the soul, "the other [way] / Is the same, not in movement/ But absten-tion from movement," he means that the twofold way, the two nights, are the same except for the passivity of the second. Both pro-ceed by purgation, illumination, and union with God. Both may pro-ceed toward union because there is a natural and a supernatural union, and indeed the natural—begun in the night of sense—may lead to-ward the "total" supernatural union possible to the saints even on earth. For while "God dwells and is present substantially in every soul, even in that of the greatest sinner," and while union of heart and soul with God in a natural way requires only that the meditant turn to Him forsaking all others, there is still beyond this the "supernatural" union "when the two wills—namely that of the soul and that of God—are conformed together in one."[6] John of the Cross thus distin-guishes the night of nature from the night of the soul.

We should not, however, think of St. John's treatises on the nega-tive way as Eliot's one source, since his early poetry shows him to be a master of the negative way some years before he referred to John of the Cross in *Sweeney Agonistes* or in fact gave any quarter to Christian spirituality in his poems. Although his Harvard reading notes men-tion both Dionysius and St. John of the Cross—especially in the cards on James's *Varieties of Religious Experience* and Underhill's *Mysticism*—

his interest in them was plainly counterbalanced by skepticism and his readings on religious neuroses. As one traces the negative way back in history one seems to move closer and closer to the negative way of the early Eliot, a way on which the dark night of St. John becomes even darker, because there is no promise of union with God at the end of the tunnel. Before turning to *Four Quartets,* we should notice the beginnings of negative theology before the period of John of the Cross.

There is no emphasis in St. John's writings which is not also in the chief theologian whom he studied at Salamanca in Spain, St. Thomas Aquinas. Eliot's Clark Lectures show that he had been reading Aquinas avidly from 1924 to 1926, and Margolis gives the precise texts. Aquinas was more appealing and accessible to Eliot than St. John was, at least until the thirties, when Christian mysticism got the upper hand over Christian rationalism in his writing. But we tend to forget that Aquinas has much to say about negative theology. Among the sources he most often cites is the Pseudo-Dionysius the Areopagite, the fifth-century Syrian monk who is the fountainhead of negative theology in the Christian world.

Aquinas makes clear that the via negativa is a way toward knowledge of God: on earth we can never know "face to face" *what* God is, only "through a glass darkly" *that* He is. Following Aristotle in describing the human mind as a tabula rasa before birth, Aquinas says that *knowledge* of God cannot be immediate, although *love* of God can be, because desire moves immediately toward God, while knowledge operates by way of sense experience:

> This being so, we have to say that love, which is an act of an appetitive virtue, even in our present state tends first to God, and from him flows out to other things: in this way charity loves God without any intermediary. The case is directly the opposite with knowledge, since it is through other things that we come to know God: as a cause, through its effects, or else, as Dionysius points out, by the way of eminence or of negation.[7]

One may note that Aquinas mentions *three* ways of knowing God here: the affirmative way, which in a commentary on Dionysius he describes as the way of recognizing God "in all things";[8] "the way of eminence," which Eliot also uses to great advantage, as we shall see; and the way "of negation."

Since Aquinas is thought by many to have altered the stricter negative way of Dionysius, we should note two other passages where he cites Dionysius. Later in the *Summa Theologiae* (II. ii, Q. 122, art. 2) Aquinas writes, "while it is true that affirmation has a natural precedence over negation, . . . in the things of God . . . because of our inadequacy, negation has greater value than affirmation, as Dionysius says [in *De caelesti hierarchia* 2]." And still later, in the *Summa Contra Gentiles,* after saying that the human intellect "cannot by itself arrive at an intuitive knowledge of God," Aquinas adds,

> Nevertheless . . . lest so noble a creature [as man] should seem to be utterly devoid of purpose, through being unable to obtain its own end, man has been given the means of rising to the knowledge of God. For, since all the perfections of things come down from God the summit of all perfection, man begins from the lowest things and rising by degrees advances to the knowledge of God: *thus, too, in corporeal movements, the way down is the same as the way up, and they differ only as regards their beginning and end.*[9]

(My emphasis points to Eliot's second epigraph for *Four Quartets,* drawn from Heraclitus but also consistent with Aquinas.)

Since the term "the negative way" derives from Dionysius, who is at least as important a figure in the theology of Eastern Christianity as in that of Western Christianity, scholars of the Eastern Church have been greatly concerned to distinguish what they consider the pure form of the negative way from what it became in the West (even for John of the Cross) because of Aquinas's teaching. Vladimir Losski, for instance, stresses that negative or apophatic theology "constitutes the fundamental characteristic of the whole theological tradition of the Eastern Church." The Western Church, says Losski (and as Aquinas's lines, just quoted, "man begins from the lowest things . . . rising by degrees," would suggest), has consistently emphasized cataphatic (or affirmative) theology and following Aquinas has used apophatic (negative) theology only *to correct* the affirmative way. Dionysius, Losski points out, refuses to accept the philosophy of Aristotle (followed by Aquinas) that God is "perfect being." For Dionysius *all* being is multiplex and disguises the absolute otherness of God. Union of the soul with God is possible only when created beings are utterly renounced for the "uncreated super-essence." Meditants must begin by saying, "God is not stone, God is not fire," but they must proceed to the final negation of saying, "God is not being, intelligence, unity or good-ness."[10]

What then of Christ? For the Christian Dionysius, Christ is the su-preme example of the negative way, emptying his humanity by the way of dispossession. (St. Paul is Dionysius's source in stressing that Christ "emptied himself" that man might be redeemed.) In Him, the hidden God remained hidden: "In the humanity of Christ, the Super-essential was manifested in human substance without ceasing to be hidden . . . in this manifestation itself."[11] Comparing the negative way of prayer to that of sculptors, stripping away stone so that the form within it may emerge, Dionysius writes,

> ascending upwards from particular to universal conceptions we strip off all qualities in order that we may attain a naked knowledge of that Unknowing which in all existent things is enwrapped by all objects of knowledge, and that we may begin to see that super-essential Dark-ness which is hidden by all the light that is in existent things.[12]

It is not clear to me that Aquinas *has* misinterpreted Dionysius, whose ascent by way of descent into Unknowing seems fully accepted by Aquinas as the best, if not the only, way of knowing God on earth. If the matter is one of emphasis in Eastern Christianity, this would, nevertheless, help to explain (for instance) Dostoevsky's Christian vi-sion manifested by way of what is furthest from God—in prostitutes, drunkards, and murderers, who find God by appalling emptying of self.

Certainly Eliot and Dostoevsky followed different negative ways, though both of their ways seem recognizable in another contempla-tive of the Eastern Church, St. Gregory of Nyssa, whose fourth-cen-tury writing inspired Dionysius. St. Gregory's portrait of the soul's anguish resembles both Eliot's Becket and Dostoevsky's Sophia Mar-meladov. St. Gregory describes the soul—even after purification and il-lumination—when "she" "rises again . . . and . . . begins to question if even the angels can apprehend him whom she loves. They give her no answer, but by their silence make it plain that he is inaccessible even to them. So . . . she abandons all that she has found there, and finds her Beloved in her very inability to grasp that which he is."[13] The three stages of the soul's journey to union (in this life) with God, de-scribed just before this passage by St. Gregory, were borrowed from

Plotinus by the earliest Christian writers. They were "purification, illumination, and union"—which Christian writers identified with the first, second, and third "heavens" described by St. Paul when he spoke of being borne to the "third heaven." It seems possible to trace these stages in Becket's "way" in *Murder in the Cathedral.* For very good reasons, though, Eliot reverses the first and second of these stages in the negative way of the poet, as conveyed in *Four Quartets.* There, as I shall later show, the "way" begins with illumination, proceeds to purification (purgation), and ends with union.

When I said that the apophatic, or negative, way grows darker or more negative the further one traces it back, I was thinking of the earliest, pre-Christian forms of it found in Eastern philosophy, especially in the Vedic songs of India, the *Bhagavad-Gītā,* and early Buddhism—all of which Eliot said were a constant influence on his poetry. His earliest poetry, one could argue, was more influenced by these writings than by any Christian literature. The Hindu Vedas, oldest of religious hymns, sang of a darkness behind created things more negative than any envisioned by the confluence of negativities from the Greek philosophers and Judaic apophaticism as they came together, for instance, in the negative theology of Philo of Alexandria (25 B.C.–A.D. 50).[14] The oldest apophaticism, impressive to Thoreau as the most complete,[15] is best revealed in the Creation Hymn of the Hindu *Rg Veda,* X, 129:

> Then even nothingness was not, nor existence.
>   There was no air then, nor the heavens beyond it.
> What covered it? Where was it? In whose keeping?
>   Was there then cosmic water, in depths unfathomed?
>
> .   .   .   .   .
>
>   At first there was only darkness wrapped in darkness.
>   All this was only unillumined water.
> That One which came to be, enclosed in nothing,
>   arose at last, born of the power of heat.
>
> In the beginning desire descended on it—
>   that was the primal seed, born of the mind.
> The sages who have searched their hearts with wisdom
>   know that which is is kin to that which is not.

And they have stretched their cord across the void,
　　and know what was above, and what below.
Seminal powers made fertile mighty forces.
　　Below was strength, and over it was impulse.

But, after all, who knows, and who can say
　　whence it all came, and how creation happened?
The gods themselves are later than creation,
　　so who knows truly when it has arisen?

Whence all creation had its origin,
　　he whether he fashioned it or whether he did not,
he, who surveys it all from highest heaven,
　　he knows—or maybe even he does not know.[16]

With such a sense of original creation at the root of his heritage, the Buddha taught (as A. L. Basham says) that "speculation on first causes was a futile waste of time." Little wonder, then, that the "basic propositions of [the great body of Buddhist literature] are not metaphysical, but psychological."[17]

The "negative way" clearly may be either a psychological discipline or a metaphysical "quest," or both. For many reasons, Eliot's poems written before "The Hollow Men" may be called psychological rather than metaphysical, whereas the poems after 1925 declare a centripetal metaphysics evident in all his plays and *Four Quartets*. Even then, of course, the stream-of-consciousness method of "Prufrock," "Gerontion," and "Ash-Wednesday" persists, though *whose consciousness* is a crucial question, since in the late poetry the consciousness is clearly Eliot's. Earlier it took a number of different identities (Prufrock's, Gerontion's, Tiresias's). The later persistence of the psychological working out of each poem, with its importance for the problem of negativity, was clear in a passage already quoted from Eliot's 1937 essay on revelation:

The human mind is perpetually driven between two desires, between two dreams each of which may be either a vision or a nightmare: the vision and nightmare or the material world, and the vision and nightmare of the immaterial. Each may be in turn, or for different minds, a refuge to which to fly, or a horror from which to escape. We desire and fear both sleep and waking; the day brings relief from the night, and the night brings relief from the day; we go to sleep as to death, and we wake as to damnation.[18]

If one takes "the dream" that shows the material and immaterial worlds as "nightmare," one comes close to Eliot's early poetic stance. After 1930, by contrast, he increasingly treated both the material and immaterial worlds as "vision." While recreating the nightmare world of his early poems, however, he found philosophical consolation in Buddhist apophaticism. "Long ago I studied the ancient Indian languages," he noted in a 1946 talk, "and while I was chiefly interested in Philosophy, I read a little poetry too; and I know that my own poetry shows the influence of Indian thought and sensibility."[19] His Indian studies at Harvard also furnished a base from which he proceeded to all the "ways" mentioned by Aquinas, "the way of affirmation" and "the way of eminence," as well as the "negative way." Having seen the changes in his poems from "Prufrock" to "Marina," we might question Grover Smith's conclusion that Eliot's poetry as a whole "developed from 'affirmative' quest to 'negative' renunciation."[20] Negation and rejection were as central to his poetry before "Marina" as afterwards, and the quest motif in fact became increasingly important after "The Hollow Men."

We can trace Eliot's development precisely by the change in his attitude toward Dante seen in his early poems and in *Four Quartets*. In 1920, while writing *The Waste Land*, Eliot wrote a short essay on Dante, arguing with a point of Valéry's and saying that *philosophy* in a poem is a vital, organizing element. He called Dante's *Commedia* "the most ordered presentation of the emotions that has ever been made."[21] Nothing in this essay, however, indicated his own acceptance of Dante's order. On the contrary, ironic echoes from the *Commedia* in all the early poems and *The Waste Land* stand as proof of his own conviction concerning the absence of any such order. Seven years after *The Waste Land* came out, he wrote his second and fullest essay on Dante, now after his conversion, speaking of the poem for the first time as bearing a close relation to contemporary thought and to his own beliefs. Thus, speaking of the *Inferno*, Eliot—whose protagonist in *The Waste Land* dreaded reincarnation—now says that "the resurrection of the body has perhaps a deeper meaning than we understand." "Dante's [poem] is one of those which we can only just hope to grow up to at the end of life." He makes another revealing comment: "It took me many years to recognize that the states of improvement and beatitude which Dante describes [in the *Paradiso*] are still further from what the modern world can conceive as cheerfulness, than are his states of damnation."[22] Dante's line "In His will is our peace" now seems to him *"literally true."* Twenty-one years after finishing this essay, Eliot wrote a third essay on Dante in which he summed up: Dante has been "the most persistent and deepest influence upon my own verse."[23] But we shall see that Dante's "way" was not exactly Eliot's.

As his poems deepened in spiritual authority, he found other writers who had made the same journey he had made, particularly Paul Elmer More, the Princeton professor who like Eliot found it impossible to follow Babbitt into a secular humanism. More had grown up in reaction against a distempered Calvinism in America, and like Eliot had turned to the *Upaniṣads* and the *Bhagavad Gītā* as a spiritual resource. Eliot read More's published account of his early development and his later Christian conversion and wrote to More in 1936: "[your]" spiritual biography . . . is oddly, even grotesquely, more like my own . . . than that of any human being I have known." Earlier he had written to More that religion had brought him "the perception of something above morals, and therefore extremely terrifying . . . the very dark night and the desert."[24] In that same year, in an essay written for Norman Foerster, who with Babbitt was founding the "New Humanism," Eliot said, "I found . . . a little intellectual discipline from a little study of philosophy. But the difficult discipline is the discipline and training of emotion . . . and this . . . is only attainable through dogmatic religion."[25]

The difficult discipline is the training of emotion. Religion is above morals, terrifying—the very dark night and the desert. These points were true for Eliot both after he committed himself to an affirmative creed and when he acknowledged none, as his 1913–14 essay on primitive religions indicated. His earliest poetry, like his latest, demanded a discipline—an *askesis* (as he called it in "A Dialogue on Dramatic Poetry") or asceticism—of emotion that translates itself immediately into poetry (when it can). *Askesis,* originally the Greek word for *the craftsman's* self-discipline, came only secondarily to mean an asceticism required for the performer of religious rites. Eliot's experience reenacted that change in meaning. Poetry is "a continual surrender" of the self "to something . . . more valuable," Eliot had said in "Tradition and the Individual Talent." In 1919 when he wrote that essay, poetry was "an escape" from a nightmare world, as well as a via negativa into a creative void. The difference between "Prufrock," "Mr. Eliot's Sunday Morning Service," and "Gerontion" on the one hand and the poems after 1927 that express a Christian's quest (from "Ash-Wednesday" forward) on the other hand is the difference between two voids explored by the ascetic, the craftsman: one in which there is no response to the poet's voice and another in which the response is "the silence of God" sought by John of the Cross. Vacuity was never for the early Eliot what it became for Sartre—a truly godlike power: "We see nothingness," says Sartre, "making the world iridescent, casting a shimmer over things." And, "Man is the being through whom nothingness comes to the world."[26] Sartre's "dark night and the desert," has its own "ray of darkness." The extremes of Eliot and Sartre approach the touching point but never meet. They come closest to meeting, perhaps, in their persistent realism, their suspicion of mythologies and "false consciousness," however differently they would interpret that phrase.

The Waste Land's closing chant from the *Upaniṣads*—"Shantih shantih shantih"—I have suggested, offered a truce to one kind of negation, the experience of life-loathing and fear. The poem had not, however, sought refuge in mythology. Eliot had used myths—the Vedas' Fisher King merged with the Fisher King legends of Europe— in quite a different way from Joyce's in *Ulysses,* though his 1923 review of that novel has been read as a wholehearted acceptance of mythology, especially when he called myth "simply a way of controlling, of ordering, of giving shape and a significance to the immense panorama of futility and anarchy which is contemporary history."[27] *The Waste Land* used myths only to fracture and finally dispense with them, leaving us with a "heap of broken images"—like the images broken by all iconoclasts. If Eliot seemed, like Pound, to repudiate the biblical word and Word before 1925, he did not even then (like Pound) find that Orpheus or Homer had any more privileged access to truth than Moses or St. Paul. Eliot never used mythology, as E. M. Forster or D. H. Lawrence or William Faulkner (for instance) used it in such works as *A Passage to India, The Plumed Serpent,* or *The Bear*—that is, as an alternative approach to reality, preferable to a modern, everyday "realism."

Even in *The Waste Land* Eliot was moving toward that realism and rejection of mythology he expressed in notes for his English 26 lectures at Harvard in 1932–33, when he said that Lawrence's use of primitive religion in *The Plumed Serpent* amounted to mindless blasphemy.[28] In these lecture notes Eliot approves of "realism" of a kind that would oppose uncritical use of mythology as romanticism. The realism he supports relies on actual objects to which the writer has most intensely responded in immediate experience. "The natural object is always the *adequate* symbol," as Pound had said in *Make It New.* For Eliot "a sense of fact"—which he called native to "classicism" as opposed to "romanticism" in his debates with John Middleton Murry[29]—led him to such "factual" sources on the inner life as the Buddha and St. Augustine in *The Waste Land,* and he adhered to factual sources from then on. After 1925, his poetry focuses on the real problems of the poet's way, and reaches its culmination in *Four Quartets,* controlled and shaped by memory rather than myth.

Such realism had been anticipated in "Tradition and the Individual Talent" when he said, "This essay proposes to halt at the frontier of metaphysics or mysticism, and confine itself to such practical conclusions as can be applied by the responsible person interested in poetry." As epigraph to this last section of the essay, he had quoted in Greek Aristotle's very Platonic statement from *De Anima,* I, iv: "Presumably the mind is something more divine and is unaffected [by these things which move or change the body]." In 1951, however, *after* writing *Four Quartets,* he concluded his essay "Poetry and Drama," "it is ultimately the function of art . . . eliciting some perception of an order *in* reality, to bring us to a condition of serenity, stillness, and reconciliation; and then leave us, as Virgil left Dante, to proceed to a region where that guide can avail us no farther."

In the first essay Eliot had proposed "to halt . . . and confine" himself to poetry, whether or not "the mind is something more divine." If it is, then "the mind [must be] something unaffected" (as the Loeb translation has it) by such things as poetry. One glimpses *Aristotle's* apophaticism in the quotation, pointing to a preserve where perfect Being resides, unaffected by finite multiplicities. This classical preserve could almost offer shelter even to a Buddhist wayfarer through the waste land. But in Eliot's 1951 conclusion, as in *Four Quartets,* there is no such area cordoned off, no barrier at the frontier between poetry and a region beyond. There is in fact a stairway (Dante's) or a method or mode by which art "bring[s] us . . . and then leave[s] us . . . to proceed toward a region where that guide can avail us no farther." The fact that the way is evidently unobstructed and continuous does not, of course, mean that it is a mythical way.

Four Quartets begins with a reflective passage on actual time and memory, reminiscent of Augustine's opening in the *Confessions* and perhaps thus signaling that the poem is a real confession—a poet's memory of *his* "way." It also summarizes Augustine's extensive inquiry into the nature of time which occupies the whole of Book XI of the *Confessions*. In this homage to Augustine, Eliot retracts his views of time given in "Gerontion" and *The Waste Land*, where history was seen as a purposeless labyrinth, returning on itself in "unreal" phases—"Jerusalem Athens Alexandria / Vienna London / Unreal." Such a view indeed had illustrated the Buddhist Nāgārjuna's negation of time in a passage that Eliot's new opening seems directly to refute. The third-century monk Nāgārjuna had written:

> If "the present" and "future" exist presupposing "the past,"
> "The present" and "future" will exist in "the past."
> If "the present" and "future" did not exist there [in "the past"],
> How could "the present" and "future" exist presupposing that "past"?
> Without presupposing "the past" the two things ["the present" and "future"] cannot be proved to exist.
> Therefore neither present nor future time exist.[30]

Eliot's opening of *Four Quartets,* by contrast, affirms the necessary reality of time and also its providential movement toward the redemption of human nature. To Augustine's analysis of time he adds that not only is what happens in time real, but also *what might have happened* is equally real. As we have seen, since writing "The Hollow Men" Eliot had been occupied persistently with the "three dreams" that cross in the human mind, and here he asserts that thoughts of "what might have been"—along with what actually occurred in time—"Point to one end, which is always present." That end is dramatically revealed to the poet as he follows a visible path toward "the door we never opened / Into the rose garden," and there looks into the empty pool of Burnt Norton:

> And the pool was filled with water out of sunlight,
> And the lotos rose, quietly, quietly,
> The surface glittered out of heart of light . . .

The juxtaposition of lotos and rose I shall mention later, but here we should simply note that more than thirty years earlier, in his Harvard notes for 1913–14, Eliot had observed that in Tendai Buddhism "the lotos alone is perfect, because it has many flowers and many fruits *at once*. The real entity is represented in the fruit, its manifestation in the flower. Mutual relation of final reality and manifestation."[31] The idea of the lotos stayed in Eliot's mind, for he mentioned it again in an unpublished paper on Bergson, also among his Harvard papers in Houghton Library. The image, or symbol, vividly embodies his point in "Burnt Norton," I, that remembering what might have been—whether it is the life unlived or the unkept promise of an Eden now in ruins—excites in the mind that momentary sense of Reality (the flower) *and* its fruit which are "always present" if we have the power to see them.

After the scene in the actual rose garden, which ends in the manifestation of the lotos in the full pool, "Burnt Norton" shifts from a visible path to the second meaning of "way" in part II, that is to the *movement* or motivating force along a path:

> The dance along the artery
> The circulation of the lymph
> Are figured in the drift of stars
> Ascend to summer in the tree
> We move above the moving tree
> In light upon the figured leaf
> And hear upon the sodden floor
> Below, the boarhound and the boar
> Pursue their pattern as before
> But reconciled among the stars.

"The way" the world and all that is in it moves is thus a dance, from the earth's axle outward in life, vegetable or animate, toward the stars. In the next stanza we see what it is that reconciles the warring elements—that is, "the still point," which draws the dance to itself by what St. Augustine called "the gravity of grace." Helen Gardner says Eliot confirmed Charles Williams's belief that Eliot was inspired by

Williams's novel *The Greater Trumps,* "where in a magical model of the universe the figures of the Tarot pack dance around the Fool at the still center."[32] If Eliot was not simply being kind to Williams, he at least had observed the ancient theories about the still point many years earlier. For instance in "The Development of Leibniz' Monadism," an essay written for *The Monist* in 1916, republished together with his thesis in 1964, he noted that Leibniz was struck in 1687 by finding in the Jewish Kabbala the theory that the universe is an "emanation from an infinite being which consists in an indivisible point." We read this with amusement beside *Four Quartets,* since in 1916 Eliot added that the theory illustrates "Leibniz' insatiable curiosity toward every sort of theological hocus-pocus."[33]

Eliot must also have encountered the theory in his Harvard classes, for as an Assistant in Philosophy he taught the Neo-Platonists, who were the first to picture God as "a circle whose center is everywhere and whose circumference is nowhere." He would have met a similar concept in Aristotle's *De Anima,* X. And it seems likely that he would also have learned that Philo of Alexandria had been the first to reconcile Aristotle's still point with the personal God, the *deus absconditus* (hidden God) of Isaiah 45. Philo had described God as a Being who can be only darkly conceived as an indivisible point without magnitude.[34] Finally, the idea of the world as a dance around this central point was not only in Dante but in Elizabethan writers, notably in Sir John Davies's *Orchestra.*

That the universal movement, or way, is toward "a white light still and moving" may be of interest in relation to Eliot's Harvard notes on Buddhism again. In Anesaki's course notes, he observed that the Buddha was compared to a white light, made up of all ten colors. But the image of white light and white rose are also in Dante's *Paradiso.* And of course the imagery for ultimate reality in *Four Quartets* is deliberately universal.

After seeing "the way" both as path and as motivating force or point, in "Burnt Norton," III, we come to the way as *means* by which the individual person responds by choice to the drawing center. Here human beings, having to choose their course rather than to obey natural laws (as do mud, tree, and stars), are directed to "the one way" of the poem's second epigraph—Heraclitus's "The way upwards and downwards are one and the same."

The concentrated summary of St. John of the Cross's *Ascent of Mount Carmel* in this part of "Burnt Norton" offers the reader a choice of the beginner's way or the contemplative's way, both being means of finding reconciliation and union with ultimate reality. Each way carries one both "upwards and downwards." In disagreeing with other readers (Preston and Smith, for example), I rely upon the whole theme of *Four Quartets* insofar as it presents us with *the poet's way* as a satisfactory way, even though it is not the way of the saint, whose "way upwards and downwards" is more concentrated—"a lifetime's death in love,/ Ardour and selflessness and self-surrender" ("Dry Salvages," V). Eliot's summary of the via negativa in "Burnt Norton," III is perfectly consonant with St. John's (if not Dionysius's) in that it promises even beginners and laymen that they will find the "way down" into dispossession, detachment, and humility, to be a "way up" to union in "the heart of light." The way of the saints provides history and mankind with *assurances* that life can be transformed by grace here and now. Their example is the "way of eminence" referred to by Aquinas as yet a third way—added to the affirmative way of approaching God through images, through perceiving His effects in nature, and the negative way of union through rejection of all that is not God. If I am right that even as a poet Eliot favors the negative way, this is so because *Four Quartets,* the poem on which he said his rank *as a poet* would stand or fall, steadily stresses "the way of ignorance" as mentioned in "East Coker," III, and does so because it is the best way that the poet can find to express his own experience in a world where

> Love is the unfamiliar Name
> Behind the hands that wove
> The intolerable shirt of flame
> Which human power cannot remove.   ("Little Gidding," IV)

The predominance of "the way" motif asserts itself, nevertheless, within a poetic structure employing images of affirmation more convincing than those in any other of Eliot's poems. The structure is built on four landscapes, drawn from Eliot's walks and memories. Though in a letter of January 4, 1941, Eliot told John Hayward he feared that *Four Quartets* lacked a powerful personal reminiscence to unify it, he obviously moves through the four landscapes in his own personality, first backward in time to the completed past (in "Burnt Norton" and

"East Coker"), then forward to a continuing past and present (in "The Dry Salvages") and finally to a perfect presence (in "Little Gidding") in which the time of the poem's writing meets timelessness, and leaves us (as Eliot would say in 1951) "to proceed toward a region where that guide [art] can avail us no longer."

Instead of Prufrock's "Streets that follow like a tedious argument," leading to an overwhelming question, each Quartet follows a visible path, and all paths lead to an answer that might also be overwhelming if Eliot's whole poetic development had not prepared us for it. The poem's method and motifs (many readers have noted) recapitulate Eliot's lifework, and thus the poem's own "way" becomes analogous to the poet's life. St. Augustine, trained as a rhetorician, had remarked on the way speech resembles our pilgrimage through time, each human event accruing its significance only by fulfilling what went before it and by pointing to what follows: "thus is our speech accomplished by signs emitting a sound," says Augustine in the *Confessions* IV, 10, "but this, again, is not perfected unless one word pass away when it has sounded its parts in order that another may succeed it." In "Burnt Norton," V, Eliot precisely points to this parallel between the way of his poem and the spiritual discipline he has just described—the movement toward "that which is not world":

> Words move, music moves
> Only in time; but that which is only living
> Can only die. Words, after speech, reach
> Into the silence. Only by the form, the pattern,
> Can words or music reach
> The stillness . . .
>
> .   .   .   .   .
>
> Before the beginning and after the end.

"Every phrase and every sentence is an end and a beginning,/ Every poem an epitaph," Eliot adds in the corresponding section of the last Quartet, "Little Gidding," V. The negative way of the poem follows the negative way of the ascetic; "any action" is a step "to an illegible stone." This was also the way of the Logos, Christ, who said, "I am the way." *Four Quartets* reminds us that this way too was toward an illegible stone: "The Word in the desert / Is most attacked by voices of temptation" ("Burnt Norton," V). The creative, ordering principle in the universe—subject of *Four Quartets'* first epigraph from Heraclitus—is analogous to the articulating power of the poet, whose words "strain, / Crack and sometimes break, under the burden" of fulfilling "the pattern." This is the poem's most persistent theme, as it is man's most insistent concern. As Augustine said, "order is that which, if we keep it in our lives, leads us to God."[35]

Many find Eliot's analogy between the poet's struggle with words and the tension between Logos and *logoi* noted by Heraclitus's fragment either presumptuous or incomprehensible, Elisabeth Schneider an eminent example of the former, Samuel Beckett of the latter.[36] Beckett's critique (for surely only Eliot fits) is less about the difficult theology than about Eliot's difficulty with mere verbal coherence, which is of course the theme of the poet's way in *Four Quartets:* "The fact would seem to be [Beckett writes in *The Unnamable*], if in my situation one may speak of facts, not only that I shall have to speak of things of which I cannot speak, but also, which is even more interesting, but also that I, which is if possible even more interesting, that I shall have to, I forget, no matter." Yet the nexus Eliot finds between the Logos and *logoi* is one that many theologians treat in just the same way. For instance Vladimir Losski writes: "All things were created by the Logos who is as it were a divine nexus, the threshold from which flow the creative outpourings, the particular *logoi* of creatures, and the centre towards which in their turn all created beings tend, as to their final end."[37]

As the first Quartet, "Burnt Norton," followed "the passage" into the rose garden of a ruined house, representing "what might have been" in the poet's finished past, the second Quartet, "East Coker" follows a "deep lane" into the village of East Coker, where Eliot's family lived until they emigrated to America in the seventeenth century. This part of Eliot's completed past appropriately becomes associated with traditions annihilated by history's onward "way" or movement, again the first two meanings of "way" employed as in "Burnt Norton." This time the movement brings no intuition of order, however, as it had when the illumination of what-might-have-been provided such an insight. The empty field where houses like the Eliots' once stood, where country people danced in midsummer midnight celebration, now reminds Eliot of the chaos and destruction—"dung and death"—to which these things came in time:

> Scorpion fights against the Sun
> Until the Sun and Moon go down
>
> . . . . .
>
> Whirled in a vortex that shall bring
> The world to that destructive fire
> Which burns before the ice-cap reigns.

Again, now, in this Quartet, "the way" of the universal movement through time leads to reflection on "the way" of poetry; and it is the negative way, by a series of rejections, or what apophatic theologians following Plotinus called *aphairesis*, a discarding of all that is not valid.

> That was a way of putting it—not very satisfactory:
> A periphrastic study in a worn-out poetical fashion,
> Leaving one still with the intolerable wrestle
> With words and meanings. The poetry does not matter.
> It was not (to start again) what one had expected.

Many besides Beckett (arguably) have ridiculed the passage as a radical rejection of the poem's *raison d'être*, but this is to forget the end of the poem, where we see the poet's way intersecting with a higher way. At this point—despite his closer and closer approach to Dante's vision and poetic "way," as I have said, Eliot explicitly detaches himself from Dante and asserts the necessity of a more negative direction or mode. Note, for instance, the reference I have italicized to Dante's opening line of the *Inferno,* which Eliot uses to illustrate precisely that Dante's "pattern" cannot be his own:

> knowledge imposes a pattern, and falsifies,
> For the pattern is new in every moment
> And every moment is a new and shocking
> Valuation of all we have been. We are only undeceived
> Of that which, deceiving, could no longer harm.
> *In the middle, not only in the middle of the way*
> *But all the way, in a dark wood . . .*
>
> . . . . .
>
> Do not let me hear
> Of the wisdom of old men, but rather of their folly.

The next lines suggest that Dante was less foolish than most "old men" (in the sense of "men of old") but that we are misled if we think we can solve our problems by clinging to the *patterns* of Dante or anyone else.

Eliot was at this time in his sixties, not like Dante imaged in his thirties in the *Commedia*. The allusion to "old men" is therefore also a compliment to Dante and is one of those reminders about the way of eminent men and women (the *via eminentiae*) which receives its full due later in *Four Quartets*. One should not be confused by the deliberate juxtaposition of allusions to old age with allusions to "the middle way" in the lines just quoted. The fifth movement of "East Coker" begins "So here I am, in the middle way," clearly *not* referring to Eliot's age but to his situation (the first definition of "way"). We are surely intended here to think of (among other things) "the middle way" of early Buddhism: the forest sage Nāgārjuna's "Fundaments of the Middle Way" where the phrase refers to a middle path between existence and nonexistence. This is clear if we remember the last movement of "Burnt Norton," where Eliot spoke of our place in time as a "form of limitation/ Between un-being and being." For Nāgārjuna the Middle Way is a way of liberation achieved by freeing oneself from all "patterns," including all fixed formulas concerning non-being or being. But while insisting that man can know no eternal reality independent of changing existences, Buddhist followers of the Middle Way focus on *the relation* between changing forms and the emptiness (sunyātā) in which forms exist. Such a "middle way" looks backward to Eliot's earlier poems. Yet it also evokes Aristotle's discussion of the "middle way" in the *Nicomachean Ethics,* II, vi–ix, as "an habitual disposition with respect to choice, the characteristic quality of which is moderation." To have the right feelings "at the right time, with reference to the right objects, toward the right people, with the right motive, and in the right manner, is to strike the mean, and therein to follow the best course . . . And in the same way our outward acts admit of excess [or] deficiency [or] the proper mean." If this construction makes Eliot appear presumptuous for saying "here I am, in the middle way," we may recall that he had chosen not only the poet's but the businessman's life and the Anglo-Catholic religion as a "middle way" and that in this poem human life itself is a middle way between "un-being and being" (a stress that, as we shall see, finally alters Nāgārjuna's position without repudiating it).

More specifically, since the journey motif of this second Quartet began by pondering the death and decomposition confronted in the empty field of East Coker, the third movement takes "the way" back to London (as in the corresponding movement of "Burnt Norton"), where images of passengers on a journey to death and darkness afflict the poet. Facing these, he calls out in the apophatic voice heard in the Psalms:[38]

> I said to my soul, be still, and let the dark come upon you
> Which shall be the darkness of God.
>
> . . . . .
>
> I said to my soul, be still, and wait without hope
> For hope would be hope for the wrong thing; wait without love
> For love would be love of the wrong thing; there is yet faith
> But the faith and love and the hope are all in the waiting.

The rejections are close to many passages in St. John's *Ascent,* for example: "the point from which the soul goes forth . . . [is] deprivation and denial . . . [T]he road along which the soul must travel . . . is faith, which is likewise as dark as night to the understanding. The . . . point to which it travels [is] God, Who, equally is dark night to the soul in this life" (I, ii, 1); or "advice must be given to learn to abide attentively and wait lovingly upon God in that state of quiet, and to pay no heed to imagination or to its working" (II, xii, 8). This "underground" jouney into the void, echoing that of the corresponding movement in "Burnt Norton," is now more insistently proffered as "the way." Eliot paraphrases St. John of the Cross exactly here; and as I have said, it seems important to note that this paraphrase is from *the way for beginners*—the middle way—of the *Ascent of Mount Carmel* (I, xii, 11), not from the way for contemplatives in the *Dark Night of the Soul:*

> To arrive where you are, to get from where you are not,
>   You must go by a way wherein there is no ecstasy.
> In order to arrive at what you do not know
>   You must go by a way which is the way of ignorance.
> In order to possess what you do not possess
>   You must go by the way of dispossession.
> In order to arrive at what you are not

You must go through the way in which you are not.
And what you do not know is the only thing you know
And what you own is what you do not own
And where you are is where you are not.

Many readers find the allegorical lyric which follows ("The wounded surgeon plies the steel") a disappointing passage. Considering that it is the first and only full treatment of the Christian kerygma in the poem, the lyric seems to them embarrassingly derivative. It imitates Andrew Marvell's "A Dialogue Between the Soul and the Body," as Sweeney noted. And surely Eliot knew that Marvell himself was imitating St. John of the Cross's "Songs Between the Soul and the Spouse." Furthermore St. John was imitating other poets (especially Garcilaso), who in turn drew from St. Augustine's *Confessions* the allegory of the dying soul seeking its cure from the wounded lover.[39] Since Eliot was probably fully aware of this free-for-all among imitators, his point that "the poetry does not matter" gains added force. Poems, like mankind, "all go into the dark." Every new poem in the tradition moves along the way of eminence laid down before, each one transforming the tradition, though each is only a partial way of expressing what words about the Word merely approximate. This too is "the wisdom of humility" mentioned earlier in the Quartet.

The last movement of "East Coker," like the second, comments on the poet's struggle for words, his "raid on the inarticulate," in a time when *logoi* are deteriorating in "the general mess of imprecision of feeling." Dead poets, like the dead in Eliot's East Coker family and their traditions, lie under "old stones that cannot be deciphered," but the decomposition marked by the stone is "burning in every moment" with the fire Heraclitus posited as the force moving along "the way upwards and downwards" in sensible and insensible nature. Having seen this, literally by touching rock bottom, after following Eliot to his family's roots in the finished past, we next turn in "East Coker" toward the evolutionary flow of life. "Old men ought to be explorers," even if their wisdom is folly. The torn arras of Mary Queen of Scots' lost cause (its motto: "In my end is my beginning") connects the Quartet's last line with its first ("In my beginning is my end"). In the Eliot family's beginning at East Coker Eliot had found one of the moments of illumination that light the negative way. Now he transforms Thomas Elyot's motto ("Do or be silent"), which he had already varied in dedicating *The Sacred Wood* to his father ("He was silent and acted"). Now, "Be still and still moving" signals passage from the dead past to the living future at this Quartet's end, from the word that "has sounded its parts in order that another may succeed it," as Augustine had said.

"The Dry Salvages," which follows, is the American Quartet, Eliot's path into it now the ocean path of explorers and the river way of inland settlers, who included his grandfather. This third landscape offers images of St. Louis on the Mississippi, where Eliot was born, and also scenes of the fishing area by the rocky coast of Gloucester, Massachusetts—a home for the Eliots in summer, but all year round the precarious home of the fishing industry that migrated from England and Portugal to Gloucester on Cape Ann. There the harbor is marked by three deadly rocks—"presumably *les trois sauvages,*" Eliot notes. The etymology wryly suggests American optimism, the transforming of savage drowners into dry salvagers. It also suggests the two faces of hope and despair that are the third quartet's main themes.

Again, from poetic evocations of "the way" as visible waterways, the poem moves to reflection on courses of action—the sea's way of tossing up the forgotten past ("earlier and other creation"); the river's way of preserving those things we try to forget in time (its "cargo of dead Negroes," its "bitter apple and the bite in the apple"). The way from the Old World to the New, like each person's hope for a new day, has long been the way of people "encouraged by superficial notions of evolution." Though evolution is only "a partial fallacy," it "becomes, in the popular mind, a means of disowning the past." The New World came to be seen as man's "last, best hope" in the words of Lincoln's Annual Address to Congress of December 1862. There is a hint of Lincoln's words as Eliot recalls "the emotionless/ Years of living among the breakage / Of what was believed in as the most reliable ..." (In *To Criticize the Critic,* p. 147, he refers to Lincoln as a great writer.) In the previous Quartet Eliot had echoed another eminent President's words, Roosevelt's Inaugural Address of 1933—"We have nothing to fear but fear itself"—in "East Coker's" "Do not let me hear/ Of the wisdom of old men, but rather of their folly, / Their fear of fear ..."[40] The American dream, to which the Eliot family contributed much, is celebrated by the homage of "The Dry Salvages" to heroic voyagers of the spirit as well as of the sea. The negative way thus follows the way of eminence when the sestina of the second movement calls the "most reliable" dream "the fittest for renunciation" *because* it was the most depended on. Aquinas's way of eminence has often been translated as "the way of transcendence" because it leads from things (and people) that are "eminent" on to better, to best, and finally points to a pre-eminence that is transcendent, one for which all eminence is renounced as merely contingent. The easy renunciations are for beginners, Dionysius had said. One progresses to renunciation of things that deceive by appearing to be divine manifestations.

We should not, however, connect this passage with Eliot's renunciation of American citizenship; for this Quartet establishes that Eliot was—as far as he could be—"a citizen of two worlds," as Henry James wrote for his own epitaph. "The Dry Salvages" reverses the view in "Ash-Wednesday" that beguiling memories of his forsaken homeland were among those things which he had to give up in the austerities of another chosen way. By the late 1950s he could say of his poetry, "in its sources, in its emotional springs, it comes from America," and that "my poetry is American ... purely American."[41]

The "breakage" drifting with the river of evolving time now serves as a reminder that nations, like men, "ought to be explorers," voyaging toward an end where there is no breakage. The lovely recollections of American scenery, so rightly praised by Elisabeth Schneider (correcting the tendency of many critics to downgrade the poetry of this Quartet), verify "the sudden illumination" that must have come to Eliot on his return to America in 1933, beautifully elucidated here. In rediscovering America, the poem also intensifies our perception of how the poet's "way" in the third sense, the way of spiritual discovery, operates in each Quartet. I suggested earlier that *Four Quartets* reveals how different the poet's way is from the contemplative's (for instance Becket's or Celia Coplestone's). One important difference, if Eliot is to be trusted, is that the poet's way of spiritual discovery begins with a "sudden illumination," proceeding from there to the discipline of purgation, and finally to the final stage of union with the object of search.[42] St. John of the Cross, following earlier mystics, accepted Plotinus's discipline for the contemplative as one that *begins* with purgation, the fruit of which is illumination, finally leading to union. (St. John describes this triad as three parts of the night, downward to the darkest, upward toward the dawn, in the *Ascent,* I, ii, 5.) Whether intentionally or not, the negative way charted in each Quartet suggests that the poet's *askesis* reverses the order of purgation and illumination, relying first on

> the unattended
> Moment, the moment in and out of time,
> The distraction fit, lost in a shaft of sunlight,
> The wild thyme unseen, or the winter lightning
> Or the waterfall, or music heard so deeply
> That it is not heard at all, but you are the music
> While the music lasts. These are only hints and guesses,
> Hints followed by guesses; and *the rest*
> Is prayer, observance, discipline, thought and action.

> ("The Dry Salvages," V, emphasis added)

Persistently Eliot differentiated between religion and literature as two separate disciplines which had become absurdly confused. In 1933 he cited and commented on a statement of Jacques Maritain's:

> "By showing us where moral truth and the genuine supernatural are situated, religion saves poetry from the absurdity of believing itself destined to transform ethics and life: saves it from overweening arrogance." This seems to me to be putting the finger on the great weakness of much poetry and criticism of the nineteenth and twentieth centuries.[43]

The "way" retraced in "The Dry Salvages" is therefore plainly not offered as an alternative to spiritual discipline, even for poets, but rather as an account of the way Eliot himself had discovered or followed.

The sequence (way) of illuminations or moments recalled in the first three Quartets (the vision of what-might-have-been in Burnt Norton's garden, the vision of what-was in East Coker's empty field, and the vision by the seacoast of what-continues-evolving) is then a sort of rule that Eliot recognized in his own life. Each illumination bears witness to a partial share of the love experienced by the saints, the measure of which is known by the experience of "happiness": "The moments of happiness ... the sudden illumination" leads to a meaning which "restores" the experience of happiness "beyond any meaning / We can assign" to it ("Dry Salvages," II). Proceeding by *aphairesis* (rejection) to define the happiness of "death in love"—

known by "most of us" only in moments—we understand this happiness in terms of what it is not. It is "not the sense of well-being, / Fruition, fulfillment, security or affection, / Or even a very good dinner"—nothing either general or particular. Aquinas, following Aristotle, considered happiness the aim of all intelligent beings and therefore of the greatest works of art. While agreeing with Dionysius that God's essence can never be "known," Aquinas said that if "the created intellect could never see God [however imperfectly on earth], it would either never attain to happiness or its happiness would consist in something else"—something, as Eliot says, like "fruition, fulfillment, security or affection, / Or even a very good dinner." Since man *can* attain to happiness (Eliot agrees) and since happiness does not consist in anything else, the essence of God is revealed to human beings in experiences of perfect happiness and love. Love for a loved one may lead the lover to perfect fulfillment even if the lover is imperfect and the loved one is only dimly known.[44] Such perfect happiness Eliot had described as a reality in 1929, when he referred to Dante's line from the *Paradiso*, III, 85—"*la sua voluntade è nostra pace*"— as "*literally true.*"[45] In "Marina" (1930) and in *Four Quartets* (1936-43) he expressed the actuality as reflected in his own experience.

The purgation that follows rather than precedes illumination in *Four Quartets* is envisioned in Part III of every Quartet. In "The Dry Salvages" it is seen in the famous negative way of the *Bhagavad Gītā*, Chapter VIII, the words of Krishna to Arjuna during battle, which Eliot renders:

> " 'on whatever sphere of being
> The mind of a man may be intent
> At the time of death'—that is the one action
> (And the time of death is every moment)
> Which shall fructify in the lives of others:
> Fare forward.
>   O voyagers, O seamen,
> You who come to port, and you whose bodies
> Will suffer the trial and judgement of the sea,
> Or whatever event, this is your real destination."

Drawing again from "the forest sages" (as he had in the first two Quartets), Eliot treats purgation both as *askesis* (the discipline of purification), ridding the mind of all that is not ultimate, and as intuition of "the darkness of God" ("East Coker," III). Philip Wheelwright's thorough analysis of this passage calls attention to Krishna's words in the *Gītā:* "In that which is night to all things, therein the self-subjugated remains awake; but where all else is awake, that is night for the knower of the self."[46] Eliot adds a new emphasis to Krishna's advice when he writes that living every moment as if it were the hour of our death "is the one action" that will "fructify in the lives of others," thus marking the social or ethical effects of the negative way, concerns that Graham Hough and others have found lacking in the *Quartets.* Giving insufficient emphasis to this passage and its reverberations in the last Quartet, we may also think there is a contradiction where there is none—between "all is always now" in "Burnt Norton," V and "here and now cease to matter" in "East Coker," V. As Augustine treated at length in the *Confessions,* XI, the present is the only actuality, since the past is gone and the future not yet come. *How* one lives the existent moment—whether as the only reality or as an intersection with a further reality—is the question in the American Quartet. Lines reminiscent of Whitman's "Song of the Open Road" and "Passage to India" add a note of modern urgency to the echoes of Krishna's song. But Eliot rounds off the passage with a phrase he recalled as the sibyl's admonition to the Visigoth Alaric on his way to Rome: "Not fare well, but fare forward."[47]

> Fare forward, travellers! not escaping from the past
> Into different lives, or into any future;
>
> .   .   .   .   .
>
> Here between the hither and the farther shore
> While time is withdrawn, consider the future
> And the past with an equal mind.
>
> .   .   .   .   .
>
>   Not fare well,
> But fare forward, voyagers.

The fourth movement of "The Dry Salvages" follows easily with a lyric prayer to Our Lady of Good Voyage, whose shrine does indeed look out to sea in the Gloucester, Massachusetts, church of that name.

As A. D. Moody has pointed out, however, Eliot did not remember having seen the church and he later told William Turner Levy that he had in mind the sailors' church of Notre Dame de la Gard in Marseilles when he wrote the lyric. Recalling both the "Ave Maria" of the Angelus and the prayer of St. Bernard in Dante's *Paradiso,* XXXIII ("Figlia del tuo figlio"), the lyric combines reflections on the constant imminence of death to remind us of the *Bhagavad-Gītā*'s words ("the time of death is every moment"), thus again focusing attention on both the perils and the ultimate aim of all voyaging.

We may be struck here with the conspicuous absence of allusion to the American tradition of religious poetry, and Northrop Frye has noted another absence in the last movement of "The Dry Salvages" of a reflection on language that would parallel the concerns in the fifth movement of the other three Quartets. We might expect the American Quartet to deal with the American language at this point, but we have found instead a return to ancient poetry followed in the fifth movement by a warning against perversions of language. No doubt Eliot recalled the reverence paid to the *Bhagavad-Gītā* by Emerson, Whitman, and America's other nineteenth-century poets. He also knew, however, that many of these writers had declared the emancipation of America's literature from a dead past, from "the sepulchres of the fathers," as Emerson said in *Nature,* or, as Whitman said in his Preface to *Leaves of Grass,* from "the corpse" of the past which must give way to "the stalwart and well-shaped [American] heir who approaches." Such prophetic claims to independence in literature led to H. L. Mencken's hailing of a separate American language in 1919, and in 1924 Eliot had protested against both claims.[48] A decade after *Four Quartets* was written he came to acknowledge both his own identity as an American poet (as we have seen) and also the existence of a separate literature in America.[49] But in 1941 his oblique treatment of language in the American Quartet owed something to his refusal to yield to Mencken or the chauvinisms of Emerson and Whitman before him.

If "The Dry Salvages" is the only Quartet that gives us no direct treatment of language, it would appear that Eliot is again making his point through the way of negation: to reaffirm its connection with the past, America must renounce false claims to a unique linguistic tradition. The fifth movement here deals not with *saying* but with *soothsay-*

ing—such things as communicating with Martians or conversing with spirits. "Superficial notions of evolution" in history lead in language to false "omens," to "Pastimes and drugs, and features of the press," as the movement says. The only true foreshadowing of the future is "an occupation for the saint." And "The Dry Salvages" here links prophecy with the one instance of it where "the past and future / Are reconciled" and foretold—that is, in the Incarnation. Human words are linked with the Divine Word but not when inspired by self-appointed prophets. The Quartet's evocations of Whitman's "April dooryard" and Twain's Mississippi, along with other reminders of the great American past, finally do end in discovery, but also in warning and rededication. To be undefeated, Eliot says, is to go on trying, but "Not too far from the yew-tree" of abiding memory.

What remains to be presented in the last Quartet is the poet's way in the actual present, intersecting with time and the river into which (Heraclitus said) one never steps twice in the same place. "Little Gidding" carries out Krishna's advice to concentrate on the present moment of action. Again the way of the poem begins as a visible road into a landscape—toward the English prayer community at Little Gidding. The concreteness of images describing the season (the shortest day of the year) and the glare of sunlight burning on ice ("no wind but pentecostal fire / In the dark time of the year") gives us objects exactly correlative to the spiritual condition St. John of the Cross urges for those seeking union with God. The paradoxes of light in darkness, heat in ice, and flowers blooming out of "the forgetful snow" (as *The Waste Land*'s despairing first movement called the barren scene) are contradictory images that Rimbaud (for instance in "Barbare") had found exhilarating for entry into the creative *Néant*. Eliot's debt to the Symbolists is paid again two movements later, when on a sort of *via eminentiae* he meets Mallarmé in the composite ghost of his dead masters. The negative way persists as the main road, however, and after the other Quartets one knows how various are the turns and intentions of this road as a course of movement:

> If you came this way,
> Taking the route you would be likely to take
> From the place you would be likely to come from,
>
> . . . . .

It would be the same at the end of the journey,
If you came at night like a broken king,
If you came by day not knowing what you came for,

·   ·   ·   ·   ·

And what you thought you came for
Is only a shell, a husk of meaning
From which the purpose breaks only when it is fulfilled
If at all. Either you had no purpose
Or the purpose is beyond the end you figured
And is altered in fulfilment.

Dionysius and John of the Cross had used the same image for their discipline on the via negativa—a stripping away of husks until there is nothing visible or perceptible left. The onion, which in a way is all husk with nothingness at the center, served the Buddha for the same purpose. Only when there is nothing left is enlightenment possible. As before, in "Little Gidding" the sudden illumination precedes this counsel "to put off sense and notion" in the stage of purgation. The "spring time . . . not in time's covenant,"[50] the icy "bloom more sudden / Than that of summer" is the hint "followed by guesses" after which "the rest / Is prayer, observance, discipline, thought and action" ("Dry Salvages," V). This poet's way is unvarying in its phases.

It is also unvarying in incorporating Aquinas's other two "ways" in the negative way. The affirmative way of seeing divine effects in nature is, of course, always present for the poet, all the more affirmative now that Eliot has abandoned the lacerating sarcasms of images turned to show the unreality of things in his early poems. "Little Gidding" is rightly praised as a triumph of poetry dealing in luminously concrete actualities from beginning to end. Aquinas's third "way"—the way of eminence—accords perfectly with this as with other intentions. "Here, the intersection of the timeless moment / Is England and nowhere." Even more than in previous Quartets, each movement of "Little Gidding" draws upon eminent men and women whose lives have contributed to revelations of "the pattern," the "dance" which is only fully revealed "at the still point of the turning world." Aquinas, indeed, meant more than great men and women by "eminence." He meant the human faculty for distinguishing superior from inferior in all things, this faculty being a judgment of the mind rather than an order sensorily perceptible in things (as with the affirmative mode). Eliot has steadily kept the eminent way in sight by his interweaving of voices, places, and things from the past. The voices of saints, presidents, kings, and poets, all point to his meaning when he promises now that these voices will speak during prayer in the eminent *ruined and restored* chapel of "Little Gidding":

> what the dead had no speech for, when living,
> They can tell you, being dead: the communication
> Of the dead is tongued with fire beyond the language of the
>   living.
>
> . . . . .
>
>   they vanish,
> The faces and places, with the self which, as it could, loved
>   them,
> To become renewed, transfigured, in another pattern.
>
> . . . . .
>
> We are born with the dead:
> See, they return, and bring us with them.
>
> . . . . .
>
>   A people without history
> Is not redeemed from time, for history is a pattern
> Of timeless moments. So, while the light fails
> On a winter's afternoon, in a secluded chapel
> History is now and England.

The purgative part of "the night" in John of the Cross dominates every Quartet and this last one most of all. Eliot's negative way in *Four Quartets* is a sombre meditation on the ineluctible way of the world into the worst war of the many wars—European, American, and Indian—alluded to in the poem. Hence the second movement, which in the other Quartets was either a "way down" to London and into the underground from the country or a return to shore from seaway and riverway, here in the last is a return to London in a crisis which was earlier unimaginable, the first bombings of 1940. Only the underground infernos of Dante or Bosch could provide analogies. In reviving memory of Dante's Inferno, Eliot reasserts the realism (even naturalism) he insisted upon for his production of *The Cocktail Party*. ("An *imposed* symbolism . . . would be painful. What I want is something superficially at least purely realistic ... [as in] a perfectly naturalistic play."[51] The war of elements, imaged in Heraclitus's Fragments 25 and 62, inspires the lyric introducing Eliot's midnight walk "between three districts," which I read as the crossing of the three dreams in "Ash-Wednesday" discussed above. The three districts may be, as some have said, Hell, Purgatory, and Heaven; but surely in this second movement they are also the poet's three worlds of illusion, actuality, and "the higher dream"—possibly related also (in this order) to the ways of eminence, affirmation, and negativity. Thus as Eliot nears the end of his great culminating poem, he gathers together the scattered leaves of his poems written from 1927 on, as well as the four elements that structure *Four Quartets* (as John Hayward noted) from its first vision of "heart of light" (air or spirit) in "Burnt Norton," of "dung and death" (earth and the Word made flesh) in "East Coker," of the Lady of voyagers (water and the baptism of desire) in "The Dry Salvages," to the vision of divine fire as purgation and love in "Little Gidding." As the last two Quartets center on evolving time and the present, their images of

> Water and fire deride
> The sacrifice that we denied.
> Water and fire shall rot
> The marred foundations we forgot,
> Of sanctuary and choir.
>   This is the death of water and fire.   ("Little Gidding," II)

The verbal way of the poet, meditated in the second movement, becomes now the poet's *aphairesis,* or farewell to his craft: "For last year's words belong to last year's language / And next year's words await another voice." John of the Cross had promised that such ultimate discardings of all attachment bring one to a part of the night just before dawn and union. This critical point in Eliot's lifework can hardly be overestimated. He had foreshadowed the as yet undeciphered stone of his own burial at East Coker ("In my end is my beginning"), and now he faced the problem of finishing "the pattern in the carpet," which he had said was discernible from the "unity in a lifetime's work [that] is one of the measures of major poetry and drama."[52] The last three movements of "Little Gidding" undertake the heroic task of disclosing not only the pattern of his own poetry and life but also the pattern of all human life in its widest context.

No new departure was needed, nor would it be tolerable since "the whole man" and "the whole pattern" are usually laid down long before the end. The first Quartet, written some years before the last three were planned, anticipates the last Quartet when we follow the visible path to the garden's empty pool, "And the pool was filled with water out of sunlight, / And the lotos rose, quietly, quietly, / . . . out of heart of light" ("Burnt Norton," I). This juxtaposition of "lotos" and "rose" forms a double entendre, merging the lotos of Indian iconography with the white rose of Dante's beatific vision, if one reads the sentence to say "the pool was filled with water out of sunlight, and [also with] the lotos rose." If the reading seems strained, its paired nouns at least have later echoes in "The Dry Salvages," I, "The salt is on the briar rose," which in turn picks up a phrase from "East Coker," IV, "the flame is roses and the smoke is briars." A merging of Indian and European figures, again centering on the rose, is also suggested in "The Dry Salvages," III: "I sometimes wonder if that is what Krishna meant . . . / That the future is a faded song, a Royal Rose." The Royal Rose is a European device for the seventh son of a king, thus symbolizing in this passage the "wistful regret for those who are not yet here to regret"—those who are a dim hope and hedge against a dim future. (Eliot was himself a seventh child and a son, from whom much was expected.) At any rate, the persistent confluence of Indian and European motifs marks their common feeding into a single stream, the negative way most clearly indicated by the flower imagery in "Little Gidding," III: three flowers

> flourish in the same hedgerow:
> Attachment to self and to things and to persons, detachment
> From self and from things and from persons; and, growing
> between them, indifference
> Which resembles the others as death resembles life.

The point of this movement and the two following ones is that the flower of attachment and the flower of detachment (like rose and lotos) grow together and work in the poet's memory "for liberation—not less of love but expanding / Of love beyond desire." The love which is attachment can lead tragically to the necessity of sacrifice or worse, the "incandescent terror" or purging warfare, when individuals and nations fail in history, in time, to find the love (the rose) that expands beyond desire, in enlightened detachment (symbolized by the lotos). Eliot's lotos is of course the Buddha's, not Tennyson's lotos of indifference and forgetfulness.

I suggested that Eliot's last poem alters the vision of early Buddhism without nullifying it. *The Waste Land* fully expressed, without modification, the forest sages' rejection of the visible world as unreal. While reaffirming their dedication to compassion and self-control, it also expressed their denial that any knowledge of ultimate reality could ever be grasped. After finishing *The Waste Land,* but without leaving the *via negativa,* Eliot moved toward the apophatic theology of St. Augustine and Dionysius. They affirmed the revealed Word but denied the validity of any absolute knowledge of its form. Augustine said, and Dionysius repeated it, that God "is better known by knowing what He is not."[53]

The Christian saints commemorated in the *via eminentiae* of *Four Quartets* all modified Dionysius's negative way by associating the still point with Christ's promises that union in the kingdom of God is actual even while one is on earth. This assertion of life's earthly reality and the possibility of union with God "now and always" is the vision Eliot brings to the last part of his poem, a non-Buddhist conclusion. He had not, however, forgotten the image of the Buddha, whose early scriptures had assisted him in recreating his own Christian tradition. That image surfaces aptly in the second-to-last line of "Little Gidding":

> When the tongues of flame are in-folded
> Into the crowned knot of fire
> And the fire and the rose are one.

"The crowned knot of fire" must surely be that which appears on the head of the Buddha in Theravāda sculpture, as well as on the heads of the Apostles in the Upper Room of Christian iconography. "The tongues of flame"—here both holocaustal and pentecostal—are "infolded," concentrating modern with ancient, Western with Oriental associations. The Buddha's fire sermon ("Burning burning . . .") is distantly heard and also the bombers' "flame of incandescent terror"—all appealing for a negative way, for extrication from the futile rotation (the ancient wheel) of hatred and false desire. From this *penultimate* vision (ultimate in *The Waste Land*), the poem moves to its final intuition, foreseen in its second epigraph: "The way upwards and downwards are the same." Heraclitus had said it; Augustine and Aquinas had repeated it; Dante had expressed it in a love poem; and St. John of the Cross had shown the way through dark nights of sense and soul to Dante's multifoliate rose. When Eliot's last line confirms that the Heraclitean fire is one with the fire of all human yearning for God, it also confirms that all yearning and the "rose" of the *Paradiso* are one in divine love. "The fire and the rose are one."

Eliot did not write this poem or any other to teach belief or theology. Whatever force it might carry he called an "esthetic sanction: that is the partial justification of [the poet's view of life] by the art to which [his views] give rise." "What poetry proves about any philosophy is merely its possibility for being lived." "Poetry . . . is not the assertion that something is true, but the making that truth more fully real to us."[54] Eliot's genius as a master of negativity, like Sartre's and Beckett's, declared itself in his power to find in the ways of negation a creative void indispensable both to art and to life.

NOTES

INDEX

Notes

Passages from T. S. Eliot's poems and plays are cited from the two-volume *Complete Plays* and *Collected Poems* published by Harcourt, Brace, Jovanovich (New York, 1969 and 1970).

Introduction

1. Terence Martin, *Scottish Common Sense Philosophy and the Origins of American Fiction* (Bloomington: Indiana University Press, 1961), pp. 50–51.

2. Martin Heidegger, *Nietzsche,* 2 vols. (Pfullingen: Neske, 1961), I, 73. I have been guided by J. L. Mehta's incisive commentary, *Martin Heidegger: The Way and the Vision* (Honolulu: University Press of Hawaii, 1976) in translating from the German. See Mehta, pp. 185 and 346, n. 9.

3. Heidegger, "What Is Metaphysics?," trans. R. F. C. Hull and Alan Crick, in Werner Brock, *Existence and Being* (Chicago: Regnery, 1949), p. 355.

4. Ibid., p. 354.

5. Heidegger, *Unterwegs zur Sprache* (Pfullingen: Neske, 1959), p. 98.

6. Heidegger, *Wegmarken* (Frankfurt: Klostermann, 1967), p. 319.

7. Heidegger, "The Onto-theo-logical Structure of Metaphysics," *Identity and Difference,* trans. Joan Stambaugh (New York: Harper & Row, 1969), p. 121.

8. Heidegger, "What Are Poets For?," *Poetry, Language, Thought,* trans. Albert Hofstadter (New York: Harper & Row, 1971), p. 138.

9. *Wegmarken,* p. 328.

10. *Poetry, Language, Thought,* pp. 105, 190. Translating the second passage, I follow Mehta, p. 47.

11. Douglas Bush, "T. S. Eliot," *Engaged and Disengaged* (Cambridge: Harvard University Press, 1966), p. 98.

12. Lyndall Gordon, *Eliot's Early Years* (New York: Oxford University Press, 1977), p. 95. See also pp. 23, 32, 35, and 69, where I should say Gordon reads the early poems as unduly positive in their religious significance.

13. I am indebted to John Margolis for setting Eliot's relation to the Action Française in the context of his intellectual development in *T. S. Eliot's Intellectual Development, 1922–1939* (Chicago: University of Chicago Press, 1972), pp. 87–99. As late as 1928, in *Criterion,* 7, Eliot supported Maurras even while acknowledging that he had ended with a different view. In this issue of *Criterion,* he described Maurras's attitude as "that of an unbeliever who cannot believe, and who is too honest to pretend to himself or to others that he does believe; if the others can believe, so much the better not only for them but for the world at large." In "Hommage à Charles Maurras" (1948), Eliot called Maurras "a kind of Virgil who led [some of us] to the doors of the temple." By 1930, however (as Margolis shows), Eliot distinguished more radically between his own view and Maurras's, saying that the latter held "grosser positive errors and far greater dangers" than, for instance, the fairly anti-Christian Irving Babbitt. (Letter to *The Bookman,* 31 March 1930—unpublished, as Margolis says, because *The Bookman* published no letters.) The next year, Eliot wrote against using Christian faith as a political credential—as Hitler and Mussolini both did. Thus in "Thoughts After Lambeth," he wrote, "One of the most deadening influences upon the Church in the past, ever since the eighteenth century, was its acceptance by the upper, upper middle, and aspiring classes, as a political necessity . . ." In the *Christian News-Letter* of 28 August 1940 he went still further: "My particular defense of the *Action Française* may or may not stand; but I believe now that the Pope understood its tendencies better."

14. T. S. Eliot, *After Strange Gods* (New York: Harcourt, Brace, 1934), p. 30.

15. Eliot, *The Use of Poetry and the Use of Criticism* (London: Faber & Faber, 1933), p. 144; Eliot, *The Sacred Wood* (London: Methuen, 1920), p. 169.

16. See *The Waste Land: A Facsimile and Transcript of the Original Drafts,* ed. Valerie Eliot (New York: Harcourt, Brace, 1971), p. 17.

17. *The Use of Poetry and the Use of Criticism,* pp. 150–51.

18. Charles Dickens, *Martin Chuzzlewit* (Saint Louis and Boston: Thompson, n.d.), p. 179 (ch. XI).

1. The Way of J. Alfred Prufrock

1. Allen Tate, "Eliot, T. S.," *New Encyclopaedia Britannica: Macropaedia,* 1974 ed., p. 725. "Masters of suspicion" is Paul Ricoeur's phrase for Nietzsche, Marx, and Freud in *Freud and Philosophy: An Essay on Interpretation,* trans. Denis Savage (New Haven: Yale University Press, 1970), p. 35. Noting how Nietzsche, Marx, and Freud applied Spinoza's concept of

"false consciousness," Ricoeur says that the "three begin with suspicion concerning the illusions of consciousness, and then proceed to the stratagem of deciphering; all three, however, far from being detractors of 'consciousness,' aim at extending it" (p. 34). Ricoeur treats Freud's essay "Negation" on pp. 313-317.

2. "Dante," *The Sacred Wood*, pp. 168-169.

3. "What Dante Means to Me," *To Criticize the Critic* (London: Faber & Faber, 1965), p. 126.

4. Stéphane Mallarmé, *Propos sur la poésie*, ed. Henri Mondor (Monaco: Editions du Rocher, 1953), p. 77. "Je suis depuis un mois dans les plus purs glaciers de l'esthétique—qu'après avoir trouvé le Néant j'ai trouvé le Beau."

5. Quoted by Martin Esslin, *The Theatre of the Absurd* (Garden City: Anchor Books, 1961), pp. 39-40.

6. Quoted by E. Martin Browne, *The Making of T. S. Eliot's Plays* (New York: Cambridge University Press, 1969), p. 233. Stanley Cavell has a similar reading of *Endgame* in *Must We Mean What We Say?* (New York: Scribners, 1969), pp. 161-162.

7. Jean-Jacques Rousseau, *La Nouvelle Héloïse*, 2 vols. (Paris: Pléiade Edition), II, 693. De Man's translation is from Rousseau's "le pays de chimères est en ce monde le seul digne d'être habité, et tel est le néant des choses humaines qu'hors l'Etre existant par lui-même, il n'y a rien de beau que ce qui n'est pas."

8. In the poem "Cousin Nancy," written about this time, Emerson appears as one of New England's "guardians of the faith," keeping watch upon "the glazen shelves"—that is, behind glass. *Sic transit* the transparent eyeball.

9. Dante, *Purgatorio*, XXI, translation mine. The original reads:

> Or puoi la quantitate
> comprender dell'amor ch'a te mi scalda,
> quando dismento nostra vanitate,
> trattando l'ombre come cosa salda.

10. Dante, *Inferno*, XXVII, translation mine. The original reads:

> S'io credesse che mia risposta fosse
> a persona che mai tornasse al mondo,
> questa fiamma staria sensa più scosse.
> Ma per ciò che giammai de questo fondo
> non torno vivo alcun, s'i'odo il vero,
> senza tema d'infamia ti rispondo.

11. I use the word "marker" throughout with the force given to it in linguistic theory, as a key word whose repetition gradually reveals significance beyond the local uses of it in a writer's work. For the theory of markers, see Umberto Eco, *A Theory of Semiotics* (Bloomington: Indiana Univer-

sity Press, 1979), and Michael Riffaterre, *Semiotics of Poetry* (Bloomington: Indiana University Press, 1978).

12. Virginia Woolf's diary for November, 1918, in fact records Eliot's comment that these lines "were a recollection of Dante's *Purgatorio.*"

13. Mario Praz, "T. S. Eliot and Dante," in *The Flaming Heart* (Gloucester, Mass.: Peter Smith, 1966), p. 366n.

2. "I Pray You Remember My Anguish": *Poems* of 1920

1. *After Strange Gods,* p. 46.

2. Elisabeth Schneider, *T. S. Eliot: The Pattern in the Carpet* (Berkeley and Los Angeles: University of California Press, 1975), p. 36.

3. Dante, *Purgatorio,* XXVI, translation mine. The original reads:
Ara vos prec per aquella valor
que vos guida al som de l'escalina,
sovegna vos a temps de ma dolor.

4. Ricoeur, *Freud and Philosophy,* pp. 314-317.

5. *The Waste Land: A Facsimile,* p. 1.

6. "The Three Voices of Poetry," *On Poetry and Poets* (New York: Farrar, Straus and Giroux, 1979), p. 107.

7. Cited in Margolis, *T. S. Eliot's Intellectual Development,* p. 142.

8. Eliot here seems to be following Mallarmé and Valéry in using this device as described by Derrida in his essay "Qual quelle," in *Marges de la Philosophie* (Paris: Minuit, 1972). Summing it up in a recent article, Michael Riffaterre says: "syllepsis consists in the understanding of the same word in two different ways at once, as *contextual meaning* and as *intertextual meaning.* The contextual meaning is that demanded by the word's grammatical collocations, by the word's reference to other words in the text. The intertextual meaning is another meaning the word may possibly have, one of its dictionary meanings and/or one actualized within an intertext. In either case, this intertextual meaning is incompatible with the context and pointless within the text, but it still operates as a second reference—this one to the intertext." "Syllepsis," *Critical Inquiry,* 6, no. 4 (Summer, 1980): 637-638. As Riffaterre shows, Derrida comments on an image—*point d'eau*—found in Valéry, which functions as a self-contradiction, an implied antanaclasis—much the way Eliot's word "springs" does. Valéry's word means both "no water" and "wellspring," as Eliot's means both "murderously attacks" and "gives new life." Derrida and Riffaterre stress that such usage is less a pun than it is a word that, in its context, tends to "veer about" (Riffaterre) to its opposite, creating an undecidability which enriches the meaning.

9. *The Waste Land: A Facsimile,* p. xviii.

10. Paul Elmer More discussed this aspect of Eliot's work in "The Cleft Eliot," *The Saturday Review of Literature,* 12 Nov. 1932. The first epigraph to "The Hippopotamus" was dropped in 1969 for the Faber edition of *The Complete Poems and Plays.*

11. Ibid.

12. *The Sacred Wood,* pp. 247, 249.

3. *The Waste Land*'s Roadway to Nowhere

1. Hugh Kenner, "The Urban Apocalypse," *Eliot in His Time,* ed. A. Walton Litz (Princeton: Princeton University Press, 1974), pp. 42–43. The persistence of the tendency to read *The Waste Land* as a "quest for regeneration," based on the Grail motif, is exemplified in the generally expert commentaries of the new *Norton Anthology of American Literature* (New York: 1979), II, 1215, 1242n.

2. Eleanor Cook, "T. S. Eliot and the Carthaginian Peace," *English Literary History,* 46, no. 2 (Summer 1979): 346 ff.

3. *The Waste Land: A Facsimile,* pp. 31 and 127–128. See also St. Augustine, *The City of God,* I, 35.

4. "*The Waste Land:* Critique of the Myth," in *A Collection of Critical Essays on "The Waste Land,"* ed. Jay Martin (Englewood Cliffs: Prentice-Hall, 1968), p. 60. Brooks's essay first appeared in his *Modern Poetry and the Tradition* (1939).

5. *Selected Essays* (New York: Harcourt, Brace & World, 1964), p. 324.

6. Conrad Aiken, "An Anatomy of Melancholy" (1923), in Martin, *Critical Essays on "The Waste Land."*

7. See Eliot's "Baudelaire" (*Selected Essays,* p. 379): "Indeed, in much romantic poetry the sadness is due to the exploitation of the fact that no human relations are adequate to human desires, but also to the disbelief in any further object for human desires than that which, being human, fails to satisfy them." This was written in 1931, when Eliot could speak about a "further object for human desires," as he could not in *The Waste Land.* It seems worth noting that Eliot's antiromanticism had two phases (at least): one in which he derided a "mystical" yearning for satisfaction beyond those available to "human relations" (a "classical" attitude) and a later antiromanticism in which he criticized desires that sought satisfaction in merely human relations. As "Prufrock" and "Portrait of a Lady" represent the first phase, "The Dry Salvages" exemplifies the second (the "partial fallacy / Encouraged by superficial notions of evolution").

8. The translation is cited by Grover Smith from Rossetti's *Works* (London, 1911, p. 240). Eliot knew his Petronius in the original Latin, of course. In his third year as a Harvard undergraduate he had read the *Satyricon* (and the *Golden Ass*) in Clifford Herschel Moore's class.

9. "Thoughts After Lambeth," *Selected Essays,* p. 323.

10. Craig Raine, "Met Him Pikehoses: *The Waste Land* as a Buddhist Poem," *Times Literary Supplement,* 4 May 1973, pp. 503–505. See also *The Waste Land: A Facsimile,* p. 125.

11. See *The Waste Land: A Facsimile,* p. 126.

12. Joseph Conrad, "Youth," *Youth and Two Other Stories* (Garden City:

Doubleday, Page, 1903), p. 37. I discussed this intertextual point in *The Political Novels of Joseph Conrad* (Chicago: University of Chicago Press, 1963). p. 129n.

13. *The Waste Land: A Facsimile,* pp. 58–61.

14. "London Letter," *The Dial,* 71 (Oct. 1921), 453.

15. *The Waste Land: A Facsimile,* p. 126.

16. Ibid.

17. Homer, *The Odyssey,* trans. Robert Fitzgerald (Garden City: Doubleday, 1963), Book X, 491–495 (p. 180).

18. See Grover Smith, *T. S. Eliot's Poetry and Plays* (Chicago: University of Chicago Press, 1956), p. 95.

19. Irving Babbitt, *Rousseau and Romanticism* (Austin: University of Texas Press, 1977), p. 126. The first edition of this book was published three years before *The Waste Land.*

20. Irving Babbitt, *Masters of Modern French Criticism* (Boston: Houghton Mifflin, 1912), p. 370. In 1941 Eliot wrote a tribute to Babbitt, saying, "I cannot imagine anyone coming to react against Babbitt. Even in the convictions one may feel, the views one may hold, that seem to contradict most important convictions of Babbitt's own, one is aware that he himself was very largely the cause of them." *Irving Babbitt: Man and Teacher,* ed. Frederick Manchester and Odell Shepard (New York: Putnam's, 1941), pp. 103–104. For calling my attention to this and many other connections between Eliot's thought and Babbitt's, I am indebted to Carey Sassower's "T. S. Eliot: A Critical Disciple" (Bowdoin Prize Essay, Harvard, 1979).

21. In his Notes, Eliot directs us to Henry Clark Warren's *Buddhism in Translation.* The passage is quoted as given here by Herbert Howarth, *Some Figures behind T. S. Eliot* (Boston: Houghton Mifflin, 1964), p. 204.

22. *The Waste Land: A Facsimile,* p. 95.

23. Frederick J. Streng, *Emptiness: A Study in Religious Meaning* (Nashville and New York: Abingdon Press, 1967), pp. 161–162.

24. B. Rajan, "The Overwhelming Question," rpt. in *Critical Essays on "The Waste Land,"* ed. Martin, p. 49.

25. *The Waste Land: A Facsimile,* p. 149. Eliot did not delete the word "feeble" until after his conversion to Christianity in 1927. Donald Gallup tells me that if the change had been made at any point before 1932, it would have been made in the 1926 edition of *Poems: 1909–25* (London: Faber & Gwyer, 1926), but the invidious comparison is retained in that edition.

26. Irving Babbitt, "Interpreting India to the West," *Spanish Character and Other Essays* (Boston: Houghton Mifflin, 1940), pp. 159–160. This essay originally appeared in *The Nation* in 1917. Again I am indebted to Sassower's "T. S. Eliot: A Critical Disciple" for the reference.

27. Robert Ernest Hume, *The Thirteen Principal Upanishads* (London: Oxford University Press, 1931), p. 101.

4. Toward Ash-Wednesday

1. Quoted by Margolis, *T. S. Eliot's Intellectual Development, 1922–1939*, p. 62.

2. *Time*, 6 March, 1950, p. 23.

3. Irving Babbitt, *The Dhammapada* (New York: New Directions Paperbook, 1965), p. 78. Eliot refers admiringly to this posthumous work of Babbitt in his essay in *Revelation*, ed. John Baillie and Hugh Martin (London: Faber & Faber, 1937), pp. 15–16. Eliot's immense regard for Babbitt as a *religious thinker* survived his conclusion that neohumanism was a "decayed form of religiosity."

4. Quoted in Howarth, *Some Figures behind T. S. Eliot*, p. 95.

5. Stephen Spender, *T. S. Eliot* (New York: Viking, 1975), p. 20.

6. Gordon, *Eliot's Early Years*, pp. 34–35.

7. "The Relationship between Politics and Metaphysics," p. 2. Unpublished typescript, Houghton Library, Harvard University.

8. Gordon, *Eliot's Early Years, p. 58.*

9. *"Introduction"* to Josef Pieper's *Leisure, the Basis of Culture* (London: Faber & Faber, 1952), pp. 14–15.

10. "Preface" to Simone Weil's *The Need for Roots* (New York: Putnam's, 1952), p. ix.

11. "Introduction" to Paul Valéry's *Le Serpent* (London: Criterion, 1924), p. 13.

12. "Paul Valéry," *Quarterly Review of Literature*, 3, no. 3 (1947): 213.

13. As noted in my Introduction, Margolis has recorded Eliot's changing attitudes toward Maurras and the Action Française in *T. S. Eliot's Intellectual Development*, pp. 87–99. My references are especially to pp. 88n. 89, and 95.

14. Untitled, unpublished essay on "the validity of artificial distinction." Case I of Philosophy Notes, Houghton Library.

15. Untitled, unpublished essay on "genesis and kinesis"—changes of form versus changes of place in Aristotle's philosophy. Case II of Philosophy Notes, Houghton Library.

16. Gordon, *Eliot's Early Years*, p. 61.

17. Unpublished notes on Russell's lectures from 17 March to 30 April 1914, in Philosophy Notebook, Houghton Library. Russell's course (Philosophy $9c^2$) was on the theory of knowledge. He was assisted by Dr. Albert Richard Chandler, who is perhaps ône model for Professor Channing-Cheetah in "Mr. Apollinax."

18. "Dante," *Selected Essays*, p. 223.

19. Helen Gardner, *The Composition of Four Quartets* (New York: Oxford University Press, 1978), pp. 43 ff.

20. Victor Hugo, "Ce que dit la bouche d'ombre" (in *Les Contemplations*), *Oeuvres Poétiques*, 4 vols. (Paris: Pléiade, 1967), II, 803, 813, 816.

21. See Edmund Wilson, "The Rag-bag of the Soul," *New York Evening*

Post Literary Review, 25 Nov. 1922, pp. 237-238; Aiken, "An Anatomy of Melancholy"; and John Middleton Murry, "More about Romanticism," *Adelphi,* 1 (Dec. 1923): 557-569.

22. I. A. Richards, *Principles of Literary Criticism* (New York: Harcourt, Brace, 1948), p. 292.

23. Samuel Hynes, "The Trials of a Christian Critic," in *The Literary Criticism of T. S. Eliot,* ed. David Newton De Molina (London: Athlone, 1977), p. 68.

24. I. A. Richards, *Science and Poetry* (London: Kegan Paul, Trench, Trubner, 1926), pp. 82-83.

25. Ibid., pp. 64-65.

26. "A Note on Poetry and Belief," *The Enemy,* 1 (1927): 16.

27. "The Pensées of Pascal," *Selected Essays,* p. 360.

28. "Dante," *Selected Essays,* p. 231.

29. *The Use of Poetry and the Use of Criticism,* pp. 96-97.

30. Ibid., p. 124.

31. I. A. Richards, "The Poetry of T. S. Eliot," *Living Age,* 329 (1926), p. 114.

32. "T. S. Eliot" (title of Eliot's essay), *Revelation,* pp. 31-32.

33. In 1959 Eliot observed that "no diligent scholarly sleuth has yet observed" the connections between his verse and the work of Kipling. He added, "I could never have thought of ["The Hollow Men"] but for Kipling's poem 'The Broken Men.'" See "The Unfading Genius of Rudyard Kipling" (1959), *Kipling and the Critics,* ed. Elliot L. Gilbert (New York: New York University Press, 1965), p. 119.

34. Friedrich W. Strothmann and Lawrence V. Ryan also read the line about the hope for empty men as intended to distinguish them from "the hollow men," but their interpretation goes beyond the limits of the poem, I think, to interpret "the desert of the last section [as] the 'delectable desert' of purgation described by St. John of the Cross." As we shall see, Eliot was still very critical of St. John's "romantic" mysticism the year after writing "The Hollow Men" when he gave the Clark Lectures.

35. Schneider, *The Pattern in the Carpet,* p. 112.

36. *The Waste Land: A Facsimile,* p. 1. See also passage cited above, note 6.

37. "The Pensées of Pascal," *Selected Essays,* p. 364.

38. *The Times* (London), 12 Jan. 1965, p. 11.

39. Unpublished notebook on "Greek Philosophy, with Especial Reference to Plato" (Philosophy 12), given by James Haughton Woods in 1911-12. Case I of Philosophy Notes, Houghton Library, Harvard.

40. Schneider, *The Pattern in the Carpet,* p. 128.

41. "Dante," *Selected Essays,* p. 231.

42. Smith, *T. S. Eliot's Poetry and Plays,* p. 157.

43. "On the Metaphysical Poetry of the Seventeenth Century, with Special Reference to Donne, Crashaw, and Cowley," eight lectures delivered at

Trinity College, Cambridge, 1926. Carbon of typescript (original at King's College, Cambridge University), Houghton Library. These quotations are from Lecture II, pp. 14 and 15, Lecture V, p. 6, Lecture II, p. 19, and Lecture III, p. 21. I have included a slight correction from the King's College MS.

44. "A Dialogue on Dramatic Poetry" and "Baudelaire," *Selected Essays*, pp. 33, 373.

45. *After Strange Gods*, pp. 56–57.

46. "A Dialogue on Dramatic Poetry," *Selected Essays*, p. 33.

47. "English Letter Writers," an unpublished lecture given at Yale in 1933, quoted by F. O. Matthiessen in *The Achievement of T. S. Eliot* (New York & London: Oxford University Press, 1958), p. 90.

5. The Stage as Still Point: Plays, 1935–1958

1. "The Three Voices of Poetry," *On Poetry and Poets*, p. 96.

2. Ibid., pp. 98, 96.

3. *The Use of Poetry and the Use of Criticism*, pp. 152–153.

4. "Tradition and the Individual Talent," *Selected Essays*, pp. 6–7.

5. *Selected Essays*, p. 40.

6. "Tradition and the Individual Talent," *Selected Essays*, p. 7.

7. "What Dante Means to Me," *To Criticize the Critic*, p. 134.

8. Quoted in Matthiessen, *The Achievement of T. S. Eliot*, p. 90.

9. "Gordon Craig's Socratic Dialogues," *Drama*, n.s. 36 (Spring 1955), pp. 19–21, 18.

10. Interview with Harold Pinter by Mel Gussow, *New York Times Magazine*, 5 Dec. 1971, p. 132.

11. Katherine J. Worth, *Revolutions in Modern English Drama* (London: G. Bell & Sons, 1972), pp. 90–91.

12. Yeats, Bernard, and Maeterlinck are quoted by May Daniels in *The French Drama of the Unspoken* (Edinburgh: Folcroft Press, 1970), pp. 4, 172–210, 48.

13. "A Dialogue on Dramatic Poetry," and " 'Rhetoric' and Poetic Drama," *Selected Essays*, pp. 45, 29.

14. "Poetry and Drama," *On Poetry and Poets*, p. 93.

15. "The Three Voices of Poetry," *On Poetry and Poets*, p. 98.

16. "A Note on the *Coriolan* Poems," in *A Political Art: Essays and Images in Honour of George Woodcock*, ed. William H. New (Vancouver: University of British Columbia Press, 1978), p. 99.

17. *Murder in the Cathedral, The Complete Plays of T. S. Eliot* (New York: Harcourt, Brace & World, 1967), p. 11.

18. Browne, *The Making of T. S. Eliot's Plays*, p. 58.

19. John Keats, letter of December 21, 27 (?), 1817, in *The Norton Anthology of English Literature*, ed. M. H. Abrams et al., 2 vols. (New York: W. W. Norton, 1968), II, 571.

20. "The Centrality of the Sermon in T. S. Eliot's *Murder in the Cathedral*," *Christianity and Literature*, 27, no. 4 (1978): 7.

21. 1849 epigraph to *Nature*, *The American Tradition in Literature*, ed. Sculley Bradley, R. C. Beatty, and E. H. Long, 2 vols. (New York: W. W. Norton, 1962), I, 1002.

22. Tom F. Driver, *Romantic Quest and Modern Query: A History of the Modern Theatre* (New York: Delacorte, 1970), pp. 333, 334.

23. *The Family Reunion*, *The Complete Plays of T. S. Eliot*, pp. 100–101. Subsequent page references will be given in the text.

24. "Poetry and Drama," p. 90.

25. Nevill Coghill, Introduction to *The Family Reunion* (London: Faber & Faber, 1969), p. 33; Helen Gardner, *The Art of T. S. Eliot* (London: Faber & Faber, 1972), p. 153.

26. Raymond Williams, *Drama from Ibsen to Brecht* (London: Chatto & Windus, 1968), pp. 186–187.

27. Letter of 4 July 1955 to Hugh Beaumont, quoted by Coghill, Introduction to *The Family Reunion*, p. 55. Coghill also quotes (p. 51) Eliot's letter of thanks to Scofield for redeeming Harry from the character of "an insufferable prig" (as Eliot called him in "Poetry and Drama," 1951).

28. Foucauld, like Harry, was drawn to a desert "cleared, under the judicial sun / Of the final eye"—in Foucauld's case the Sahara, where he served the Tuareg tribes and was much loved by them.

29. "Gordon Craig's Socratic Dialogues," pp. 19–20.

30. Helen Gardner, "The Comedies of T. S. Eliot," *Essays by Divers Hands* (Oxford: Oxford University Press, 1965), 34:55–73.

31. Browne, *The Making of T. S. Eliot's Plays*, p. 174.

32. Robert B. Heilman, *"Alcestis* and *The Cocktail Party,"* *Comparative Literature*, 5, no. 2 (Spring 1953): 109n.

33. See Browne, *The Making of T. S. Eliot's Plays*, p. 233.

34. American readers who lack access to the letter Eliot wrote to Geoffrey Faber about Lavinia's pregnancy often miss the clues to this symbol of the ultimate union between Lavinia and Edward. The letter, quoted in Nevill Coghill's edition of *The Cocktail Party* (London: Faber & Faber, 1974), p. 192, says, "I thought it was obvious, from one line at the end of Act III [finally Act II] and one line in the opening dialogue of Act IV [finally Act III], that Lavinia was going to have a baby. At her age, I fear it will be an only child."

35. D. W. Harding, "Progression of Theme in Eliot's Modern Plays," *Kenyon Review*, 18, no. 3 (Summer, 1956): 337–360.

36. Note on back of envelope addressed to his house, 9 Clarence Gate Gardens, in Vivien Eliot's ledger for 1924. Bodleian Library (Oxford) collection of Vivien Eliot's papers and diaries.

37. Van Wyck Brooks, *The Confident Years* (New York: E. P. Dutton, 1952), pp. 603–604. Brooks's whole last chapter is a fevered attack against Eliot on religious, political, and economic grounds for breaking with American tradition.

38. Eliot, *The Idea of a Christian Society* (New York: Harcourt, Brace & World, 1940), p. 96.

39. Eliot here uses the same phrase he used in the Clark Lectures for the tendencies of Saints Teresa and John of the Cross, as well as John Donne, to confuse divine and earthly lovers—at least in their imagery—but by now their imagery has been validated by his own uses of the rose garden in *Four Quartets* and in *The Family Reunion*.

40. Unpublished letter to Michael Sadleir, dated 9 May 1930, folded with a typescript of "Marina" in the Bodleian Library. Quoted by permission of Valerie Eliot.

41. *The Idea of a Christian Society*, p. 13.

42. As remarked above, note 34, readers may miss the hints in the "Guardians'" gnomic toasts and Edward's attentions to Lavinia, but Eliot's letter to Geoffrey Faber makes Lavinia's pregnancy clear, and her altered figure should convey it on stage. In Act 2 Edward cries "O God" three times, but one recognizes his unconscious use of the words.

43. *The Idea of a Christian Society*, p. 97. Grover Smith points to this parallel with "the Guardians" in *T. S. Eliot's Poetry and Plays*, p. 220.

44. Letter to Geoffrey Faber, quoted by Coghill in his edition of *The Cocktail Party*, p. 192.

45. See for instance William Arrowsmith, "Notes on English Verse Drama, II: *The Cocktail Party*," *Hudson Review*, 3 (Autumn 1950): 411-430.

46. Sagittarius, "Nightingale Among the Sweeneys," *New Statesman and Nation*, 29 July 1950, p. 118.

47. Leonard Lyons, "The Lyons Den," *The Boston Herald*, 11 Jan. 1952, p. 32. I have slightly abbreviated the anecdote.

48. David E. Jones, *The Plays of T. S. Eliot* (Toronto: University of Toronto Press, 1960), p. 175.

49. Interview with John Beaufort, *Christian Science Monitor*, 20 Feb. 1954, p. 16, cited in Carol H. Smith, *T. S. Eliot's Dramatic Theory and Practice* (Princeton: Princeton University Press, 1963), p. 185n.

50. Review in the *Herald-Tribune*, cited by Browne, *The Making of T. S. Eliot's Plays*, pp. 293-294.

51. Gardner, "The Comedies of T. S. Eliot," pp. 67-69.

52. *The Idea of a Christian Society*, pp. 77-78, 80.

53. Ibid., p. 103: "I know that it is wrong for me to speculate," Eliot says here, "but where the line is to be drawn between speculation and what is called legitimate investment is by no means clear. I seem to be a petty usurer in a world manipulated largely by big usurers . . . And I believe that modern war is chiefly caused by some immorality of competition which is always with us in times of 'peace'; and that until this evil is cured, no leagues or disarmaments or collective security or conferences or conventions or treaties will suffice to prevent it."

54. "John Ford," *Selected Essays*, p. 179.

55. Brien Alan, "The Invisible Dramatist," *Spectator*, 5 Sept. 1958, pp. 305-306.

56. Hugh Kenner, *The Invisible Poet: T. S. Eliot* (New York: McDowell, Obolensky, 1959), p. 331.

57. Smith, *T. S. Eliot's Dramatic Theory and Practice,* p. 216.

58. Eliot's letter of December 1959 is reprinted in Coghill's edition of *The Family Reunion,* p. 15.

59. *Oedipus Rex: An English Version,* trans. Dudley Fitts and Robert Fitzgerald (New York: Harcourt, Brace, Jovanovich, 1969), pp. 160, 163.

60. Browne, *The Making of T. S. Eliot's Plays,* p. 311.

61. Jones, *The Plays of T. S. Eliot,* p. 200.

62. See Howarth, *Notes on Some Figures behind T. S. Eliot,* pp. 293–296; and William V. Spanos, *The Christian Tradition in Modern British Verse Drama: The Poetics of Sacramental Time* (New Brunswick: Rutgers University Press, 1969), pp. 249–250.

63. "Seneca in Elizabethan Translation," *Selected Essays,* p. 68.

64. William Turner Levy and Victor Scherle, *Affectionately, T. S. Eliot* (Philadelphia & New York: J. B. Lippincott, 1968), p. 41.

6. "At the Top of the Stair": *Four Quartets*

1. These studies are found in Leonard Unger, ed., *T. S. Eliot: A Selected Critique* (New York: Russell & Russell, 1966).

2. St. John of the Cross, *Ascent of Mount Carmel* in *Complete Works,* (Westminster: Newman, 1964), p. 24.

3. *The Living Flame of Love, Complete Works,* p.169.

4. Ibid., p. 28. The translation I have used, however, is that of David Lewis, *The Living Flame of Love* (London: Baker, 1934), p. 20.

5. "Ash-Wednesday," in Unger, ed., *T. S. Eliot: A Selected Critique,* p. 350.

6. *Ascent of Mount Carmel,* p. 76. Eliot was aware that even for meditation (as contrasted with contemplation), St. John called for a passive waiting upon the event of grace. Eliot wrote that meditation requires "tireless activity and tireless passivity." See his Preface to *Thoughts for Meditation,* ed. N. Gangulee (London: Faber & Faber, 1951), p. 13.

7. Thomas Aquinas, *Summa theologiae,*II:ii, ques. 27, art. 4, trans. R. J. Batten, O.P. (New York: McGraw-Hill, 1975), xxxiv, 171.

8. Raymond Preston has called attention to this passage, which was translated by Martin D'Arcy. Thomas Aquinas, *Selected Writings* (London: Dent, Everyman, 1939), p. 186.

9. Aquinas, *Summa contra gentiles,* trans. English Dominican Fathers (New York: Benziger, 1929), IV, 1.

10. Vladimir Losski, *The Mystical Theology of the Eastern Church,* trans. Fellowship of St. Alban & St. Sergius (London: Clarke, 1957), pp. 26, 40.

11. Dionysius's Epistle III, quoted by Losski, ibid., p. 39.

12. Dionysius the Areopagite, *The Divine Names and the Mystical Theology,* trans. E. E. Rolt (London: Society for Promoting Christian Knowledge, 1971), pp. 195–196.

13. St. Gregory of Nyssa, *In canticum canticorum,* VI, quoted in *Cambridge History of Later Greek and Early Medieval Philosophy,* ed. A. H. Armstrong (Cambridge: Cambridge University Press, 1967), p. 454. Raymond Preston has already suggested Gregory of Nyssa as an early proponent of the negative way Eliot followed. See Preston's essay in *T. S. Eliot: A Symposium for His Seventieth Birthday,* ed. Neville Braybrooke (New York: Farrar, Straus & Cudahy, 1958). My other references to Preston are to his *Four Quartets Rehearsed* (London: Sheed & Ward, 1946) except where otherwise noted.

14. See Henry Chadwick, "Philo," in *Cambridge History of Later Greek and Early Medieval Philosophy.*

15. Henry David Thoreau, *Cape Cod* (New York: Crowell, Apollo Editions, 1961), pp. 141-142. I am indebted to Lawrence Willson for pointing this out to me.

16. *Rg. Vedas,* X, 129, trans. A. L. Basham, *The Wonder That Was India* (New York: Grove, 1954), pp. 247-248.

17. Basham, *The Wonder That Was India,* pp. 249, 268.

18. *Revelation,* ed. John Baillie and Hugh Martin, pp. 31-32.

19. "Reflections on the Unity of European Culture," *Adam* 14, no. 158 (May 1946): 1-3, cited by Howarth, *Notes on Some Figures behind T. S. Eliot,* p. 95.

20. Smith, *T. S. Eliot's Poetry and Plays,* p. 298.

21. "Dante," *The Sacred Wood,* p. 168.

22. "Dante," *Selected Essays,* pp. 212, 223.

23. "What Dante Means to Me," *To Criticize the Critic,* p. 123. For further discussion of Eliot and Dante, see my forthcoming "T. S. Eliot's Virgil: Dante" in the *Journal of English and Germanic Philology.*

24. Quoted by Margolis, *T. S. Eliot's Intellectual Development,* pp. 145, 144.

25. "Humanism without Religion," *Humanism and America,* ed. Norman Foerster (New York: Farrar & Rinehart, 1930), p. 110.

26. Jean-Paul Sartre, *Being and Nothingness,* trans. Hazel E. Barnes (New York: Philosophical Library, 1956), pp. 23-24.

27. "Ulysses, Order, and Myth," *The Dial,* (Nov. 1923): 483.

28. Manuscript notes in Houghton Library, Harvard, for a course in Modern British Literature, given by Eliot at Harvard as English 26 in 1932-33.

29. See Margolis, *T. S. Eliot's Intellectual Development,* p. 57. Eliot is quoted as saying, "So important [the sense of fact] seems to me, that I am inclined to make one distinction between Classicism and Romanticism of this, that the romantic is deficient or undeveloped in his ability to distinguish between fact and fancy, whereas the classicist, or adult mind, is thoroughly realist." This passage originally appeared in "The Function of Criticism" in 1923, but it was excluded from the reprinted essay in 1932 (in *Selected Essays*)—largely, I suspect, because in 1923 Eliot went on to say that the classicist is "without illusions, without day-dreams, without hope,

without bitterness, and with an abundant resignation." As his poems from "The Hollow Men" on show, Eliot was convinced after 1927 that "dreams" and "illusions"—when controlled by "facts"—are testimonies to "the higher dream." And of course hope was fundamental to the Christian convert.

30. Nāgārjuna, "An Analysis of Time [kāla]," *Fundamentals of the Middle Way* (*Mūlamadhyamakakārikās*), trans. Louis de la Vallee, in Streng, *Emptiness*, p. 205.

31. Notes for Philosophy 24a, given by Masaharu Anesaki in 1913–14. Case III, Houghton Library.

32. Gardner, *The Composition of Four Quartets*, p. 85.

33. Eliot, "The Development of Leibniz' Monadism," *Knowledge and Experience* (London: Faber & Faber, 1964), p. 179.

34. See Chadwick, "Philo," p. 149.

35. Augustine, *De Ordine*, I, 9, 27.

36. See Schneider, *T. S. Eliot: The Pattern in the Carpet*, pp. 184–185, and Samuel Beckett, *The Unnamable* (London: Calder and Boyars, 1973), p. 294.

37. Losski, *The Mystical Theology of the Eastern Church*, p. 26.

38. For example, see Psalms 27, 37, 45, 46, 53, 54, and 62.

39. St. John of the Cross, *Complete Works*, p. 411.

40. Roosevelt was quoting Thoreau, who wrote in his journal in September 1851, "Nothing is so much to be feared as fear."

41. Interviews in *Paris Review*, 21 (Spring/Summer 1959): 70; and "Reawakened: The Heart of Eliot the Austere," *Scottish Daily Mail*, 26 Aug. 1958.

42. In his reading notes on Evelyn Underhill's *Mysticism*, Eliot had noted many years earlier that Underhill recorded *five* steps: "1. Revelation of Divine Reality, 2. Purgation, 3. Illumination, 4. Dark Night of the Soul, 5. Union." He also noted that "Oriental mysticism insists on a further stage—absorption. Western mysticism insists on activity." On his own reduction of the steps to three, see also Gordon, *Eliot's Early Years*, p. 115. As to St. John of the Cross, we must assume that *some* preliminary illumination would have to precede the motive to purgation.

43. "The Modern Mind," *The Use of Poetry and the Use of Criticism*, p. 137.

44. *Summa theologiae*, I, ques. 12, arts. 1–4, and II, i, ques. 27, art. 4.

45. "In His will is our peace." The line spoken by Piccarda Donati, a nun forced to be untrue to her vows, is quoted with Eliot's comment in "Dante," *Selected Essays*, p. 231.

46. *Bhagavad-Gītā*, ch. II, 69; quoted by Wheelwright in "Eliot's Philosophical Themes," *T. S. Eliot: A Study of His Writings by Several Hands*, ed., B. Rajan (London: Dobson, 1948), p. 103.

47. Eliot mentions the sibyl's words in a letter of 4 January, 1941, which is in the John Davy Hayward Collection, King's College, Cambridge.

48. In a letter to Ford Madox Ford, published in *The Transatlantic Review*, 1, no. 1 (Jan. 1924): 95–96, Eliot called himself "an old-fashioned Tory" and said, "The present age . . . is the age of a mistaken nationalism and of an equally mistaken and artificial internationalism . . . a genuine nationality depends upon the existence of a genuine literature, and you cannot have a nationality worth speaking of unless you have a national literature." He added that "there can only be one English literature; . . . there cannot be British literature, or American literature."

49. In his essay "American Literature and the American Language" (1953) in *To Criticize the Critic,* pp. 50–51, Eliot describes Mencken's *The American Language* as "a mistaken assimilation of language to politics," but says there has recently occurred a "revolution" in literature, and "we are now justified in speaking of what has never, I think, been found before, two literatures in the same language." The language, of course, is English.

50. Concerning the unusual division of "spring time," see Mallarmé's syllepsis *"point d'eau"* ("spring" *or* "no water"), mentioned in Chapter 2, note 8. Reading this line in "Little Gidding" as an intertextual echo of the line I have considered in "Gerontion" adds force to it. Another syllepsis in this Quartet's first strophe is "Zero summer." The summer is both absolute and exists in no time.

51. Letter of July 1949 to E. Martin Browne, in *The Making of T. S. Eliot's Plays,* p. 232.

52. "John Ford," *Selected Essays,* p. 171. Schneider, in *The Pattern in the Carpet,* has drawn together Eliot's most important comments on order and unity in poetry (including his own), especially on pp. 1–4, 149–159. Eliot made unity of vision the test of a great poem as early as 1920 in his essay on Dante of that year.

53. Augustine, *De Ordine,* II, 16, 44.

54. "Poetry and Propaganda," *Literary Opinion in America,* ed. Morton Dauwen Zabel, 2 vols. (New York: Harper & Row, 1962), I, 106.

Index